"Thatcherism will leave next Labour Government trial base; the other wil fare state. Never since extensive a need for reconstruction. But the problems will, in one respect, be more severe than those created by six years of war. In 1945, Labour had some remedies to hand. Nationalisation of basic industries, the creation of a national health service, the replacement of the poor law, the establishment of social welfare, the relief of poverty, all these presented themselves as opportunities in a world in which it was possible to make things new.

Tomorrow will not be the same. The Labour administrations of the 1960s and the 1970s provided very few fresh insights into the way socialism should develop in the 1980s and 1990s. The old Labourism will not do. The problems are different, the future is more dangerous, the structures of national and international society have changed."

This stimulating and important book is a thoughtful contribution to the considerable debate about the first steps to be taken to build a socialist society in the cold climate of the 1980s. It is not a handbook for immediate revolution or an instant blueprint for policy, nor does it assume that the remedies will be quick and easy — or orthodox. It is a book of ideas for the intelligent lay-person interested in politics and society whether of a socialist view or not. It covers topics as diverse as concepts of equality and fairness, sex discrimination, economic policy, health and urban policy, pensions, poverty and the economics of the welfare state, defence and internationalism.

The book will be essential and rewarding reading to all those interested in British politics, in the Labour party or in socialism generally.

# Socialism in a Cold Climate

# COUNTERPOINT
# SOCIALISM IN A COLD CLIMATE

Tony Atkinson – Colin Crouch
Meghnad Desai – Howard Glennerster
John Griffith (Editor) – Chris Husbands
Julian Le Grand – Jane Lewis – Michael Mann
Doreen Massey – Robert Power
Mike Reddin

London
UNWIN PAPERBACKS
Boston          Sydney

First published by Unwin Paperbacks 1983

**UNWIN® PAPERBACKS**
40 Museum Street, London, WC1A 1LU, UK

Unwin Paperbacks,
Park Lane, Hemel Hempstead, Herts HP2 4TE, UK

Allen & Unwin Inc.,
9 Winchester Terrace, Winchester, Mass 01890, USA

George Allen & Unwin Australia Pty Ltd.,
8 Napier Street, North Sydney, NSW 2060, Australia

---

**British Library Cataloguing in Publication Data**

Socialism in a cold climate.
  1. Socialism in Great Britain
I. Griffith, J.A.G.
335′.00941    HX246
ISBN 0-04-335050-X

---

**Library of Congress Cataloging in Publication Data**

Main entry under title:
  Socialism in a cold climate.
Includes index.
1. Socialism—Great Britain. 2. Great Britain—
Economic policy—1945–    . 3. Great Britain—
Social policy. 4. Great Britain—Politics and govern-
ment—1964–    . 5. Labour Party (Great Britain)
I. Griffith, J. A. G. (John Aneurin Grey)
HX249.S63  1983    335′.00941    82–22731
ISBN 0-04-335050-X (pbk.)

---

Set in 11 on 12 point Garamond by
PREFACE LTD, Salisbury, Wiltshire, UK
and printed in Great Britain
by Guernsey Press Co. Ltd, Guernsey, Channel Islands

# Contents

|  | The Authors | *page* | viii |
|---|---|---|---|
| 1 | Introduction  *John Griffith* | | 1 |
| 2 | A New Start for Labour  *Howard Glennerster* | | 6 |
| 3 | The Commitment to Equality  *A. B. Atkinson* | | 22 |
| 4 | Economic Alternatives for Labour, 1984–9 *Meghnad Desai* | | 37 |
| 5 | Privatisation and the Social Services *Julian Le Grand* | | 65 |
| 6 | Income Maintenance  *Mike Reddin* | | 81 |
| 7 | Conceptualising Equality for Women  *Jane Lewis* | | 102 |
| 8 | Industrial Relations  *Colin Crouch* | | 124 |
| 9 | A Politics of Location  *Doreen Massey* | | 144 |
| 10 | Race and Immigration  *Christopher T. Husbands* | | 161 |
| 11 | Nationalism and Internationalism: a Critique of Economic and Defence Policies  *Michael Mann* | | 184 |
| 12 | Provision and Choice in Housing  *Robert M. Power* | | 207 |
|  | Index | | 226 |

# The Authors

John Griffith is Professor of Public Law at the London School of Economics, a Fellow of the British Academy and from 1956 to 1981 was Editor of *Public Law*. He has published numerous articles and books on law and on politics, including (with H. Street) *Principles of Administrative Law* (5th ed. 1973), *Parliamentary Scrutiny of Government Bills* (1974), (with T. C. Hartley) *Government and Law* (2nd ed. 1981), *The Politics of the Judiciary* (2nd ed. 1981) and *Public Rights and Private Interests* (1981); he also edited *From Policy to Administration* (1976).

A. B. Atkinson is Professor of Economics at the London School of Economics. He was previously Professor of Political Economy at University College, London, and Professor of Economics at the University of Essex. He was a member of the Royal Commission on the Distribution of Income and Wealth, 1978–9 and is also the author of *Poverty in Britain* (1969), *The Reform of Social Security* (1969), *Unequal Shares* (1972), *The Economics of Inequality* (1975), *The Distribution of Personal Wealth in Britain* (1978), *Lectures on Public Economics* (1980) and *Social Justice and Public Policy* (1982).

Colin Crouch is Reader in Sociology at the London School of Economics and a former Chairman of the Fabian Society. He is the author of *The Student Revolt* (1970), *Class Conflict and the Industrial Relations Crisis* (1977), *The Politics of Industrial Relations* (1979) and *Trade Unions: The Logic of Collective Action* (1982).

Meghnad Desai was educated at the Universities of Bombay and Pennsylvania. He worked at the University of California, Berkeley, before coming to the London School of Economics, where he is Reader in Economics. He has written *Marxian Economic Theory* (1974), *Applied Econometrics* (1976), *Marxian Economics* (1979), *Testing Monetarism* (1981) and is assistant editor of the *Cambridge Economic History of India*, vol. 2 (1982).

Howard Glennerster worked as a Research Officer for the Labour Party from 1959 to 1964 before coming to the London School of Economics, where he is currently Reader in Social Administration. He is also the author of *Social Service Budgets and Social Policy* (1975) and has edited a forthcoming book, *Remaking Social Policy*, for the Fabian Society.

Christopher Husbands conducted his doctoral research at the University of Chicago into the electoral support for George Wallace in 1964 and 1968 and has lectured in sociology at the London School of Economics since 1978. He co-translated, edited and introduced the English-language version of Werner Sombart's *Why is There no Socialism in the United States?* (1976), and his book on urban support for the National Front is shortly to be published.

Julian Le Grand is Lecturer in Economics at the London School of Economics and has previously taught at the Universities of Sussex and California. He has long worked on the economics of social policy and has published (with Ray Robinson) *The Economics of Social Problems* (1976) and *The Strategy of Equality* (1982).

Jane Lewis has taught in the Social Science and Administration Department at the London School of Economics since 1979. She is the author of *The Politics of Motherhood: Child and Maternal Welfare in England, 1900–39* (1980), editor of *Women's Welfare/Women's Rights* (1982) and has written a number of articles on various aspects of the history of women.

Michael Mann is Reader in Sociology at the London School of Economics and previously lectured at Essex, Yale and New York Universities. He has published *Workers on the Move* (1973), *Consciousness and Action among the Western Working Class* (1973) and *The Working Class in the Labour Market* (1979).

Doreen Massey is now Professor of Geography at the Open University and was Senior Research Fellow at the London School of Economics in 1981–2. She is currently the SSRC Fellow in

Industrial Location Research and also a member of the Labour Party NEC Home Policy Sub-committee on Town and Country Planning. Her publications include (with Alejandrina Catalano) *Capital and Land* (1978), (with Richard Meegan) *The Geography of Industrial Reorganisation* (1979) and (with Richard Meegan) *The Anatomy of Job Loss* (1982).

Robert Power studied the sale of council houses for his Ph.D. at the London School of Economics and is currently teaching at a London comprehensive school.

Mike Reddin is Lecturer in Social Administration at the London School of Economics. His major teaching and research interests concern the redistributive effects of social policies, particularly in the field of income maintenance. His special interest in recent years has been in the 'pension partnership' of state and occupational pension systems. He is author of *Universality and Selectivity: Strategies in Social Policy* (1977) and has contributed to the *Year Book of Social Policy* (1976 and 1982) on the subjects of pensions and occupational welfare, to *Taxation and Social Policy* (1981) on the tax treatment of pension systems and, most recently, to *The Wealth Report*, vol. 2 (1983) on the growing inequalities among the elderly.

# 1

## Introduction

John Griffith

Thatcherism in 1979 seemed very like the standard Conservative product: tax cuts, promises of a review of the social services to eliminate extravagance and wastage, law and order, curbs on trade unions, reduction in Government intervention and in subsidies – down with nationalisation, up with free enterprise. These were the slogans believed to be election winners in those constituencies where winning and losing mattered. Then, after victory, very large hand-outs followed to those with the highest incomes, while VAT increases cancelled out the tax reliefs at the lower levels.

It was to be expected that standard Conservatism, like too much standard Labourism, would then sit back, contemplate the real world and see, from day to day, what might be done to move some way towards the fulfilment of some election pledges. No need to be over-literal; a week's a long time; circumstances alter cases; the business of government is a private affair; the Civil Service pulling back Ministers to that central consensus; no cause for drastic action; hope for the best and accommodate to the worst.

But Thatcherism departed from the standard and, to a very considerable extent, despite the protests from right, left and centre, persisted in its aim of seeking to improve the competitiveness of British industry by deflating the economy, creating huge unemployment, weakening the trade unions and forcing small firms into bankruptcy.

Today we are witness to an unusual phenomenon in British politics: a Government which not only has no positive social policies but takes pride in having none. We have no idea how it is planned that major state responsibilities in housing, roads, land use, education, health and welfare services will develop over the next few years because the Government has no plans,

except in a few instances to transfer some of those responsibilities to private ownership. Ministers for the social services
stand like figureheads at the prows of the becalmed ships of
their Departments, saying and doing very little except considering how further financial cuts may be imposed. No attempt is
being made to consider how the social well-being of the nation
may be improved.

All this was not achieved without help from elsewhere. But
Thatcherism has no wish to excuse the consequences of its own
policies by blaming the world recession. On the contrary, it
wishes to claim the credit for everything except unemployment.
So there is much wringing of hands in public about the jobless,
while in private the policies which deprive people of work, over
and above those attributable to external causes, continue to be
directly and deliberately pursued.

Governments like to publicise some economic aim which is
both easy to understand and almost certainly attainable. Wilson
used the balance of payments and then the voluntary control of
wages. For Thatcher the trick was initially to pursue policies
that boosted the rate of inflation and then to justify public-
expenditure cuts over the years by the need to reduce that rate,
all of this, and more, being subsumed under 'monetarism'.

But these are means not ends. And the end is to collapse the
economy.

In this sense, Thatcherism has been a highly interventionist
type of Conservatism. In addition, partly by legislation but
much more by changing the political, ideological and economic
climate, it has contained trade unionism and greatly reduced
the standard of living of the poor by keeping percentage
wage increases far below the level of inflation, holding down
supplementary benefit payments and weakening the social
services.

One of the five 'tasks' which the Conservative party set itself
in its 1979 Election Manifesto was 'to support family life, by
helping people to become home-owners, raising the standard of
their children's education and concentrating welfare services on
the effective support of the old, the sick, the disabled and those
who are in real need'. The transparent ambiguities of that last
phrase are not a sufficient defence to the charge that this state-

ment was dishonest. Reducing the level of the social services was an inevitable, intended and central part of the economic and financial strategy.

For these reasons, appeals to Thatcherism to indulge in modifications of its policy, to effect even a modest U-turn, mistake the nature of that policy. Governments have hitherto sought to manage the economy. Thatcherism seeks to change it. Thatcherism seeks not to help industry but to create the harsh economic conditions in which industry will be forced to make the changes necessary to keep itself alive.

This is most obvious when we consider what will happen if the Conservative Party is returned to power at the next general election. Mrs Thatcher has said many times that she needs a second term. But there is no suggestion that in that second term, continuing until nearly the end of the 1980s, there will be any change in policy. Indeed, the promise is for more of the same. There is no suggestion that, having put the country on a sounder footing (as the Conservatives would claim), Government will seek through positive action to reduce unemployment, to restore the social services, to improve the conditions of the poor. Thatcherism is unable to offer any alleviation. All those policies which socialists must insist on — an increase in industrial activity, the reduction of unemployment, the improvement of social services — are bound to militate against the strategy of Thatcherism.

The more Western capitalism changes, the more it remains the same. Its considerable successes over the last 200 years have always been accompanied by its consequent calamities. In economic terms, profit-seeking in the short term has resulted in unwillingness and inability to plan for the future and in collapse. In political terms, the need to centralise power and to resist democratic developments in industry has resulted in monopoly and in authoritarian structures. In social terms, its operation has, because of all these other factors, resulted in widespread unemployment which, from time to time, has gone out of control and helped to accelerate the periodic collapses. But until now Governments in this country and in other Western democracies have considered it a part of their function to give positive support to those industries they wished to nurture. This

is not the approach of Thatcherism, despite its total commitment to private capitalism.

The politics of self-destruction which Thatcherism has pursued means that the devil takes the hindmost. It is a drastic and
radical policy and has one strongly religious tenet: that out of
the funeral pyre of industry a phoenix will arise. It is obvious
that this cannot be assured. This is why it is proper to describe
the politics of the last four years as the Thatcher experiment. It
is the beginning of a policy, in every sense highly individualist,
that in its own terms might work. British industry might be
thus rejuvenated. Or the policy might be catastrophic. Purifica-
tion by fire always carries its own obvious dangers. The freshly
feathered eagle, in its red and gold plumage, may not rise from
the ashes.

For socialists Thatcherism is not a possible way of proceed-
ing. The price paid in human suffering is already far too high
and will greatly increase. But, even more, the political philosophy that believes the welfare of the mass of the population will
be promoted by the profit motive of private enterprise, financed
by private investment and supported by a cheap labour force, is
rejected by socialism. Thatcher's way, socialists believe, must
depend on exploitation, on greed, and that is what Thatcherites
meant when, in the Conservative Manifesto of 1979, they spoke
of working 'with the grain' of human nature. Socialists believe
that this mistakes and debases human motives. They believe
that representative democracy can, through its control of the
principal means of production, so organise the economy that it
works designedly for the general good. They believe that the
power of private capital to employ and to dispose of labour, to
make investment decisions affecting the livelihood of tens of
thousands of workpeople, to make political decisions of the
utmost significance, must be brought under public scrutiny
and, where necessary, transferred to public management. Collapsing the economy, creating unemployment, cutting social
services is not the way to recovery for the mass of the people.

Thatcherism will leave two appalling legacies for the next
Labour Government. One will be a crippled industrial base; the
other will be a severely damaged welfare state. Never since 1945
will there have been so extensive a need for reconstruction. But

the problems will, in one respect, be more severe than those created by six years of war. In 1945 Labour had some remedies to hand. Nationalisation of basic industries, the creation of a national health service, the replacement of the poor law, the establishment of social welfare, the relief of poverty, all these presented themselves as opportunities in a world in which it was possible to make things new.

Tomorrow will not be the same. The Labour Administrations of the 1960s and the 1970s provided very few fresh insights into the way socialism should develop in the 1980s and 1990s. The old Labourism will not do. The problems are different; the future is more dangerous; the structures of national and international society have changed.

The socialist solutions to the problems faced by a post-Thatcherite Britain will not be those of the previous years. We believe that Thatcherism will have greatly damaged the productive strength of the country, antagonised large sections of the working population and weakened the social services. In January 1980 I suggested to colleagues of mine at the London School of Economics and Political Science who were Labour supporters that we might put forward some analyses, propose some ways in which the task of reconstruction might be begun. Over the next months we met each week during term and discussed each other's draft chapters. Final drafts were produced during the summer of 1982. This is not a handbook for immediate revolution; nor does it assume that the remedies will be quick or easy. No attempt has been made to cover the whole field of government policy. Each contributor has written on his or her own subject, and, not surprisingly, none of us agrees with all that the others have written.

This book of essays is meant as a contribution to the considerable debate within the Labour movement about the first steps to be taken to begin to build a socialist society in the cold climate of the second half of the 1980s.

# 2

## A New Start for Labour

Howard Glennerster

At various points in their history political parties must examine their fundamental assumptions. Surely this is such a time for the Labour Party and its social policies. Their intellectual origins were varied but not particularly socialist. They have been undermined by practical experience, by wide-ranging attacks not only from the far right but also from the Marxist left and by self-doubt about the achievements of the welfare state by erstwhile supporters. To renew its momentum, the Party must develop an alternative social as well as economic strategy (Meacher, 1982), having honestly faced these criticisms. The essence of such a new strategy should lie in an extended interpretation of the ideal of full citizenship in modern Britain, building upon and extending institutions like the National Health Service, which in themselves embodied initially a deeper conception of what it meant to be a British citizen.

How has the world changed since the foundations for Labour's social policies were laid in 1945?

### Keynesianism and full employment

In the 1920s and 1930s Labour relied on a mystical belief that something called socialism would solve the unemployment problem, but it had no practical substance (Skidelsky, 1967). Hence Keynesian theory came to fill a theoretical vacuum, to be embraced as the final justification for a mixed economy. This is best illustrated in the 1944 full employment White Paper (Cmd 6527), which the postwar Labour Government took as one of its articles of faith. It formed the premise for Crosland's *The Future of Socialism* (1956). Rereading that book, one is amazed by the confidence of the first section. Indeed, most of the later chapters depended on this logical foundation. The problem of unemployment was permanently solved; Britain's growth rate was high and assured; and inflation was barely mentioned until the end of the book, where the problem is seen entirely as one of demand management and the stimulation of an adequate supply of savings: 'It simply means that under normal peacetime conditions, progress and efficiency require, amongst other things, the avoidance of periodic crises of serious excess demand (though it may be that a continuing mild inflation is inseparable from full employment)' (Crosland, 1956, p. 401).

It was precisely this misjudgement that lay at the root of the problem that successive Labour Governments faced. It was a Labour Government, after 1966, that began the process of trading higher levels of unemployment for lower levels of inflation. In some ways it is surprising that this 'crisis of Keynesianism' should have taken so long to become obvious (Crouch *et al.*, 1979). The problems posed by organised labour and large-scale employers in a fully employed economy were clearly appreciated not only by Keynes himself in *How to Pay for the War?* (1940) and Beveridge (1944), who advocated permanent wages and price controls after the war, but also by socialists such as Barbara Wooton (1954).

## The presumption of growth

A presumption of the inevitability of growth and of its benefits became an integral part of Labour's social policy in the 1960s. Just as in the 1920s and 1930s the Labour Party had no real policy for full employment, so in the 1960s and 1970s it had no real basis for its belief that it could affect the growth rate. There was virtually no economic analysis to explain Britain's relatively poor economic performance, although this dated back to the late nineteenth century, if not before (see chapter 4).

## Universality and redistribution

Just as Keynes had filled the vacuum in Labour's economic policy in the 1930s, so Beveridge supplied coherence for many of Labour's disparate social policy objectives. The Labour movement came only gradually to accept the principle of social insurance. It was born, after all, out of Liberal and Bismarckian parentage and was extended by a Conservative Government. Beveridge went to great pains to point out that his proposals were designed not to promote redistribution between the classes but to provide a means of redistributing income through the life cycle, to give minimum, adequate support in periods of misfortune and interrupted earnings. The social welfare schemes of the interwar period were selective in scope. Many were received only by sections of the manual classes and lower-income groups. Other services (like secondary education), from which the middle classes did benefit, carried charges. Labour's postwar legislation was frequently all-embracing or universal. All employees were members of the National Insurance scheme. All citizens could use the National Health Service. All children were to have secondary education. The legislation embodied what T. H. Marshall (1963) was to call a third level or dimension in citizenship. From the time of Magna Carta onwards the British people had won certain civil rights — freedom from arbitrary arrest, free speech and equality before the law — at least in theory. In the nineteenth and twentieth centuries they won another element in British citizenship — one person one vote. But the Second World War and its aftermath were to add a third dimension: 'the right to a modicum of economic welfare and security, to share to the full in the social heritage and to live the life of a civilised being according to the standards prevailing in society' (Marshall, 1963, p. 72).

The practice fell short of the ideal. Benefits were never enough to ensure the universal right to such a standard of living, but since the Second World War the commitment to a high standard of public services has become the one really distinguishing feature of Labour policy. Indeed, until Mrs Thatcher's administration, the Conservative Party played an important part in extending the scope of social policy and the scale of benefits provided under postwar legislation. There is no reason to be apologetic about the scale of these achievements. In 1951 three-quarters of all households were living in accommodation that lacked basic amenities like lavatories or hot water, or were statutorily overcrowded or homeless. Today the figure is still too high, but at less than 15 per cent it is far lower than it was thirty years ago. In the 1940s classes of fifty in the state schools were common, and only one child in twenty stayed on at school beyond 16. Today classes of thirty or below are the norm, and one child in five stays on. Despite the attacks of this Government, the minimum standard of living we tolerate, the supplementary benefit level, has risen in real terms by more than two and a half times since 1948. If it were not for social security benefits of various kinds, over 6·5 million people would be living below this poverty line, and one in five of the population would literally be starving. As late as 1960 most old people in local authority care who were not living in their own homes were accommodated in vast old workhouse accommodation that dated from the Poor Law. Today these institutions have virtually gone. These improvements have been achieved despite the substantial shift in the population structure to the dependent age groups.

So one may go on. Yet, as Cole (1954) put it, although the welfare state may be necessary to socialism, it is not sufficient. Social policy on its own cannot transform society. Part of the current disillusionment with social policy derives from the unrealistic ambitions set for it by people like Crosland. Moreover, there is real and understandable resistance on the part of rate- and tax-payers and trade union members to the continuous extension of collective as opposed to individual spending. More of the same is not a viable strategy.

The problem is more complex than simply persuading the electorate to accept a manifesto which fails to contain any pledge to reduce taxation, or contains a pledge actually to increase it – difficult as that would be. Individuals and groups in society have considerable power to avoid paying direct taxes. This is made possible by an array of tax allowances on mortgages, life assurance and pension schemes. For the most part these allowances or 'tax expenditures' are claimed by the higher-income groups and are one of the main reasons why our tax structure is not effectively progressive. Business has pressed Governments, including the last Labour Government, to calculate corporation tax in such a way that it becomes virtually a voluntary system. Total corporation tax in 1979 raised only £4,000 million out of a total tax revenue of central government of about £60,000 million.

If industry, in a corporate sense, can reduce its tax burden, so can organised labour. There is econometric evidence to prove that as direct tax rates rise, people seek to preserve their standards of living by seeking compensating wage increases. Professions and corporations do the same. The market converts direct into indirect taxes. This seems to hold in other member countries of the Organisation for Economic Co-operation and Development as well as in Britain (OECD, 1978). The process merely becomes inflationary. As Hirsch (1977) has argued, it is this above all which sets limits to collective social spending. Other democratic socialist parties are wrestling with the same issues (Strasser, 1979).

So far I have reviewed what seem to me to be reasons for much disillusionment with Labour's record on social policy despite what are, in fact, many major achievements. What this review reveals, in my opinion, is that it is the old Croslandite approaches that have been most undermined. Merely to raise a new standard with a strange device on the electoral field will not solve these problems: hence the appeal of the far right and the far left to many today. Yet do they have alternative strategies that add up?

## The attack from the right

The first prong of the attack from monetarist economists was on traditional demand management. Governments that sought to sustain employment above its 'natural' level had produced inflation. Moreover, Governments had tended to intervene to gain electoral advantage, thus accentuating the underlying cycles. Since spending is popular and paying taxes is not, there is a systematic tendency for Governments to run budget deficits, and these produce inflation.

Some of these claims are more factually disputable than others. They do correctly emphasise the political character of demand management — which is far from the neutral technical process some Keynesians described. What is so strange about the monetarist diagnosis, however, is that the proposed cure has almost nothing to do with this element in its analysis. 'Restraint in the rate of monetary growth is both a necessary and sufficient condition for controlling inflation,' we are told (Friedman, 1980). But if demand management failed because of the temptation to do the electorally popular thing, how is controlling *monetary* aggregates (as opposed to national income aggregates) supposed to be easier? In practice, the Conservative strategy seems to turn on the proposition that unemployment must remain high enough, social benefits low enough and anti-union legislation tough enough to destroy the power of organised labour. But if over 3 million unemployed is barely enough to induce 'acceptable' levels of wage claims, what happens when the economy expands again? The unspoken elements in the monetarist strategy are a deep distrust for democracy and a contempt for the suffering of ordinary people that were alien to much of postwar Conservatism.

Where growth is concerned, the far right seems as naively optimistic about its inevitability and its benefits as the moderate left was. Yet 'growth' in conventional terms — a rise in private incomes and in the Gross Domestic Product — are poor measures of 'welfare'. Some of the most important elements in an individual's command of resources — health, education and other non-marketed goods — are measured in the national income statistics by their expenditure, not by their output. Thus no productivity gain can be shown statistically. The more a society spends on health and education, the *lower* its growth rate will be for that reason alone. But that is a pure statistical artifice. The cost of economic growth — environmental pollution — is not measured, and attempts to minimise it (for example, through clean air and water regulations) increase a product's costs and tend to reduce the crude 'growth' rate: hence their rejection by Reagan's administration. This is to mistake statistics for substance.

On public spending the monetarists' position is equally simple and equally naive: let the state withdraw from the provision of services and confine its activity to cash aid for the poorest. In its less extreme form, charging for existing publicly provided services is advocated as a way of reducing the net cost to the taxpayer. The last turns out not to be a solution at all. Most recipients of the personal social services, the health service and day nurseries, the usual candidates for charges, turn out to be very old, very poor or very young and are either excluded from paying or have their fees paid by the Supplementary Benefits Commission — not a saving to the public purse at all (Parker, 1976; Judge and Matthews, 1980). The revenue raised from the remainder turns out to be trivial by comparison with total public expenditure and only about 8 per cent of local authority rate-fund spending. The Conservative Government's own Green Paper on local government finance (Cmnd 8449) argues that 'it would be either impracticable or inefficient to try to charge customers the economic cost of the services they consume' in many cases in which the benefits are indivisible and would defeat the purpose of social service provision in most others. It concludes: 'Education, law and order, highways and the social services together account for 70 per cent of rate-fund expenditure and offer little scope for additional charging' (para. 11. 8).

Even less of a solution is a return to the private market. Paradoxically, in countries that have private insurance-based systems of social and health care, the services turn out to be more expensive and not more effective (Royal Commission on the National Health Service, Cmnd 7615). It is precisely because the caring professions in particular monopolise expertise and deal with vulnerable people that the market is a poor (indeed, perverse) vehicle. The provider is both proxy demander and supplier of service. Health care is the classic example. It is not the patient who carefully weighs what kind of treatment to demand. That is done on the professional advice of his medical adviser, the GP or specialist, who has an interest in the diagnosis he makes. In private insurance the disciplines of the market are absent but are not replaced by public scrutiny.

In short, while the neo-classical iconoclasts on the right have put their finger on major institutional weaknesses in the modern 'mixed' economy by showing how the pursuit of self-interest in large organisations and the professions can pervert the wider public interest, they have failed, for ideological reasons, to perceive that the criticisms apply with even greater force in the private than in the public sector. The rampant pursuit of professional self-interest is far more apparent in the US medical market than in the National Health Service, where public countervailing power has contained it.

## The attack from the left

For many years Marxists have held conflicting views on the scale of public spending and the extension of social services. By many it had been seen as an extension of the state's apparatus of control. More recently, some Marxists have developed a more coherent dialectic. High and growing public expenditure is necessary to sustain productivity in a capitalist economy, to maintain a high level of demand, to contain social unrest and to mollify working-class demands. But it also has a tendency to outgrow the political system's capacity to finance it without undermining individualist values and incentives and running into severe inflation. This process cannot be reversed because of the working class's power to defend its gains. The system is therefore driven remorselessly to collapse, as cuts in public spending produce a working-class backlash (O'Connor, 1973). (The French Marxist Castells' account is essentially the same, though the terms are different.) Ian Gough has extended O'Connor's thesis to Britain (Gough, 1979). The first part of the argument makes considerable sense, the conclusion less so. The powerful working class with jobs and bargaining power is quite likely to acquiesce in the diminution of welfare benefits and services to the weak and elderly and loses much of its power when faced with a severely depressed economy. The really striking inequalities between manual and non-manual workers are not those of income or even of wealth but those in the workplace, where conditions of work, fringe benefits associated with work and the simple human dignities are denied working people, let alone any say in or control over their working lives. We know that those recruited to apprenticeships are, by conventional measures, little different in ability from those who enter university, and that the more able university students tend not to enter industry. We therefore have a situation in which some of the most able and critical people in our society enter jobs in which they are treated as inferior beings and have the organisational capacity and willingness to retaliate. However, this is a recipe for industrial stalemate rather than revolution, and that is what we have.

The cuts in public spending have scarcely produced a radical protest. Whenever mainstream universal services like health and education have been attacked there has been some popular reaction just because they have become rights of citizenship to many people. When income-related unemployment benefits were cut there was little protest.

Nevertheless, it is true that the values that motivate an individualistic economy are widely held in our society and are incompatible with many of the social goals that Labour Governments have pursued since the Second World War. Indeed, both value systems are reflected in our social institutions. The point of compromise we have at the moment is an unstable one. As Hirsch argues, it is the pursuit of collective objectives within an individualistic economic structure that helps to produce inflationary pressure and collective frustration (Hirsch, 1977). It may be that in some societies which have a longer history of democratic socialist Governments collective values are more pervasive than in Britain, and the scale of the public sector can be extended further before these contradictions (Marxist terminology) or limits (Hirsch's) are met. In Sweden and other Scandinavian countries and in Austria the scale of the public sector in relation to the economy as a whole is about half as big again as it is in Britain. These countries have achieved this because they have been able to reach some collective agreement on the scale of private incomes and the size of the social wage. Such an approach to incomes policy involves a higher conception of collective citizenship than our society has been able to sustain. But Marxists, like the far right, have no answer to this basic problem. They reject incomes policies, and Eastern Europe has just suppressed free trade-union bargaining as its 'solution'.

Democratic socialists cannot merely hope for catastrophe. They must seek to foster wider democratic support for the values in which they believe. Social policy has a central role to play in creating the kind of society in which it may be possible to develop a 'non-corporatist' basis for incomes policies – a socially fairer and more democratic society, in which there is an alternative to accelerating inflation other than 3 or 4 million unemployed.

If the far right and the far left provide no solutions to the dilemmas with which we began, they do draw attention to some key issues, as we have seen. I have argued that if we are to avoid continuing to pay a high price in unemployment for restraining inflation, an acceptable incomes policy will have to involve a more integrative social policy and the involvement of working people in its content.

Where nationwide service and benefit extensions are sought, the case for higher taxes or tax changes must be made and the battle fought head-on. There is, for example, a strong case for abolishing the married man's tax allowance and translating it into a higher level of cash child benefit. Much more could be done to reduce the wide range of tax allowances that are such an inefficient way of targeting aid. Within the existing levels of spending much could be done to make public services more responsive to the needs of poorer members of society, to women and to social groups that are not effectively served. Other contributors to this book deal with some of these topics; here I wish to concentrate on what seems to me a central feature of any extended notion of citizenship – the fostering of a sense of local citizenship and involvement with the delivery of services.

The more pervasive and equal national services become, the more local disagreements there tend to be with a centrally determined norm. This is reflected in more general resentments about taxation and 'excessive' government. The more freedom and flexibility that can be built into local services and the more citizen involvement that can be achieved, the less such resentments may be reflected in a general attack on public services. Yet some basic rights of national citizenship, and some strong national controls on the economy, are crucial if local authorities are to retain their freedom of action in an economy in which large private institutions play such an important role. To a considerable extent, the argument between the localists and the centralists seems to me misplaced. It is a strong *dualism* that we require.

The case for dualism (as I call it) is this:

- The achievement of the collective restraint on private consumption that is necessary to sustain and improve social provision without rapid inflation will demand a much greater measure of perceived fairness in access to jobs, incomes and wealth and in the sharing of the tax burden required to finance the social service sector. None of these can be achieved without powerful central government policies designed to create jobs, and tax income and wealth more fairly. Central government is the only agency powerful enough to ensure an equitable geographical distribution of revenue and a fairer treatment of groups which society has systematically stigmatised or disadvantaged — racial minorities, the handicapped, the elderly infirm or women.
- At the same time, excessive central control over service provision can alienate ordinary people from those services. People become frustrated if their local priorities for more or fewer services have no tangible effect. If central government lays down an average or standard level — and discourages provision beyond it, as is now the case — local pressure to innovate, to extend the scope of services or make them less costly or to participate in their provision, is largely taken away. Long-term corrosion of interest and support will result.

How can excessive central control be reduced and local citizenship extended?

## Greater financial independence of local government

Governments of both parties have accepted the Treasury orthodoxy that it was necessary for macro-economic policy reasons to control closely the level of local authority spending. There is a case for limiting global sums of capital expenditure in times when there are strong inflationary pressures. Local and central government and private industry are then in competition for investment funds, and excessive competition pushes up interest rates. It is far from clear, however, that the same is true of revenue spending. It holds good only if you believe that 'marketable' goods and services are somehow more productive than services not produced for the market (Blackaby, 1979). If people choose to spend their incomes collectively rather than privately in an area, should this concern the Treasury? As Foster and his colleagues put it:

Is, for example, an increase in the number of restaurants, or clothes shops, of concern for macro-economic policy on the grounds that part of the money spent in such establishments may come out of private savings and so the total demand for resources will increase? But why would this be any different from the provision of additional services for residents of some locality by the local authority and financed by the rates? . . . if people employ private contractors to clear away rubbish there is no effect on aggregate demand. But if the local authority provides the service, total demand is thought to increase. . . . a household's decision on how much to save is determined by the balance between current and future living standards, and will not be significantly affected by whether the goods and services that contribute to its standard of living are provided by the public or private sector (Foster *et al.*, 1980, p. 375).

There is a valid point in the argument that high rates raise costs to employers in an area, and the present system that gives an Exchequer subsidy to hold down householders' rates but not those of commerce and industry is perverse in this respect. In my view, it ought to be possible to devise a fee-for-service scheme for local services to industry and commerce, even if only a rough-and-ready one, whereby they paid that portion of the rate poundage that related to 'public goods' such as roads and sewers and public health.

If local communities were faced more directly with the consequences of reduced spending or its converse and could see more directly what they were purchasing, as well as what it cost, this would breed not financial irresponsibility but the reverse.

A Labour Government should repeal the present legislation on local government finance and the rate support grant, with all its complex system of penalties and recommended levels of spending. It makes local democracy purposeless. The central government grant should cease to try to ensure that every rate-payer pays the same rate in the pound for comparable services, taking into account arbitrary and complex national formulae. Instead, grants from the centre should first seek to compensate for the differential incomes of those living in different areas and hence their taxable capacity. This would require annual information from the inland revenue on incomes by area — a much needed piece of social information for other purposes. (All we have now are sample earnings data for employers in an area.) Second, an age factor could be added to the population figures, taking account of the national average cost of services devoted to those under 16 and those over 65. People could understand that. Further complexity is counter-productive. Housing finance should be transferred to a national system giving support directly to households. The total level of rate support grant could be reduced as a share of the average council's income and replaced by a local income tax meeting perhaps a third of the average local authority income, with rates continuing to meet another third. Rates are well adapted to payment for benefits (excluding housing) that county-district authorities provide, like public health, roads, parks, which add to property values.

The snag with this proposal is that a local income tax could not be introduced — at least cheaply — until the 1990s, and it would best be linked to a new system of end-of-year self-assessment for income tax. Even a sales tax would take eight years to introduce. On the other hand, local authorities would need time to adjust to their greater freedom, and the fact they knew it was coming would be a stimulus.

## Local diversity

Since we know so little about what constitutes effectiveness in social services – about what the right form of provision is – it is highly dangerous to force local services into common patterns or levels of provision in order to confine services to those provided by local authority employees and credited professionals. Aid to local community groups should be encouraged by Labour councils. There is, in fact, a great deal of innovation going on in local authority services and in voluntary groups working with local authorities. These experiments have tended to be the first to suffer from the enforced public-spending cuts.

## Breaking down local bureaucracy and professional control

The sheer conservatism of the medical profession apart, it is difficult to see why, with a system of local income tax and a reformed grant structure, it would not be possible for the National Health Service to be administered by the same local authorities that administer education and personal social services. Schools, colleges and hospitals might be given their own budgets to administer, which would be controlled by governing bodies comprising, among others, elected representatives of local people – parents, staff and pupils. The size of the allocation would be determined by the statutory body, though it could be added to by voluntary effort. The rigorous monitoring of service outcomes would then be the local authorities' function.

Nor should the idea of neighbourhood or ward committees that G. D. H. Cole (1954) advocated many years ago be lost. He argued that people identify most closely, in a collective sense, both with their workplace and with very local neighbourhoods. When we lived in North Kensington we occupied a flat in an old Victorian terrace that backed on to a common garden. All the properties were covered by a Victorian Private Act of Parliament which permitted the owners of the properties to mandate the local council to levy a discretionary 'garden rate' on top of the basic rate for the upkeep of the garden and other communal purposes. We had great arguments about the provision of playgroup facilities, I remember. However, the principle of a voluntary additional rate decided on by an annual meeting open to all the residents, like a parish meeting with an elected committee, has always attracted me as an example of direct democracy, and one that could be used to involve local communities in improving their estates or neighbourhoods, in setting up visiting services for old people, even in employing their own community worker or playgroup organiser. Moreover, now that we are in the age of computerised rate demands, why not introduce a discretionary element into the rate bill? It would be possible to allocate the equivalent of a penny rate by indicating what portion should be devoted to, say, six proposals put up by the local council or voluntary bodies in the area. It would be up to local organisations to put up schemes for short-listing by the council.

A number of Labour councils have experimented with schemes for devolving the management of their estates and have turned their estates into co-operative housing developments. The notion of old people running their own residential accommodation is spreading. The use of volunteers in hospitals and homes for the mentally handicapped is also growing, and all these changes could help people to see that the social state is theirs to shape and control.

Taken together, these measures could foster a value system that would sustain, defend and be prepared to extend the boundaries of the social state and would permit some communities with a more individualistic cast of mind to pursue their own priorities.

I have argued that a strong central Government is necessary to control private economic power, to pursue a set of social priorities that will make some form of incomes policy possible and to redistribute income. The despairing diagnoses of the extreme right and the extreme left fail to lead to consistent solutions. A strong parliamentary Government is necessary and would not be incompatible with more devolved responsibility for some areas of social policy, notably education, health, housing and the personal social services. Within a fairer geographical and personal distribution of resources more diversity in service provision and greater lay involvement would become possible. It is inequality that constrains such freedom and variety.

# References

Beveridge, W. (1944) *Full Employment in a Free Society* (London: Allen & Unwin), pp. 198–207.

Blackaby, F. (ed.) (1979) *Deindustrialisation* (London: Heinemann)

Cmd 6527 (1944) *Employment Policy*

Cmnd 7615 (1979) *Royal Commission on the National Health Service* (London: HMSO)

Cmnd 8449 (1981) *Alternatives to Domestic Rates*, Department of the Environment (London: HMSO)

Cole, G. D. H. (1954) 'Socialism and the welfare state', *Dissent*, Autumn

Crosland, C. A. R. (1956) *The Future of Socialism*, (London: Cape), p. 401

Crouch, C. (ed.) (1979) *State and Economy in Contemporary Capitalism* (London: Croom Helm): see contributions by Crouch, Skidelsky and Martin

Foster, C. D. *et al.* (1980) *Local Government Finance in a Unitary State* (London: Allen & Unwin), p. 375

Friedman, M. (1980) 'Friedman on Britain', *Observer*, 6 July

Gough, I. (1979) *The Political Economy of the Welfare State* (London: Macmillan)

Hirsch, F. (1977) *Social Limits to Growth* (London: Routledge & Kegan Paul)

Judge, K., and Matthews, J. (1980) *Charging for Social Care* (London: Allen & Unwin)

Keynes, J. M. (1940) *How to Pay for the War* (London: Macmillan)

Marshall, T. H. (1963) *Sociology at the Crossroads* (London: Heinemann)

Meacher, M. (1982) 'Socialism with a human face', *New Socialist*, March/April, pp. 18–21.

O'Connor, J. (1973) *The Fiscal Crisis of the State* (New York: St Martin's Press)

OECD (1978) *Public Expenditure Trends* (Paris: OECD)

Parker, R. A. (1976) 'Charging for the social services', *Journal of Social Policy*, vol. 5, no. 4, pp. 359–73

Skidelsky, R. (1967) *Politicians and the Slump* (Harmondsworth: Penguin)

Strasser, J. (1979) *Grenzen des Sozialstaats?* (Cologne: Europaische Verlagsunstalt)

Wooton, B. (1954) *The Social Foundation of a Wages Policy* (London: Allen & Unwin)

# 3

# The Commitment to Equality

## A. B. Atkinson

The commitment of the Labour Party to equality is rather like
the singing of the 'Red Flag' at its gatherings. All regard it as
part of a cherished heritage, but those on the platform often
seem to have forgotten the words. It serves to rally Party confer-
ences but would not be regarded as appropriate for meetings
with the EEC Council of Ministers or the International Monetary Fund. As Tawney once remarked, 'the degeneration of
Socialist parties on assuming office is now an old story' (1932,
p. 325). This observation, which the subsequent half-century
has done little to modify, is particularly true of the commitment to equality. Whatever the achievements of recent Labour
Governments, no one could claim that the elimination of
inequality has been a dominant theme. In this respect perhaps
more than any other, the Labour movement appears to have lost
its sense of direction.

Why has the story always turned out this way? Why has the
principle of equality retained merely ritual significance? Why
do commitments to 'bring about a fundamental and irreversible
shift in the balance of power and wealth' (Labour's 1974 Manifesto) turn out to be empty? One answer that is frequently
given points to the lack of accountability of Labour Cabinets
and the subordination by Ministers of long-term objectives to
short-run events. The leaders of Labour Governments have seen
their job as that of governing, an activity in which Manifesto
commitments are a handicap and socialist principles of academic
significance. Crossman described the Labour Party as having lost
its way 'not only because it lacks a map of the new country it is
crossing, but because it thinks maps unnecessary for experienced
travellers' (1956, p. 36).

But there may be another explanation, and the responsibility
may not be that of the 'experienced travellers' alone. There may

have been a lack not only of political will but also of intellectual momentum behind principles such as equality. The case for a commitment may not have been made sufficiently forcefully. We may have neglected the egalitarian theory which is the foundation for political practice. If Labour Ministers had looked for a map, they might have found it to be missing or at best faded.

Where does one turn to find a clear statement of the case for equality? Almost invariably, the answer is Tawney's classic essay *Equality* (1964), first published in 1931. For its powerful prose and telling argument this essay can scarcely be bettered. But Tawney himself would surely have been the first to recognise that his conception and statement of the problem were very much products of his times. The case for equality has to be made in terms of current concerns and circumstances. There is therefore a need to restate the case for the commitment to equality so that it occupies a central position in Labour Party policy. Those concerned that a future Labour Government should pursue this objective with greater resolution than in the Wilson–Callaghan years must rehearse the intellectual arguments for equality and their relevance to modern times. The ways in which the commitment to equality could and should influence the whole range of policy issues which will confront a future Cabinet must be demonstrated. This is the more necessary to the extent that the Social Democratic Party is seeking an alternative distributional policy (as well as claiming Tawney for its own).

The first part of this chapter seeks to restate the case for equality and to identify the distinguishing features of a socialist approach to economic justice. The second part develops some of the guidelines for a future Labour Government.


## The case for equality

Clarity about the nature of the objective is the first essential. Sweeping references to the 'reduction of inequality' or to a 'shift in the distribution of wealth and power' are not sufficient. Their generality renders such goals largely vacuous and means that they are too easily ignored when it comes to the reality of government. Moreover, it is only by making the objectives more precise that we can distinguish a socialist vision of a fair and equitable distribution from that of other political parties.

The objective of economic justice can be pursued at different levels, and we may consider increasing degrees of commitment, with the stakes rising at each stage. The Conservatives tend to opt out when the stakes are low, the Liberals to hang on to the next stage; as far as can be discerned, the Social Democrats intend to quit well short of egalitarianism.

### Freedom from want

Most people are in favour of abolishing poverty. But poverty means different things to different people. One view is illustrated by the following passage:

> A family is poor if it cannot afford to eat. It is not poor if it cannot afford endless smokes and it does not become poor by the mere fact that other people can afford them. A person who enjoys a standard of living equal to that of a mediaeval baron cannot be described as poor for the sole reason that he has chanced to be born into a society where the great majority can live like mediaeval kings. By any absolute standard there is very little poverty in Britain today. (Joseph and Sumption, 1979, pp. 27–8)

The position of Joseph and Sumption is an extreme one, even by the standards of Conservatives – and many of them would probably prefer a higher standard by which to judge the existence of 'want', the level being determined by a blend of historical precedent and political judgement. The key feature, however, is that the poverty line is viewed as a specific level of resources. Thus people talk about the unemployed now being much better off than those in the 1930s – a debatable proposition – on the implicit assumption that the criterion should be independent of incomes elsewhere in society.

Freedom from want, in terms of food, housing, medical attention, etc., is evidently an important goal, but it represents a very limited conception of the problem of poverty. It means, for instance, that social security benefits have only to be maintained in real terms and not increased in line with rising prosperity elsewhere. According to this view, poverty will disappear with economic growth – indeed, according to Joseph and Sumption, it already has. This restricted perception of the problem is unlikely to be acceptable to the Labour Party.

Before considering the alternative of a relative concept of poverty, we should note that the implications of an absolute approach are more far-reaching than its supporters recognise. Joseph and Sumption argue that by their standards there is little poverty in Britain, but surely the same does not apply to low-income countries? Concern for freedom from want should not stop at the boundaries of the nation state. It may be claimed that Britain can do little on a world scale – for example, that overseas aid is ineffective and goes only to those not in need. But that is another argument and points to the need for measures to improve the effectiveness of assistance rather than to the abdication of responsibility. The formulation of the objective in terms of securing a basic minimum may be seen by Conservatives as grounds for limiting the welfare state in Britain, but if the objective is to have any moral validity, then by the same token it implies a much more active policy for world redistribution.

## A 'participatory minimum'

The case for a more radical approach to poverty in Britain, concerned not only with an absolute subsistence level but also with contemporary living standards, has been well put by a succession of Labour writers. In the *Future of Socialism* Crosland argued:

> we should not behave like medical officers of health, concerned only to provide sufficient food and clothing to ward off starvation and ill-health. We are surely concerned with happiness and social justice also. This demands a relative, subjective view of poverty [taking account of] the enforced deprivation not of luxuries indeed, but of the small comforts which are really 'conventional necessities'. (1964, p. 89)

More recently, the authors of *Manifesto* wrote:

> The minimum we seek might be called a 'participation' stan-
> dard to distinguish it from the subsistence standard adopted
> after the war [which] fails to recognise that needs are social,
> and not merely physical. We want a new right for all to share
> fully in the life of the community. (Cripps *et al.*, 1981, p.
> 184).

The adoption of such a relative standard has several implications. It means that social security benefits have to be linked to
the general level of incomes; that unemployment benefit (for
example) should be maintained in relation to incomes at work;
that the low-pay target should be set in relation to average earnings and not kept at the levels set by the Trade Boards of 1909;
that participation should be open to all groups, regardless of sex
or race.

Of particular importance is the fact that the 'participation'
standard has to be viewed not just in terms of cash incomes.
Income and wealth have been the variables of primary concern
in economic theories of inequality, and it is their — still more
narrow — counterparts which are reflected in official statistics.
But they capture only part of the problem. The objective is also
to secure a minimum standard for the quality of housing, of
medical facilities, of education, of safety at work, of the environment and so on.

The need for this wider view of minimum standards was recognised in the concept of the 'social wage' which made a brief
appearance under the Labour Government of 1974–9. This was
a welcome advance, emphasising that improvements in public
provision could be set against higher taxes, but it is wrong to
seek to combine everything in a single number. £1,000 of earnings cannot necessarily be added to £500 of housing benefits. It
may be that the lack of adequate medical facilities cannot be
compensated by wage increases or, conversely, that a family
short of cash cannot be compensated by increased spending on
schools.

The 'participatory' minimum should therefore be interpreted
in terms of specific targets for each of the different dimensions

of need with which we are concerned. These targets should be *relative* and should be defined in terms of *outcomes*. (For example, in the field of medical care we are aiming not to provide a minimum allocation of resources but to ensure a standard of health, where this is determined by the current conditions and expectations of society.) Moreover, it should be emphasised that the achievement of these specific targets is not an alternative to the guarantee of incomes; the objectives are complementary.

## Poverty and justice

Crosland's case for a relative poverty standard was based on an appeal to social justice. Recent writing on the theory of justice seems to have had relatively little to say explicitly on the definition of poverty, but we can draw on their wider discussion of the distributional problem. It would, for example, be possible to see concern with poverty as a minimal function of Nozick's 'night-watchman' state (1974), although this is most obviously applicable as a justification for the absolute approach. The case for a relative standard can be based more directly on the social contract theory of Rawls (1971), in which the 'difference principle' leads to concern with the position of the least advantaged, a concern which — given a crude interpretation of his ideas — may be seen as 'insurance' against an income which is low in relation to that of others in the society.

The Rawlsian approach brings us to the question of inequality. What is the relation between the twin goals of abolishing poverty and reducing inequality? In much discussion of Labour policy these are spoken of in the same breath, as if they were complementary. But that need not be the case. The argument by the right that reducing inequality may mean lower living standards for all is not an empty one. A choice may have to be made. For Rawls the answer is straightforward. It is the maximisation of the benefit to the least advantaged that has priority, according to his 'difference principle'. If fiscal incentives for the sunrise industries of Britain improve the earnings prospects of the low-paid, then they are distributionally justifiable — even if their main consequence is the creation of large fortunes by the entrepreneurs.

*Egalitarianism*

The example just given is an important one, since it allows us to draw a distinction between the Labour perspective and that likely to be adopted by the Liberals or Social Democrats. For the latter distributional concern appears to be focused solely on those below the poverty line. For the socialist, on the other hand, there is a broader concern with inequality.

The espousal of an egalitarian position means that we regard as relevant the question of how incomes are distributed above the povery line. It may be necessary to accept that incomes are lower for everyone as the price for narrowing differences. This would not apply where it is a matter of starvation — meeting such urgent needs evidently comes first. But the concept of relative poverty, explicitly directed at the relation between incomes, would have no such claim for priority. The emergence of large disparities may be seen as too high a price to pay for a modest improvement in the living standards of the low-paid.

Egalitarianism — or the concern with the extent of economic distance — should be a major element in Labour's approach to distributional policy. It is, indeed, the principal feature which marks it out from its rivals. But it will not be easy to convince the electorate. On what arguments should its case be made? What it is *not* based on, as frequently alleged by the right, is envy. Such negative considerations have no role to play. Quite the reverse: the case should be founded on the vision of the kind of society which should inspire people, calling not on feelings of dissatisfaction but on an identification with the lot of others. To elicit such a response — in the face of powerful opposing forces — is the challenge that the Labour Party faces.

The most straightforward argument for reducing economic and social distance is that these are, on their present scale, incompatible with a full sense of participation. The point was made by Tawney in a frequently quoted passage:

What a community requires . . . is a common culture, because, without it, it is not a community at all. . . . But a common culture cannot be created merely by desiring it. It must rest upon practical foundations of social organisation. It is incompatible with sharp contrasts between the economic standards and educational opportunities of different classes. . . . It involves, in short, a large measure of economic equality – not necessarily in the sense of an identical level of pecuniary incomes, but of equality of environment, of access to education and the means of civilisation, of security and independence, and of the social consideration which equality in these matters usually carries with it. (1964, p. 43)

Should we not, like Plato's legislator, 'announce the acceptable limits of wealth and poverty', allowing a person to have up to four times the lowest level of income? Such a limit would help to prevent the divisions in the style of living which destroy the sense of community. Just as we are not willing to tolerate a situation in which people lack the resources to participate, so too we want to avoid the emergence of a privileged group able to opt out of common problems through the private provision of facilities such as medicine and schools and through the corporate welfare system.

The distinctive nature of the egalitarian approach may be seen from a consideration of the plans for economic recovery that have been advanced. It appears that the Conservative programme for expansion is based, on the one hand, on the creation of low-paying jobs and, on the other, on the hope that large financial gains for businesses will generate new employment. The Alliance position, as indicated by such statements as 'We must . . . start to put far greater emphasis . . . on recognising throughout British society the commercial and competitive imperatives on which our prosperity depends' (Owen, 1981, p. 81), suggests that financial incentives at the top would again play a major role. The Labour Party, by contrast, should surely be opposed to such a widening of economic disparity – to both the worsening of the position of the low-paid and the gains to the highly privileged.

Finally, we must return to the international dimension. Do not the arguments apply equally between countries? Plato's four-to-one ratio is obviously violated many times over on a world scale. This poses a clear dilemma. One resolution, proposed with considerable reservations, is that the objective of freedom from want applies at a world level, but that notions of relative poverty or distance are essentially national in application. The concept of a common community is based on the nation state, with only absolute standards applying across frontiers. It is with participation in British society today that the argument is concerned and with the extent to which economic distance leads groups to be excluded from that society. (This, of course, raises issues related to the ethics of immigration.) Thus measures which benefit low-paid workers in Britain might be considered justified despite the fact that they worsen the relative distribution of income worldwide, providing that they do not put workers elsewhere in risk of starvation.

The essential features of a commitment to equality have been identified as: freedom from 'want' worldwide; the securing of a participation minimum standard in Britain; the setting of specific targets for particular dimensions of disadvantage; the limitation of the distance between the top and the bottom of the economic scale. We turn now to how these can be translated into action.

## Guidelines for policy

The conversion of the commitment to equality into a concrete programme for policy is a major task requiring a great deal of preparation, as was illustrated by the 1974–9 Labour Government's 'success' story of the new pension scheme and its 'failure' to implement the proposed wealth tax. It is not the aim here to discuss policy in detail, however, for such a discussion would have to take account of the circumstances in which a future Labour Government is likely to take office and of the constraints that it will face. Now, perhaps more than at any other time in the postwar period, it is hazardous to venture to predict such circumstances. That the economic situation will pose problems can scarcely be doubted, but events of recent years have shown that these can change dramatically in scale within the time that it takes a book to proceed from manuscript to printed page.

The aim is instead to describe *guidelines* which can be used to judge policy questions which are likely to arise, criteria which are mid-way between general principles of justice (as discussed earlier) and specific policy proposals. What has so often seemed to be lacking is a touchstone by which reactions to events may be assessed. What should be the criteria which future Labour Ministers should bring to bear on the particular issues that confront them? How should they react when faced by the latest economic or social crisis? All too often Labour Governments, when blown off the course charted by manifesto pledges, have appeared to lack principles of navigation.

## *The need to understand the problem*

The first suggested guideline is that it is crucial to understand the nature and extent of inequality. We need both quantitative measures of the distribution of income and wealth and theoretical analyses of the forces that tend to intensify or moderate inequality.

This may sound like a job-creation scheme for academics, but the contribution of knowledge should not be undervalued, as has been recognised by the Social Democrats: 'The only way of achieving a more equitable distribution in a democracy is to secure a greater awareness by the mass of the population of the facts about poverty' (Owen, 1981, p. 247). The Conservatives, to their shame, have set about systematically dismantling the apparatus to collect key distributional information. The Royal Commission on the Distribution of Income and Wealth was abolished on the grounds that the statistical information had been improved, but within two years the Rayner Review of the Government Statistical Service announced that work on estimates of the distribution of wealth was being stopped and recommended that estimates of the distribution of income be prepared only every three years.

As has long been recognised by reformers, statistics are a powerful weapon. The Labour Party should give priority to the establishment of an independent body – not subject to temporary political whims – which would have the resources to collect and to analyse distributional information.

*Distribution and not just redistribution*

If Labour and the Social Democrats are likely to agree on the need for information, they are bound to part company on the question of the measures that should be adopted to achieve lesser inequality. Most fundamentally, whereas the Liberal approach sees the market as having primacy in the determination of gross incomes (wages and profits), the socialist approach sees the distribution of economic rewards as a proper subject for intervention. The Alliance seems likely to confine its activities to redistribution through taxation and public spending: 'There is a strong case . . . for leaving redistribution to tax and social security policy' (Owen, 1981, p. 105). By contrast, a Labour Government should act to secure a distribution of wages and profits which, taken together with the tax and benefit system, will ensure its distributional objectives.

The first (and most obvious) application of this guideline is to Labour's policy for economic recovery. The successful pursuit of higher employment will in itself contribute to the reduction of inequality, but the design of this policy should be set in a specifically distributional context. The choice of measures should be based on their implications for equity objectives – aspects which cannot be read from the computer printouts of the Treasury forecasting model.

The return to full employment has typically been discussed in terms of conventional Keynesian measures, but there are strong grounds for believing that a major change in economic strategy is required if unemployment is to be tackled in a serious way. In this context a revitalised distributional policy may have a significant role to play. Tawney, writing in the 1930s, referred to the fact that Britain needed a common culture

in a special degree at a moment like the present, when circumstances confront it with the necessity of giving a new orientation to its economic life, because it is in such circumstances that the need for co-operation, and for the mutual confidence and tolerance upon which co-operation depends, is particularly pressing. (1964, p. 43)

The Labour Government would, for instance, be ill-advised to attempt to conceal from the electorate that real wages for those in work are unlikely to rise in the foreseeable future. Would it not be better to make a virtue of this necessity? After all, equality conveys obligations as well as benefits.

The policy emerging in these new circumstances is bound to involve some form of collective agreement on incomes, both wages and profits. This means that the Labour Party will have to seize the nettle of incomes policy. It need not be of the past type, nor need it bear that name, but some kind of consensus will be necessary. There is no reason why the market economy should lead to an equitable distribution between labour and capital; nor is there any reason to suppose that free collective bargaining will ensure an equitable distribution of earnings. What would distinguish Labour's policy on incomes is an explicitly redistributive bias. The Social Democrats' tax-based incomes policy, for example, eschews any bias in favour of the low-paid, since it is felt that it 'should be dealt with through taxes and transfers' (Layard, 1982, p. 229).

In the design of the policy towards gross incomes, two aspects warrant close attention. The first is the role of private capital. This applies both to individual claims to assets, and their transmission through inheritance, and to the function and reward of capital in the process of production. The ineffectiveness of, for example, the Capital Transfer Tax in limiting the conveyance of inherited wealth would be staggering to those such as Josiah Wedgwood, who concluded many years ago that 'the ethical arguments in favour of claims to inherit . . . are extraordinarily weak' (1939, p. 207). Second, the structure and organisation of industry is usually discussed, as part of the alternative economic strategy, in terms of its contribution to the development and employment of output. But this structure may have profound implications for the distribution of resources. The scale of enterprises and the associated managerial hierarchies affect the pattern of earnings, as do their links through the international economy. (President Nyerere is reported to have favoured nationalisation on the grounds that domestic pay levels could then be divorced from those of multinationals.)

*Effective progressive taxation*

The weight attached above to the distribution of gross incomes does not mean that redistribution via progressive taxation is redundant. On the contrary, an essential element in Labour's strategy must be the reform of the tax structure. The fiscal history of the postwar period is a sorry one as far as socialists are concerned. The tax threshold has fallen markedly, and the tax base has been eroded by the extension of tax allowances and reliefs. These developments have combined to shift the burden of income taxation towards lower- and lower-middle income groups.

In any attempt to redress this situation, two factors will be important. The first is that the tax structure must be sufficiently flexible to allow the burden to be shared more equitably. In the case of the income tax there is in effect a choice between a 'simple' system with a single basic rate, progression being ensured by the allowances (and higher rates for a few tax-payers), and a 'complex' system with rates of tax that start low and build up gradually. The former has administrative advantages but implies a loss of flexibility. For those whose distributional concern is limited to the position of the people at the bottom, the simple structure may suffice; but if one is concerned with the question of how the burden is shared between those just above the poverty line and those higher up, then greater flexibility may be needed.

The second ingredient is an analysis of the reasons why the fiscal system has changed in the way it has and why it has been impervious to reform. Economists have rightly been criticised for ignoring the functioning of the state. Ministers may not always regard themselves and their officials as proper objects for study — but it is clearly foolhardy to embark on further tax changes without an understanding of the causes of previous failures.

*Social insurance*

Social insurance will be an essential element in realising Labour's commitment to equality. It will be necessary to ensure a guaranteed minimum, defined in relation to the level of incomes elsewhere. At the same time, it is part of the wider vision that Labour brings to bear that social insurance will not be only a transfer of income.

First, it is crucial that the guaranteed income should be provided as of right and not subject to a means test. The evidence of means tests, over many years, is that this approach — central to Conservative welfare policy — is incompatible with dignity and self-respect. People should see themselves as entitled to social insurance and treated as such; it is the great achievement of the National Insurance system that this is felt to be the case with the universal benefits. What is required is a strengthening of the insurance scheme, not the retreat we have witnessed in the past few years.

Second, the receipt of benefit should be linked with clearly identified contingencies. The uncertainty which is otherwise generated in the minds of recipients reduces the sense of security provided; the uncertainty in the minds of the public engenders hostility towards claimants.

## A world perspective

In seeking to put its commitment to equality into effect through the extension of social insurance and other measures, the Labour Party will have to work hard to carry the electorate, and in no respect will this be harder than in the field of world redistribution. As a minimum, there is a commitment to ensure freedom from want in all countries, and it can be argued that even more extensive redistribution is implied by Labour's principles of economic justice.

Moreover, the political difficulties lie not only with the voters. The position just described requires that the Labour Party adopt an internationalist stance which runs counter to much of the 'alternative economic strategy'. It is understandable that people faced by a world economy dominated by multinational companies and financial institutions have argued for an independent, nationally orientated policy. But there is the other option: that of seeking to change the world economy. Britain's potential contribution to the world transfer of resources is bound, by the force of arithmetic, to be small, but her contribution to the securing of a socialist international order could be of prime importance. This aim may be ambitious, but it seems to be the only way in which the goals of abolishing poverty at home and abroad can be secured.

## Last words

Much of what has been written above will appear far removed from the realities of a future Labour Government, from the world of White Papers, NEDO and Brussels. To many it will appear naive, even wholly unrealistic. But if that is so, it is at least considerably less dangerous than the cynicism and world-weariness that constrains and confines much discussion of economic and social justice today. As the title of this book indicates, a Labour Government will almost certainly take office in a hostile economic climate. This will limit what can be achieved in the way of securing distributional objectives. However, it is important to recognise that the constraints lie as much in perceptions as in resources, and that they are not immutable. The act of making a positive commitment to equality, with its emphasis on full participation, may in itself transform attitudes and ease the solution of Britain's economic difficulties.

## References

Cripps, F., *et al*. (1981) *Manifesto* (London: Pan)

Crosland, C. A. R. (1964) *The Future of Socialism*, rev. ed. (London: Cape)

Crossman, R. H. S. (1956) *Planning for Freedom* (London: Hamish Hamilton)

Joseph, K., and Sumption, J. (1979) *Equality* (London: Murray)

Layard, R. (1982) 'Is incomes policy the answer to unemployment?', *Economica*, vol. 49, pp. 219–39.

Nozick, R. (1974) *Anarchy, State and Utopia* (London: Basic Books)

Owen, D. (1981) *Face the Future* (Oxford: OUP)

Rawls, J. (1971) *A Theory of Justice* (Cambridge, Mass.: The Belknap Press)

Tawney, R. H. (1932) 'The choice before the Labour Party', *Political Quarterly*, vol. 3, pp. 323–45

Tawney, R. H. (1964) *Equality*, 4th ed. (London: Allen & Unwin)

Wedgwood, J. (1939) *The Economics of Inheritance* (Harmondsworth: Penguin)

# 4

# Economic Alternatives for Labour, 1984–9

Meghnad Desai

A Labour Government that comes to power in 1984 (or before) will face the biggest challenge that a new Government has faced for years – a challenge comparable to that of 1945.[1] The economy will be in a critical condition after five years of dry monetarism; unemployment is likely to be between 4 and 5 million; the decline in output in 1980–2 is unlikely to have been substantially reversed. Barring upheavals in the Conservative Party leadership, the most likely estimate is that an election-winning budget from the present Government will take the form of tax cuts – for the middle- and upper-income groups, for the private corporations and for the wealthy. There will probably have been little substantial economic recovery, and it is unlikely that the economy will be back to its postwar trend level of output below which it has operated since 1974.

Unemployment, bankruptcies and loss of production capacity are not the only problems. The potential for future growth has been harmed by a persistent decline in output and the senseless cutting of expenditure on education, research and development. But the most serious matter for an incoming Labour Government to consider will be that the welfare state launched by the policies of the Coalition Government and the Labour Government of 1945 will have been severely damaged. The Keynes–Beveridge design for welfare capitalism fell short of a socialist alternative; even so, inadequate as it was, its implementation was niggardly, and its full potential was never realised.[2] Despite this, it is only now, when it has been rejected as official policy, that we have begun to appreciate how much we took it for granted. In abandoning full employment as an objective, in jettisoning even a nominal commitment towards a guaranteed minimum standard of living, in running down the health and social facilities provided under the state's aegis and, above all, in attacking the ideology that sustained the arrangement, the present Tory Government has precipitated a radical departure from the postwar policy consensus. In many ways, policies since 1979 (if not those before that year, as we shall see below) have been a replay of the deflationary episode of 1921 which inaugurated the long interwar period of high unemployment and conflict that lasted until 1939. Only the outbreak of the war made it imperative that mass support be secured for a successful war effort; full employment and a substantial welfare state were the almost inevitable consequences of the nation's total involvement in the war — as if there had been a social contract between the Government and the people.[3] That a reversal of such a long-standing policy could come about raises questions about the sources of political as well as economic power and about the best way of guaranteeing that such reversals do not recur.

Thus a new Labour Government will not only face the immediate short-term tasks of restoring and rehabilitating the economy after five years and more of devastation. It will also have to regain the ground that has been lost in the public provision of health, education and social services. But it cannot be desirable — nor is it feasible — to see the task as one of restoring the *status quo ante*: there will have to be a restructuring of the economy.


## Diagnosing the British disease

In diagnosing the British disease, it is tempting to rake over recent failures of economic policy. The backsliding by the Wilson and Callaghan Governments from their avowed promises, a panic boom inaugurated by the Heath Government, the mistiming of the devaluation decision by the Wilson Government — all these can be rehearsed. The postwar period saw both an unprecedented quarter-century of full employment, with real income growth, and the realisation that such could not be the permanent condition of the British economy. 'You Never

Had it so Good' was true in 1959 but could not be repeated a decade later. The realisation that full employment and growth were difficult to achieve simultaneously crystallised during Maudling's years as Chancellor of the Exchequer. At first the problem seemed to be the balance of payments and the overvalued pound, then high wages which were causing inflation, then the expanding share of public sector or the un-restrained growth of money supply. These were not unrelated, but each surfaced at various times as the fashionable explanation of the British disease.

What they hid, however, was the deeper structural reasons for the predicament, which go back to the 1870s. Indeed, what needs to be explained is the miraculously easy period of 1948–63. Various conjunctures – the growth of world trade that resulted from the simultaneous adoption of full employment policies in all developed capitalist countries, the preoccupation of Britain's potential trade rivals with the immediate task of postwar construction, the sluggish growth of the US economy in the 1950s, etc. – helped to ease the British problem. The structural causes of British economic stagnation were thus hidden for a while, but it is on these that we must focus.

By the 1870s it was clear that the British economy was no longer the most dynamic capitalist economy. Its growth rate, its rate of innovative activity, its international competitiveness had all suffered, and it was facing competition from the USA and Germany in all the markets to which it exported. The response of the political and economic community in Britain in the years 1870–1900 determined the course of the long-run stagnation.

The first Industrial Revolution took place in the second half of the eighteenth century, preceded by an Agricultural Revolution, and between 1790 and 1840 the British economy witnessed tremendous expansion and structural transformation. The dominant pattern of industrial organisation was the privately owned firm managed by the owner. While there were many competing firms in each industry, internationally Britain was in a monopolistic position. She did not face any serious competition from domestic or foreign rivals in the various countries where she sold goods. Captive markets were also created by the policy of imperial expansion — the loss of the American colonies was quickly recouped by the gain of the Indian Empire — and these markets were immediately penetrated by British textile and engineering firms. This was the period during which Britain exported new manufactured goods as well as new technology.

But the second Industrial Revolution, which occurred in the 1870s and 1880s with the introduction of electrical-mechanical technology, passed Britain by. The favoured form of industrial organisation in Britain was unsuitable for exploiting the economies of mechanised production, and it hindered the adoption of new managerial practices. The American economy, by contrast, underwent this technological-managerial revolution, which encouraged the growth of large, vertically integrated firms managed by personnel who could use new methods of cost accounting and production control. The British firms in many ways revealed their crafts origins and remained small-scale. From the 1870s onwards the British economy began to lose its competitive edge in third markets to the USA and Germany.[4]

This loss was noticed by contemporaries, and many attempts were made to identify the ingredients of the foreigners' success. But the responses of the Establishment were exactly the opposite of what was needed. Instead of responding to this new challenge by changing the structure of industry, the economy increasingly took the character of a *rentier* economy. The domination of finance capital over industrial capital dates from this period, when banking became concentrated in and around London, at the expense of country banks. The educational system, far from changing over to technical and scientific subjects, inculcated the anti-industrial values of the landed aristocracy. There was no democratic spread of education as there was in the USA. Workers learned their craft skills on the job and not at polytechnics. There was no managerial education, and even if there had been, there would have been no opportunities for the employment of the graduates of such education, since firms continued to be owner-managed.

The *rentier* economy flourished by specialising in the export of capital. There was a shift from direct investment abroad to passive equity or fixed-interest debenture participation. The City of London could raise money from British savers for almost any project anywhere in the world, and much of this was in debenture form. The gentleman who drew his income from interest on past investment was ranked above the industrialist. The heirs of industrialists preferred to become gentlemen if they could buy their way into the gentry by education and marriage.

Faced with international competition, one political response was to rely on imperial expansion to assure markets. The idea was to keep the imperial territory as a protected area from which competition could be shut out, as Joseph Chamberlain urged. While the protectionists did not win the argument, there were many ways of excluding rivals from imperial markets, not least important of which was to instruct the natives of India and the African colonies that British was best.

The Empire provided an area of effectively (though not formally) protected markets, and in the functioning of the Gold Standard India was pivotal. Her trade surplus was transferred by means of a complex web of financial arrangements to finance the British balance of payments deficit, which arose from the large volume of capital exports that exceeded the commodity trade surplus. Freedom to export capital was vital to the *rentier* economy and to its nerve centre – the City of London.

The *rentier* economy experienced high and cyclical unemployment in the 1860–1914 period, but in the absence of political pressure *laissez-faire* policies could be maintained. The trade union movement had won over skilled craft workers but was spreading to general industrial workers only slowly. Nevertheless, all workers, skilled or otherwise, benefited from the Victorian arrangements, since Britain could import cheap consumables and raw materials from the Colonies and could export finished manufactures at prices which were favourable to herself.

It was precisely this delicate compromise that fell apart in the 1914–40 period. The inadequacy of the compromise in dealing with poverty and distress had already been apparent in the discussions following the Boer War. The increased electoral pressure after the 1884 extension of the franchise, the growth of union activities evidenced by the Taff Vale retaliation and the débâcle of the Boer War had led to a pressure for a welfare state. The Liberals conceded this in the Lloyd George budgets, but the advent of the First World War changed the entire political context in Britain.

The year 1915 was perhaps the first since recorded unemployment statistics began to be kept that unemployment fell under 1 per cent. The war effort required mass co-operation, and this meant giving the trade unions official recognition in tripartite committees. The full employment prevalent in the 1914–20 period boosted Labour's share in total income from a 60 per cent average between 1860 and 1913 to 65 per cent. Another extension of the franchise had taken place, so that all adult males were now entitled to vote.

The war prompted a tremendous structural change in the *rentier* economy. During the war many of the Empire countries and other markets in which Britain used to have dominance (e.g. Argentina) began to industrialise. The USA emerged as a creditor nation and New York as a rival financial centre to London. The response of the British Establishment was to renege on the wartime compromise with workers. A severe deflation designed to restore the pound sterling to its old parity of $4.86 was inaugurated without any consultation with trade unions in 1921. This was followed by various wage-cutting exercises and an end to tripartite co-operation. The interwar period saw a higher level of unemployment on average than in the prewar period. The British economy was squeezed through a long deflation from 1921 until 1939 in order to restore the City of London to its former prominence. The period from 1921 to 1932 was perhaps the worst because much of the unemployment was concentrated in the traditional export industries which were adversely affected by the high exchange rate. Despite the squeeze, however, no fundamental restructuring of the economy took place in terms of managerial or industrial organisational change.

The Second World War forced the Establishment to revive the contract of the First World War, but this time firm guarantees had to be given that there would be no backtracking. Also since 1928 full adult franchise had been established and now the obsolete economic and political machine had to cope with mass democracy. The war not only prompted much egalitarian sentiment; it also encouraged modernising tendencies. The economic orthodoxies were shown to be those not of a dynamic competitive economy but of protective, inefficient cartel arrangements behind which reactionary owners hid. The needs of war – manpower planning and the application of new techniques – showed what could be done if this moribund capitalism were modernised. But the war had also shown that the regulation of production and of labour allocation increased rather than reduced production efficiency, just as the rationing of consumer goods improved nutrition and health. War conditions enlisted egalitarianism and change in the service of a spirit of community, playing down conflict.

Postwar reconstruction thus consisted of the guarantee of full employment and the carrying out of a package of reforms in welfare provision – health, social security, pensions, unemployment benefit. The rationalisation of industry took the form of the nationalisation of the most obsolete and reactionary of the old industries, especially coal-mining. But the financial structure was unchanged, and the City was left in private hands except for the nationalisation of the Bank of England. Instead of the abolition of the privileged private educational system, or even its reform, a binary system was adopted whereby state education grew up side by side with public schools. But the much more drastic plans of industrial reconstruction proposed in the war years were never realised. The tripartite equilibrium between Government, employers and unions was re-established and cemented by the employers' willingness to concede some public ownership and the closed shop; the state's guarantee of full employment and the adoption of an orthodox scheme for financing the welfare state; and the unions' display of interest not in the control of production but only in free collective bargaining.[5]

Even so, some fundamental change in the industrial structure on the managerial and on the union side was inevitable. With the loss of India, it was obvious that colonial markets were no longer secure. But there was a temporary reprieve. Although the financial burdens of the war weighed more heavily on Britain than on the defeated countries, for a while there was not much

competition from Germany and Japan. Much of Europe was
recovering from war damage. There was also a sustained growth
in world trade because of the full employment policies that were
being followed in the developed capitalist countries. Britain's
*rentier* economy faced no immediate crisis; it faced instead easy
conditions in the world markets. After the immediate
problems of physical shortages in the period 1946–9, the
economy began to enjoy growth of exports and income, with full
employment, through much of the 1950s.

The pivotal position of India in the financing of British
capital exports has been mentioned above. Once India had
gained independence, this benefit disappeared. There were also
large wartime credits due to India as well as to other Empire
countries. To stave off immediate repayments, it was essential
to preserve the sterling area. This and the creation of the
Commonwealth gave a breathing space to the *rentier* economy
and the City of London.

With the re-establishment of free convertibility of European
currencies, the revival of the Western European economies and
the establishment of the Common Market, the breathing space
came to an end. From the beginning of the 1960s the economy
faced severe challenges, which took the form of an inadequate
growth rate, incipient inflation and growing concern about the
burden of sterling as a key currency.

Rapid economic growth became the universal solution to the
problems of the *rentier* economy. It was needed to preserve the
wartime social contract. In fact, as Crosland clearly saw, it also
obviated the need for any drastic redistribution of income. But
even if it had been achieved, more was asked of rapid growth
than could be delivered. Indeed, it became the only way to
avoid hard choices.

But the breathing space of the 1950s had revived the City of
London, which adjusted remarkably well to the decline of sterling as a key currency and regained its status as the major banking and financial centre of the developed capitalist world. It was
assisted by the fact that the now prospering Western Europe
economies had weak banking sectors and that despite the
growth of New York as a financial rival, proximity to Europe
helped London to hold its own. The City had thus an abiding

interest in strengthening its links with Europe and in resisting any drastic change required for, and contingent upon, rapid growth.

The real problem in the 1960s, however, was international competition. While world trade was still growing, the British economy faced many industrial rivals. The development of new products which could cut costs, investment in research and innovation, the rapid retraining of the work force as demands for new skills emerged – all these were important. But nothing had been done in the 1950s (or indeed during the previous years of the twentieth century) to instil a culture of industrial capitalism in this *rentier* economy. The relative position of the British economy in the growth league began to slip badly from the early 1960s onwards. All those postponed decisions of the previous hundred years had now to be taken. But as the pressure on sterling, the subsequent abandonment of the National Plan and the resort to short-term fiscal and monetary manipulations since 1966 show, the decisions have still not been made.

## Future policy and prospects

What lessons can be drawn from this conspectus of long-run problems? Much discussion today, on the left especially, about the problems of the British economy holds international economic forces responsible for the British decline. Thus multinational corporations, the EEC, the ideology of free trade which leaves British markets open to competitive imports, the free flow of international capital in and out of the country, competition from the newly industrialising countries of the Third World are all blamed for de-industrialisation and the loss of economic and political sovereignty. The openness of the economy is seen as the major structural weakness by many writers on the left. Those who argue along these lines would not much dispute the main lines of my narrative above, but precisely because of that I wish to make explicit my departures from their interpretation (see Cripps *et al.*, 1981; Singh, 1980).

The growing internationalisation of the world economy (and not merely of the capitalist First World) has been evident since

1945. In this respect the world economy has resumed the course on which it embarked after the Napoleonic Wars, which was interrupted by the First World War and its aftermath. In the nineteenth century national sovereignty in economic affairs could be afforded by very few countries. Britain's economic and political sovereignty was sustained by her Empire abroad and her lack of democracy at home. But in the recent period every country, including the USA, has increasingly felt that its economic autonomy is being compromised. Multinational corporations and the other international forces mentioned above are not peculiar to Britain. If their impact on the British economy is more severe than on (say) that of West Germany, the reasons lie precisely in the structural weaknesses outlined above. To blame Britain's economic decline on foreign economic forces is once again to evade the question of the responsibility of deep-seated historical and institutional forces for the present malaise.

It is also to demonstrate a signal failure to learn from history. The imperial props of Britain's much vaunted sovereignty are now gone. Indeed, it was the presence of the Imperial Alternative that lured Britain down the path of compromise which created the *rentier* economy. The various devices used to preserve British prosperity at home and imperial hegemony abroad reflected the wrong choices. Instead of revolutionising educational institutions and industrial practices, restructuring the pattern of trade to meet competition from abroad, defensive attitudes were adopted which postponed change. The culture of industrial capitalism was never inculcated, either on the factory floor (indeed, the expression 'shop floor' betrays its pre-industrial origins) or in the educational institutions. The costs were borne by the natives of the imperial colonies or by the poor at home who were beyond the Pale of industrial employment.

Whatever the outcome then, it would be a mistake now to use again the same devices, even with a radical rather than an imperial-chauvinist rhetoric. The decline in living standards, the erosion of social capital and the rapid obsolescence of industrial capital all point to the limited room left for manoeuvre in the urgent task of restructuring the economy. It would be a mistake to cocoon the economy against change once more. The cost of any new attempts to resist change and innovation, no matter how radical the language in which they are clothed, will have to be borne entirely by the domestic population, and societies have many ways of shifting such costs inevitably on to the poorest. If one is to fashion a socialist economic programme, such evasions must be made explicit and avoided. The achievement of a socialist economy must remain the ultimate goal, and in devising short-run and medium-run policies we must be on our guard against foreclosing socialist options. The need for a modernising, innovative economic strategy is profound, however. In what follows I shall concentrate on policies that would enhance the chances of successful restructuring while at the same time ensuring that short-term economic policies generate as much employment and income as possible.

Whatever reservations one may have about specific details, the Alternative Economic Strategy (AES) has been discussed very widely in Labour and left-wing groups.[6] Although its beginnings go back to the discussions preceeding the 1974 Labour Government, since 1979 there has been a veritable explosion of debates, articles and books on the AES. Seldom before have so many different groups taken part in an economic debate, but even now there is need to involve more people.

There seems to be general consensus that AES involves five ingredients:

- reflation through increased public expenditure or devaluation
- the expansion of public ownership and the extension of control over the industrial sector via planning agreements
- import controls and restrictions on capital exports
- policies for job creation, worksharing, early retirement and a 35-hour week
- price control.

In what follows I wish to assess the adequacy and the feasibility of the AES as it now stands, to make explicit some of the implicit assumptions about the nature of the economy that a Labour Government will wish to achieve by means of the AES and to fill out a skeletal statement of general principles with some illustrative macro-economic projections.

The full-employment aspect of the AES strategy is in the Maudling–National Plan tradition. Thus the notion is that of expanding aggregate demand by higher government expenditure, or by devaluation, or by tax cuts. While higher government expenditure, especially on the capital side, will be absolutely essential, if only to replace what has been depreciated, what is not clear is that reflation would lead to more jobs rather than to higher imports or, if import control is imposed, to higher prices and profits. Such doubts persist in the absence of any detailed plan for correcting the structural weaknesses of the British economy.

Although no detailed projections have been made in any of the AES publications, work is now available which clarifies the structural constraints on any reflation plan. In recent years a number of studies has been carried out with econometric models which have some common features. These exercises were undertaken on the Treasury Model by the Fabian Society group coordinated by David Blake and Paul Ormerod in 1980 (Blake and Ormerod, 1980); again in 1981 in a series of articles in *The Times* by David Blake (Blake, 1981); by Terence Barker using the Cambridge Multisectoral Dynamic Model (Barker, 1982); and, in early 1982, Peter Shore launched a five-year alternative plan for full employment.

David Blake's 1981 calculations are of the most immediate interest to us. Barker's analysis with a more detailed interindustrial model does not in any way contradict Blake's conclusions, so let me summarise Blake's conclusions first. Blake's calculations are given as alternatives to the current strategy over the 1981–4 period. Barker also concentrates on alternative policies for generating extra employment, but he looks at the short run (1982–5) as well as at projections to 1990.

David Blake tried three separate policy packages, all consistent with the AES. These were:

- a reflation package of £4 billion, comprising (i) an investment programme costing £1 billion; (ii) an income tax cut of £1.25 billion, obtained by indexing threshold levels; (iii) a cut in the National Insurance Surcharge by 1.75 percentage points

- 20 per cent devaluation, bringing the pound down from the June 1981 level of $2.07 to a level of $1.60
- protection plus public spending: a £6 billion increase in demand, plus a 30 per cent tariff on all imports of manufactured goods as well as of semi-manufactured goods.

The effects of these policies on output growth, unemployment, inflation and consumption growth are shown in Table 1.

One can only say that the results make terribly depressing reading. None of the three packages cuts unemployment by even 0.5 million by early 1984. Taking into account the increased participation in the labour force that such job creation entails, the net reduction in unemployment is at most 400,000 compared with present policy in Option III. Given that all these estimates are surrounded by a penumbra of error, the difference between II and III can hardly be significant. The major difference, then, between a purely reflationary policy without import controls/devaluation (I) and a mixed policy with import controls (II/III) seems to be of the order of between 250,000 and 450,000 jobs, with unemployment above 3 million in all cases.

The import control/devaluation strategy, however, involves a reduction in the standard of living of between 4 and 4.5 per cent more than the purely reflationary strategy. On the other hand, the purely reflationary strategy generates a lower output growth rate than the mixed reflationary strategy. Indeed, the output level is between 1.5 and 2 per cent higher by 1984 under II/III than under I. As against this, the inflation rate is between 3.5 and 4.5 per cent higher in II/III as compared with I.

What this calculation reveals is that a mixed strategy such as II or III succeeds in achieving growth and high employment but also redistributes income in favour of profits. Thus the real wage decline is much more pronounced in the case of such policies than in that of the purely reflationary strategy, as can be seen by comparing the figures for the standard of living. Thus import control or devaluation is a way of generating growth by increasing the share of profits (i.e. it is a method of cutting real wages).

This is said not to detract in any way from the merits of the

Table 1 *Likely impact of alternative economic strategies*

| | Present Policy | I | II | III |
|---|---|---|---|---|
| Output (percentage growth of GDP) | −1% by summer 1982 0% 1982–3 +1.5% 1983–4 | 0% 1981–3 1.5% 1983–4 (on average 1% above present policy) | 0% until end 1982 2% 1983–4 (on average 3% higher than present policy) | 1.5% growth by early 1982, followed by stagnation (2.4% above present policy by 1984) |
| Inflation | Falls slowly to 9.6% by early 1984 | Falls faster over mid-1981 to end 1982 but is 10.3% in early 1984 | Up to 14% by end 1981. 19% by end 1982 but falls to 13.8% by early 1984 | 17% in winter 1981/2 19½% by summer 1982, then down to 14.7% by early 1984 |
| Living standards | Stagnant to end 1983, then rises to early 1981 level | On average 1% higher than present policy | Falls by 3.5% by late summer 1982, then rises by 2% by autumn 1983 and by 3% by summer 1984 (on average 3% below present policy by 1984) | Falls by 3.5% in summer 1982, rises by 1% by summer 1982 then at rate of 2% per annum until early 1984 (on average 3.5% below present policy by 1984) |
| Unemployment, including school-leavers | More than 3 million in winter 1981/2, then rising gently to 3.5 million by 1984 | Just over 3 million in winter 1981/2, rising to 3.38 million by early 1984 | Over 3 million in winter 1981/2, rising to 3.265 million by late 1982, then falling to 3.185 million by early 1984 | Rises very gently to above 3 million in late 1982, then falls during rest of the year but rises to 3.05 million in early 1984 |
| Extra jobs created | | 175,000 | 420,000 | 600,000 |

*Source:* Blake (1981).

import control strategy but to make explicit the effects of the policy. Since profitability is a problem in British industry (and this is so for the private sector as well as for nationalised industries), one way in which to examine the political aspects of any policy is to see how it deals with that problem. An import control policy allows domestic firms to increase their prices in relation to import prices net of tariffs. This depresses real wages (in terms both of product and of wage goods) and increases profits. These profits are presumably invested in output expansion, and this gives the extra output.

The best alternative with which one should compare such a policy is a reflationary package with an incomes policy. Incomes policies have been used as short-term devices for cutting real wages. Unfortunately, this was not simulated by David Blake, but it is clearly another way of altering the relative share of wages and profits. It would be interesting to examine whether it would have milder effects on standards of living or equally severe ones. Incomes policy is one issue on which AES has been coy, since unions take a stand on free collective bargaining and other radical analysts have castigated it as merely a wage-cutting device. We are aware that an import control policy is also a wage-cutting strategy: the choice between them should be made on the grounds of their contribution to the other objectives of the overall economic plan.

Terence Barker, using the Cambridge Multisectoral Model, arrives at similar conclusions. After considering a variety of policies such as import controls, National Insurance and tax cuts, investment projects and employment subsidies, he writes: 'The conclusion is that the changes required to reduce unemployment appreciably are probably too large to be feasible within the life of the present Government and represent a daunting task for the next one' (Barker, 1982, p. 19). Barker tried ten different policies separately in a simulation exercise. The aim was to find the change in the policy instrument that would generate 100,000 jobs by 1984 (starting in 1982) and then to project the result to 1990.

In Table 2 I have provided information on the ten policies with regard to their effect on employment, inflation, income and consumption growth as well as on PSBR as a proportion of

Table 2 Effectiveness of alternative employment-creation policies

| Measure | To generate 100,000 jobs by 1984 | Increase in employment (000) | | Inflation (%) | | GDP Growth (%) | | Consumers' expenditure (%) | | PSBR as % of GDP | | |
|---|---|---|---|---|---|---|---|---|---|---|---|---|
| | | 1982–4 | 1990 | 1982 | 1984 | 1982 | 1984 | 1982 | 1984 | 1982 | 1984 | 1990 |
| Tariff on manufactured imports | 22.2% | 355 | −73 | 14.1 | 12.4 | 2.1 | 1.8 | −2.3 | 0.1 | 1.3 | 0.7 | −2.3 |
| Permanent incomes policy | 3% | 156 | 621 | 9.1 | 9.2 | 1.1 | 1.9 | −1.3 | 0.7 | 3.3 | 3.3 | −0.8 |
| Temporary incomes policy | 3.3% | 162 | 178 | 8.9 | 9.6 | 1.1 | 1.9 | −1.3 | 0.9 | 3.3 | 3.4 | 2.4 |
| Devaluation | 3.5% | 224 | 128 | 9.9 | 11.5 | 1.4 | 1.9 | −1.2 | 1.0 | 3.4 | 3.7 | 3.4 |
| Import quotas on engineering and motor vehicles | 12.4% | 160 | 250 | 10.9 | 11.1 | 1.1 | 1.8 | −0.8 | 1.2 | 3.4 | 3.7 | 2.7 |
| Employment subsidies | 76,000 jobs | 294 | 109 | 10.8 | 11.0 | 1.0 | 1.6 | −0.7 | 1.2 | 3.5 | 4.1 | 4.4 |
| Current government expenditure | 1.9% | 242 | 112 | 10.9 | 11.1 | 1.1 | 1.7 | −0.8 | 1.2 | 3.4 | 4.1 | 4.4 |
| National insurance surcharge | −2.8% | 231 | 171 | 9.8 | 10.7 | 1.5 | 1.9 | 1.4 | 1.6 | 4.0 | 4.6 | 5.0 |
| Investment projects | extra £1.37 billion | 226 | 197 | 10.9 | 11.1 | 1.4 | 1.9 | −0.7 | 1.2 | 3.8 | 4.8 | 5.2 |
| Income tax: standard rate | −3.8% | 264 | 113 | 10.7 | 11.1 | 1.7 | 1.9 | 1.3 | 2.2 | 4.7 | 5.6 | 7.4 |
| Present policy | | | | 10.9 | 11.1 | 1.0 | 1.6 | −0.8 | 1.0 | 3.4 | 4.0 | 4.2 |

Source: Barker (1982).

GDP. Each policy was tried separately, but their effects are not additive. It is clear that for short-run employment creation tariffs are the best policy by far. Incomes policies and import quotas generate about 160,000 jobs over three years, whereas tariffs generate 355,000 jobs. In terms of long-run job creation, tariffs do worst and incomes policies do best. Import quotas also show a high job-creation rate in the long run.

Tariffs achieve the best GDP growth rate, though the effect declines over the next two years, whereas with all other policies the 1984 growth rate exceeds the 1982 one. Tariffs also require a large drop in consumption growth and again the long-run effects are better with all other policies. In terms of inflation, incomes policies do best and tariffs worst.

The investment project policy steps up government expenditure each year from 1982 to 1984 to inject an extra £1,370 million into the economy by 1984. This creates 226,000 jobs over three years or about £6,000 per job. This is considerably less than the cost implicit in David Blake's calculations, which is about £20,000 per job. Barker directed the extra investment to public construction projects, which have higher employment multipliers than manufacturing industries. It is a typical result of many of these calculations that the generation of extra jobs in manufacturing is much more costly than in non-manufacturing industries, especially services.

If one is to plan a full-employment strategy, then, it would seem that on present information employment effects are likely to be higher if the final demand is such that the non-manufacturing sector will have a greater share. Similarly, public goods have a lower import content than private goods. Since construction, public utilities, transport and communications are all non-manufacturing, initially demand will have to be directed at these sectors. Indeed, expenditure directed mainly at capital investments in the public sector – schools, hospitals, sewers, roads – will seem to be a good way in which to achieve low import content and high employment-generating growth.

This means, however, that initially it will not be possible to promise increases in the consumption of private goods and that industrial revival will have to come from directions other than a reflationary package. These are both quite drastic implications of a capital construction programme, and we need to look at them.

The emphasis on import control in AES is justified by the need to afford British industry breathing space while it reverses its decline of the last fifteen years. This is to be supplemented by an industrial strategy which relies on planning agreements to force the private sector to direct investments into channels laid down by the Government. As David Blake's calculations show, import control will increase profits. One question remains, however: should they be allowed to be ploughed back in the old declining industries? To some extent, the strategy of affording protection to existing industry from competing imports conflicts with the need to restructure the economy. The industries which have lost their competitive edge have done so, to some extent, because of their inability to provide products at low cost. By channelling resources into them, other activities would have to be starved.

It is best at this stage to confront the issue of profitability openly. Should a Labour Government be following a policy designed to restore profitability, or should it be launching a socialist policy designed to abolish the capitalist system? Should a Labour Government be managing capitalism or smashing capitalism and building socialism? It must be strongly contended that such a dilemma is a false one. There is no immediate prospect that an incoming Labour Government will have the electoral strength, the mass support or the objective conditions that would be conducive to launching a fully socialist economy. Indeed, any incoming Government will be taking over when the economy is in a dire condition (but not propitious for a socialist revolution) and, as any left-wing Government would, it will face immense international pressures. It will have to manage capitalism in order to put through even a reformist or transitional programme. (The analogy with the Mitterrand Government's actions in its first year, especially as regards the speculative pressure on the franc, is very instructive.) The real test will be the extent to which such immediate pressures do not detract from the transitional/reformist tasks which such a Government should be engaged in.

The test of any AES is, then, not the narrow question of

whether profit share is restored but how it looks upon the role of profit in a long-run perspective and how different elements of the policy add up to a left-wing policy. Since the British economy will be a mixed one, even after a Labour victory, profits will continue to constitute a crucial determinant of investment and output growth. Consequently, low profitability will mean low growth of output and employment. The crucial issue is not whether profits will be raised but the extent to which the Government can ensure that profits are channelled into investment and not into consumption, exports or speculation. It will also matter whether the Government can channel them into areas which, in its long-term view, have priority. The only justification for profits in a modern economy is as a source of investment funds. But since market forces can be myopic in channelling investment, the Government will have to take over the task of controlling the direction of investment. Profitability (in terms of size and rate of profits) will continue to signal, in a majority of cases, the desirability of continuing to pursue a certain activity. If the economy pursues a loss-making activity continuously, it will only be taxing other sectors of the economy. Such a decision may still be the correct one according to some criteria (social need, long-run viability), but it should be made explicit that losses are a tax on the economy, and such losses are frequently visited on the least well-off sections of society.

The merit of an AES, then, is to be judged by the extent to which it alters the shape of the economy by using the profitability generated by sacrifice on the part of the mass of workers. It should also make explicit how much sacrifice will be made by other groups (i.e. what concomitant tax policies are followed). Thus if profits are to be channelled into investment, businessmen's consumption privileges afforded by the tax system must be taken away and corporation tax must be at a level which will enable the Government to channel these resources either into priority investment (e.g. a hospital building programme) or into increasing the social wage.

The need for import control should be therefore argued as a part of an overall macro-economic plan — a medium-term strategy. Such a strategy would need to generate surpluses for investment into a whole range of new industries which could afford growing employment, competitive advantage and, eventually, a rising real wage. Thus import control has to be seen as *a strategy for regulating the growth of private consumption*. The profits generated in the protected industries should be diverted, via taxation or other arrangements, into new growth industries such as micro-electronics, biotechnology or other R & D-intensive industries. The UK has a work force with high literacy and an educational establishment which has a good record in basic research. It would be part and parcel of any policy for restructuring the economy to reshape the educational system to take more advantage of the opportunities in these R & D-intensive industries. Hence what is needed is a phased withdrawal from the products with which the UK has lost her competitive edge and the establishment of new industries. This will require massive investment in the retraining of workers as well as in the training of new entrants into the work force (school-leavers, for example) into new skills. To freeze the present employment pattern will not lead to the creation of new jobs or to any rise in real wages.

I acknowledge that any proposal that there be phased withdrawal from existing, uncompetitive industries is bound to raise much resistance on the part of the unions as well as the management of these industries. Extensive experience of high unemployment, except for brief boom periods between 1870 and 1940, has ingrained certain defensive practices concerning job preservation in union bargaining. Even the long period of high employment in the postwar period did not alter these practices, perhaps because this period, though quite long by previous standards, was still short in relation to any cohort's working life. Thus if we consider man's working life as stretching from 15 to 65 years of age, the longest period of full employment in recent decades has been thirty years (1940 to 1970) or, more usually, about twenty years (1946 to 1966). Thus it is probable that every working man (to say nothing of working women, whose experience is much worse) born in any year since 1900 has experienced one or more spells of unemployment in his life. It is not surprising, therefore, that unions who represent workers' interests are conscious of job losses and resistant to the introduction of new technology that may threaten jobs.

But these defensive practices are an endogenous response to the long-run stagnation of a *rentier* economy. Workers have long been fobbed off with a high level of real income but have suffered from a low growth rate of income (relative, say, to the USA), and in terms of lifetime income – i.e. weighted by spells of low-income unemployment and high-income employment – they have lost out by comparison with workers in other countries. British wage-bargaining practice is to settle for a regular overtime component in the pay packet, though with a low regular real wage and job protection. The final effect on lifetime income is still adverse; the working week continues to be long; and the investible surplus generated by such activities remains small. Management practices are equally influenced by the *rentier* economy psychology – snobbish aloofness from the shop floor, lack of technical or professional knowledge of industrial practices, the appointment of managers by reference to old school tie considerations, the failure of top management to work as hard as their counterparts elsewhere and so on.

To understand these practices is not to assign blame, nor to seek to perpetuate them. There is much that is undesirable about them, and it is no defence to say that they are justified by the nature of capitalist social relations. We have frequently noticed in the past that socialists have condoned workers' resistance to new technology when capitalist relations have prevailed, only to turn around after the 'revolution' and insist on these very practices as progressive (Lenin on Taylorism is a good example of this). If we are to inaugurate the long period of transition to socialism, we have to affirm that many of these pre-industrial labour practices are obstacles to the restructuring of the economy. We have to welcome new technology and to speed up its invention and introduction. The fear of new technology is related to the threat of job loss. But we can generate jobs which afford high real income with a shorter working week only if we adopt new technology and restructure the economy. The need to generate investible surpluses and to invest them in new technology would be paramount even if the entire economy were collectively owned; otherwise the stagnations of real incomes and the precarious nature of employment will never be cured.

It is precisely for these reasons that arguments for thinking again about work and income are the strongest. It is quite likely that micro-electronics will make small production units viable and will allow both for work to be decentralised and for firms to be smaller. Working from a home base or from a small industrial unit will have obvious advantages in terms of work satisfaction. In addition, the possibility of the work stoppages and industrial conflicts to which large multiplant units are prone will be reduced (Prais, 1977). Small units of this type will also afford the possibility of new patterns of ownership – they might be co-operatives or enterprises that are owned by the Government, by a private individual, by the workers or jointly by workers and management.

Arguments for reducing the length of working week and for early retirement have been made mainly along the negative lines of work-sharing. But if such work-sharing is to mean not the reorganisation of the work process but only a lower real income, then there is bound to be resistance. One radical proposal in this area, from the women's movement, has been to rethink the nature of income from work. It has been argued by Anna Coote, for instance (Coote, 1981), that AES has been pursuing a male-oriented strategy of full employment with high real wages without having explored more radical arrangements of the work process.

The need to organise the working week or even the working year around the social needs of child-rearing, work satisfaction and some autonomy over the work process means that once again the arguments for new small-scale industrial units with high potential productivity and decentralised locations are very strong. Thus flexitime, the abolition or blurring of the distinction between full-time and part-time work (say, by reducing the working week to thirty hours), the provision of sabbatical leave for everyone in the active labour force, arrangements for day-release or short-term leave for taking up educational opportunities – all these must be important ingredients of any AES. They are not idealistic, but neither can they be implemented except through a planned medium-run strategy over perhaps ten or fifteen years. They are of great importance because they raise fundamental questions about the purpose of jobs and wages and economic activity in general.

A concomitant of these arrangements would be some down-grading of the role of private consumption and a boost for the role of publicly provided consumption goods. Such a rearrangement in favour of public consumption makes sense on several grounds. First, the need to restrict the growth of private consumption is imperative if funds are to be available for investment and if growth is not to lead to heavy imports. The strategy of increasing public investments in non-manufacturing industries and concentrating on new growth products dovetails with this. Second, the need to channel profits from existing protected industries to new growth industries will require a planned incomes policy which regulates wages, salaries, perks and prices. This will mean not only regulating the overall rate of growth of wages but also implementing a policy whereby wages in the protected industries do not grow more rapidly than in other sectors. A planned incomes policy should also tax managerial consumption privileges and surplus profits, and it should fashion a plan for wage income which will regulate its growth over the period of ten or fifteen years that will be needed to work through a restructuring of the economy. Thus the fiscal policy needed to redirect resources from consumption to investment and from old to new industries will require a downgrading of private consumption and the regulation of the growth of personal incomes.

The growth of public consumption, on the other hand, is necessary both to achieve traditional egalitarian aims and to facilitate the emergence of new work practices which treat women and men on an equal footing. Publicly provided meals, crèches, medical facilities available at places of work, access to educational opportunities at work or away from it, the financing of sabbaticals and short holidays as well as the adequate provision for the many income assistance schemes — all these will be necessary. Any medium-term plan will also need to stipulate a growth in leisure facilities — libraries, theatres, art galleries, museums, etc.

Thus a plan for restructuring the economy would require the growth of both public and private investment and public consumption over a period of five to ten years, if not longer. This would entail a planned incomes policy, an industrial restructuring policy, and an import-control policy (though with the proviso described above concerning the ploughback of profits). It would also require a fiscal package for raising resources through taxation and borrowing. It is best, therefore, to provide some detailed calculations for such a five-year plan.

## A five-year plan for full employment

If we accept the multiplier pessimism illustrated by some of the projections discussed above, a plan which could create 500,000 jobs per year for five years would require a public investment programme of £10 billion per annum, growing cumulatively to £50 billion by the end of the fifth year. Public investment will be 6.5 per cent of GDP by 1989. Along with private investment, this would take up 20 per cent of GDP. Such a high rate of investment would be necessary if each extra job cost anything up to £20,000. The economy would have to grow at a rate of 6.5 per cent per annum over this period to allow room for productivity growth as well as extra employment. This is an extraordinarily high growth rate and would put a strain on wages and prices if these were not made part of a plan. But the regulation of take-home income is also necessary because the needs of investment – public and private – and of public consumption mean that *there would be virtually no room for the growth of real take-home pay in the five years required to achieve full employment.*

This contention is based on the very crude illustrative macro-economic calculation which is given in Table 3. It is based on the figure of £20,000 per job as a necessary investment. The numbers involved assume a steady rate of inflation, 10 per cent per annum. The share of capital formation in government expenditure rises from its 1979 level of 6.5 per cent to its 1966 level of 13 per cent by 1989. Allowing for 20 per cent of GDP as investment's share, 25 per cent for exports and imports and government consumption at 25 per cent, there is only 55 per cent left for private consumption. If we translate this into the share of disposable income in GDP, it comes to 62 per cent by 1989. It is currently in the region of 80 per cent. So all the income growth has to be taken out of personal incomes

Table 3  Hypothetical projections for a maximal growth plan

| | Actual GDP (1975 prices) | Potential GDP (1975 prices) | Actual GDP (current prices) | Price level (1975 = 100; 1980 actual, other years projected) | Government expenditure (current prices) | Government consumption and investment (current prices) | Government consumption plus investment (1975 prices) |
|---|---|---|---|---|---|---|---|
| 1980 | 101 | | 193 | 200 | 105 | 64 | |
| 1981 | 98 | | 215 | 220 | 118 | 69 | |
| 1982 | 96 | | 230 | 242 | 128 | 76 | |
| 1983 | 98 | | 260 | 266 | | | |
| 1984 | 101(102) | 104.7 120 | 280 | 293 | 140 | 95 | 33 |
| 1985 | | 108.6 | | 322 | | 110 | |
| 1986 | | 112.6 | | 354 | | 128 | |
| 1987 | | 116.8 | | 389 | | 150 | |
| 1988 | | 121.1 136.7 | 570 640 | 470 | | | |
| 1989 | | | | | 315 | 205 | 44 |

*Note:* All absolute figures are in £ billions.

and put into investment and public consumption. There is just no room for a real wage explosion if full employment is to be achieved and the economy is to be restructured. The growth of public consumption (social wage), however, will be about 3.5 per cent per annum over the five years under this plan. Private income can grow by no more than 10 or 11 per cent — barely up to the assumed rate of inflation.

This is obviously a drastic proposal, but there is no reason to believe that it exaggerates the difficult situation that Labour will face when it comes to power. As the French resort to price freeze and devaluation in June 1982 showed, an employment-creation plan can rapidly run into trouble if such difficulties are not foreseen. These difficulties have to be made explicit and subjected to the widest public discussion if they are to be visited on the people. The promise of full employment, a restructured economy, the room that it will afford us for a drastic rethinking of income, work and leisure are the benefits. They will have to be delivered, of course, and this means no short-run blowing off course. The political task of the Labour Party is to discuss these questions openly and honestly with its supporters and to arrive at broad, democratic agreement that the sacrifices are worth the benefits. It can then begin to define the next step in the reshaping of the economy which will mark its progress towards a socialist society.

## Notes

1 Comments by Jane Lewis, Julian Le Grand and Henry Neuberger as well as members of the 'Labour Seminar' are gratefully acknowledged. Christine Wills was patience itself in the production of each of the four drafts through which the paper went. To her my thanks.

2 Upon reading Beveridge and Keynes again, one realises how much tougher they were on the kinds of reform that private capitalism had to undergo to become welfare capitalism. Thus Keynes' views are even today far ahead of the policies pursued in his name by postwar Governments: 'The state will have to exercise a guiding influence in the propensity to consume partly through its scheme of taxation, partly by fixing the rate of interest, and partly, perhaps, in other ways. Furthermore it seems unlikely that the influence of banking policy on the rate of interest will be sufficient by itself to determine an optimum rate of investment. I conceive, therefore, that a *somewhat comprehensive socialisation of investment* will prove the only means of securing an approximation to full employment. . . . If the state is able to determine the aggregate amount of resources devoted to augmenting the instruments and

the basic rate of reward to those who own them, it will have accomplished all that is necessary' ('Concluding Notes on the Social Philosophy Towards Which the General Theory Might Lead', *The General Theory*, ch. 24, p. 378; emphasis added). Beveridge had envisaged that, with full employment, the central direction of the labour force along the lines of wartime manpower budgeting would be required. He also clearly saw the case for state regulation of the wage bargain. See 'The war time triangle, 1941–5', ch. 10 in Middlemass (1979).

3  'There existed, so to speak, an implied contract between Government and people; the people refused none of the sacrifices that the Government demanded from them for the winning of the War; in return, they expected that the Government should show imagination and seriousness in preparing for the restoration and improvement of the nation's well-being when the War had been won. The plans for reconstruction were, therefore, a real part of the war effort' (Hancock and Gowing, 1953, p. 541).

4  For the US experience of the second Industrial Revolution, see Chandler (1977, 1978). For British experience in this period, see Payne (1978). The transformation in British attitudes towards industry has been charted in Weiner (1981) and also Hutchison (1951).

5  Middlemass (1979).

6  Publications on AES are appearing at a steadily accelerating rate. The main references are: CSE London Working Group, *The Alternative Economic Strategy*, and articles by Adam Sharples, Terry Ward, Sam Aaranovitch and Pat Devine in Currie and Smith (1981). Among these the Sharples paper is a very good overall survey and critique of AES, and it also contains a full bibliography. See also Glyn and Harrison (1981) and Aaranovitch (1981). There have been articles in *New Socialist* by Sapper (1981) and Coote (1981).

# References

Aaranovitch, S. (1981) *The Road to Thatcherism* (London: Lawrence & Wishart)

Barker, T. (1982) 'Long term recovery: a return to full employment?', *Lloyds Bank Review*, Jan., pp. 19–35

Blake, D. (1981) 'Is there an alternative to the Government's economic strategy?', *The Times*, 1–3 June

Blake, D., and Ormerod, P. (1980) *The Economics of Prosperity: Social Priorities in the Eighties* (London: Grant McIntyre)

Chandler, A. (1977) *The Visible Hand: the Managerial Revolution in American Business* (Cambridge, Mass.: MIT Press)

Chandler, A. (1978) 'The United States: evolution of enterprise', in Mathias and Postan (1978), Part 2, pp. 70–133

CSE London Working (1979) *The Alternative Economic Strategy* (London: Conference of Socialist Economists)

Coote, A. (1981) 'The AES: a new starting point', *New Socialist*, Nov./Dec., pp. 4–7

Cripps, *et al.* (1981) *Manifesto: A Radical Strategy for Britain's Future* (London: Pan)

Currie, D., and Smith, R. (1981) *Socialist Economic Review* (London: Merlin Press)

Glyn, A., and Harrison, J. (1981) *The British Economic Disaster* (London: Pluto Press)

Hancock, K., and Gowing, M. (1953) *The British War Economy* (London: HMSO)

Hutchinson, K. (1951) *The Decline and Fall of British Capitalism* (London: Cape)

Keynes, J. M. (1936) *The General Theory of Employment, Interest and Money* (London: Macmillan)

Mathias, P., and Postan, M. (eds.) (1978) *The Cambridge Economic History of Europe*, vol. 7 (Cambridge: CUP)

Middlemass, K. (1979) *Politics in Industrial Society: The Experience of the British System since 1911* (London: Deutsch)

Payne, P. (1978) 'Industrial entrepreneurs and management in Great Britain', in Mathias and Postan (1978), Part 1, pp. 180–230

Prais, S. (1977) *The Strike Proneness of Large Plants in Britain*, Discussion Paper No. 5 (London: National Institute of Economic and Social Research)

Sapper, A. (1981) 'The Alternative Economic Strategy', *New Socialist*, Sept./Oct., pp. 19–24

Singh, A. (1980) 'UK industry and the less developed countries: a long-term structural analysis of trade and its impact (Department of Applied Economics, University of Cambridge)

Weiner, M. (1981) *The Decline of the Industrial Spirit in Britain* (Cambridge: Cambridge University Press)

# 5

# Privatisation and the Social Services

## Julian Le Grand

Among the colder of the elements affecting the current climate
for socialism is the wind of privatisation. In almost every area of
public activity the present Government has proposed, advocated
and, in some cases, implemented policies for substantially
reducing the role of the state. The profitable parts of nationalised industries and state services are being sold off to the private
sector. Currently unprofitable parts are being ruthlessly cut so
as to facilitate their eventual sale. And state subsidies to the
private manufacturing and services sectors are being systematically withdrawn.

Nowhere has this phenomenon been more pronounced than
in what are commonly considered to be the 'social' services: housing, education, the National Health Service, public transport
and the personal social services. The Government is forcing
through the sale of council houses while at the same time reducing the subsidies to those remaining in public ownership. The
Department of Education and Science has actively considered
ways in which the present system of grants for students in
higher education could be replaced by some form of loans
scheme. In the recent past both Sir Keith Joseph and Margaret
Thatcher have expressed considerable interest in the idea of education 'vouchers'; indeed, the present assisted places programme
can be viewed as a form of voucher scheme.[1] In 1982, a widely
leaked think-tank report recommended the replacement of the
National Health Service by compulsory private insurance. The
Department of Health and Social Security has been investigating
the possibilities of 'contracting out' hospital catering and clean-
ing services. A combination of eccentric legal decisions and of

Government reluctance to countenance further increases in public expenditure is forcing public transport operators to pursue break-even policies, while regulations restricting the competition they face from private operators are being removed. Old people's and children's homes are being cut back, and the care of their current and prospective inmates is being forced on to the 'community'.

The standard reaction to such proposals from many on the left is to condemn them root and branch. For them, any attempt to reduce public control and expenditure (particularly by a government of the stripe of the present one) is anathema and to be resisted at all costs. The welfare state is among the pinnacles of socialist achievement; its boundaries are to be defended to the death, come what may.

But such a view is short-sighted. The welfare state is far from perfect. Its services are often inefficient, inegalitarian and undemocratic. Reforms are necessary in many areas, and these reforms may involve elements of so-called 'privatisation'. What is needed is a method of sorting out good reforms from bad ones, where 'good' and 'bad' are defined in terms of socialist principles. To provide such a method, and to make some effort at the actual sorting out, is the aim of this chapter.

There are two essential preliminaries. The first is to specify the principles by which the reforms are to be judged. To provide, and to justify in a suitably comprehensive fashion, a full list of socialist principles is a task well beyond the scope of this chapter. Instead I shall simply state in very general terms what I take to be the principles underlying socialists' support of the welfare state. These are the promotion of social justice; the attainment of economic and social efficiency; and the furthering of the sense of community. The concepts involved (justice, efficiency, community) are broad; where appropriate, more specific interpretations will be offered as the discussion proceeds.

The second preliminary is a classification of the privatisation proposals that have been put forward in the context of the social services. These may be divided into three. First, there are those involving a reduction of state *provision*. These require a reduction in the assets and institutions owned by the state and in the numbers of people it employs. Examples are the sale of council houses, the closing of local authority residential establishments and most education voucher schemes.[2] Second, there are proposals involving a reduction in state *subsidy*. These require users of the service concerned to pay more towards its cost and hence to make it more self-supporting. Examples include the raising of council house rents, the replacement of student grants by loans and 'break-even' requirements for public transport. Third, there are proposals for reducing the amount of state *regulation*; an example is the removal of restrictions on the operation of private bus companies.

In what follows I shall concentrate upon those proposals that involve a reduction in provision and in subsidy. This is partly because there are fewer of the third kind of proposal – reduction in regulation – in the context of the social services, and partly because it seems important to emphasise the distinction between state provision and state subsidy. It appears to be widely believed, at least within the social services, that if the state provides a service, the service must be provided free – or at least at a heavily subsidised price. But there is, of course, no such necessity. It is perfectly possible to have state ownership without state subsidy (an example is British Gas) and equally to have state subsidy without ownership (examples are tax subsidies for owner-occupiers and private education, discussed below). Moreover, it is possible to argue for one without necessarily supporting the other. The merits and demerits of expanding or contracting state provision are quite different from those of increasing or reducing state subsidy. Much of the rest of this chapter will be devoted to establishing this proposition.

## The case for state provision

State provision of a social service is justified if the outcome is more efficient, more just and more socially cohesive than either private provision on its own or private provision coupled with some other form of state intervention such as regulation or subsidy. There are a number of reasons why private provision of the social services, or private provision with state regulation or subsidy, might fail in this sense when compared with state provision. Of these, the major ones concern the exploitation of monopoly power and the promotion of social divisions, and it is on these I shall concentrate.

The exploitation of monopoly power is undesirable because it is inefficient and because it leads to an unjust distribution of rewards. If the social services were run entirely privately, the opportunities for such exploitation would be legion. They would derive from a number of sources.

First, certain groups have a monopoly on essential skills. The classic example here is the British Medical Association, which, through its influence over the numbers entering medical schools, the graduation requirements of those schools and the entry requirements for foreign doctors, can control the numbers of people who practise as doctors in this country.

Second, there may be 'natural' monopolies within some parts of the social services — cases where private competition would be uneconomic and where, if it existed, it would rapidly degenerate into private monopoly. Natural monopolies arise when there are economies of scale in production; the major example of this within the social services is the railways, with their high fixed costs of track installation and maintenance.

A third source of monopoly power is the difficulty that users of a service often face in obtaining information. This problem is particularly acute in the case of health care, education and personal social services. Because of the specialised nature of medical knowledge, it is difficult for patients adequately to assess the value of the advice that doctors give them. This confers considerable power on medical personnel, for if they choose (and in a private market they have a strong incentive so to do), they can recommend only marginally beneficial operations or other expensive courses of treatment with little fear that their recommendations will be challenged. Similarly, it is often difficult for parents adequately to assess the quality of the education being offered by different schools or colleges, and private institutions do not find it difficult to exploit this ignorance. Private residential homes, particularly those for the elderly, also offer many opportunities for exploitation because of ignorance: the ignorance of the residents themselves, often half-anaesthetised through lack of stimulation, and the ignorance of their relatives, who know little of what actually goes on in the home outside visiting hours.

A fourth source of monopoly power prevalent in the areas with which the social services deal is the cost of finding alternatives. In many cases, if one is dissatisfied with the service received it is difficult, if not impossible, to 'shop around'. Patients in hospitals, parents of children taking exams, families in privately rented accommodation, all find it difficult to move to an alternative, even if they know of one, and all are to that extent locked into their situations. Here again there are obvious opportunities for exploitation by private entrepreneurs.

Now, the existence of (or potential for) monopoly exploitation is not in and of itself an argument for state provision. Private monopolies can also be controlled by the regulation of standards and profits. Thus private hospitals, schools and residential homes can be monitored by inspectors; profits can be regulated, so that if they rise above a certain level, the institutions or individuals concerned are forced to lower their prices. Indeed, there is already much regulation of this kind. The rent of most privately rented accommodation has been controlled in Britain since 1915. Inspectors monitor both the public and the private sectors of education. And private residential homes are subject to a system of licensing.

But regulation entails a number of pitfalls. First, because no one else has the necessary expertise, members of regulatory agencies are commonly drawn from the service they are regulating. For instance, in some states of the USA the state medical regulation board is actually the local branch of the American Medical Association! As a result, these agencies often operate more in the interest of those whom they are supposed to be regulating than in the public interest. Second, the regulation of monopoly profits faces an intrinsic dilemma: if the regulation permits too high a return to the monopolists, this is obviously unsatisfactory from the point of view of social justice; but if the regulated return is too low — that is, if it is set below the return that could be earned elsewhere — capital will be withdrawn from the service concerned, leading to its eventual demise. The classic case of the latter is rent control. At the end of the First World War, when rent control was introduced, about 90 per cent of all dwellings were rented; now the proportion is less than 16 per cent, and it continues to shrink.

So state provision seems preferable to regulation as a means of preventing the private exploitation of monopoly power. But that is not its only merit. Another advantage is that it permits a degree of control over the service that private provision cannot match. This control can be used for a number of purposes, perhaps the most important of which is the promotion of a sense of community. A clear case is that of education. As Blaug (1970, p. 118) argues, some agreement on some fundamental values is necessary for the very existence of society, and state education can contribute to this through the inculcation of those values. The private provision of education encourages the setting up of schools by religious and other groups with values at variance with those of the wider society. Also social stability depends in part on different groups' knowledge and awareness of each other; but extensive private education is more likely even than the present system to lead to schools segregated according to parental class, income or race. State ownership and control of schools thus seems an essential tool for the preservation of the community.

Nor is this advantage confined to education. Under the National Health Service the middle and working classes find themselves in the same hospital wards and in the same out-patient clinics, and — to some extent — they use the same GP surgeries. All this makes a small, but not insignificant, contribution to social mixing. More important, state ownership of housing can be used to create more heterogeneous communities through the building or purchase of properties in areas otherwise dominated by owner-occupation. Admittedly, it rarely has been used in this way; local authorities apparently prefer to create large estates of which the chief characteristic is homogeneity rather than variety. But this is not a necessary consequence of public housing policy; rather, it is the outcome of the unimaginative exercise of that policy.

Moreover, private provision can hinder the growth of community in a yet more fundamental way. The mainspring of private markets is competition; and, by its very nature, competition is antithetical to the spirit of fellow feeling that is an essential ingredient of a viable community. A system that uses self-interest as its major motivating force both legitimates and encourages insensitivity to the concerns of others. Hence, as Richard Titmuss has argued in his celebrated book *The Gift Relationship* (1970), any extension of the private market's role into areas from which it is currently excluded diminishes the opportunity for the spread of values and behaviour of which society approves, such as altruistic acts, while at the same time encouraging the expression of attitudes that in other contexts it condemns, such as selfishness and greed.

Thus state provision appears to have significant advantages over private provision in terms both of its ability to restrain the inefficiencies and injustices created by the exercise of private monopoly power and of its contribution to social stability and community. But this is not to say that state provision is without problems of its own. State services can be inefficient and wasteful. They are often bureaucratic and insensitive to the needs of their users. And their contribution to the sense of community is purchased at the expense of certain liberties − the freedom of parents to send their children to schools of their own choice, the freedom to choose one's own doctor, the freedom to live next to, and to mix with, one's own kind.

But although these difficulties are real, it is important not to be over-impressed by them. Popular mythology, fuelled by anecdote rather than by scientific investigation, has exaggerated the relative inefficiency of state enterprises. A study by Robert Millward (1982) of the relative efficiency of public and private corporations around the world that are engaged in the same activity concluded that management in private enterprise was, with the exception of refuse disposal, *less* efficient than its counterpart in the public sector. Of course, there is inefficiency in the social services; given the general inefficiencies of the UK economy, it would be very surprising if they were immune. But there is no evidence to suggest that they are more susceptible than private industry. Bureaucratic insensitivity is also undoubtedly prevalent in the social services; but this seems to be a function more of the size of the relevant institutions than of the fact they are state-owned. Decentralisation and a greater degree of democratic accountability would seem to be the solution here rather than a return to the private market.

The problem concerning the erosion of liberty by state provision is rather different from the others. For it concerns the aims of the welfare state themselves rather than the ability of different forms of organisation to achieve those aims. Libertarians commonly define liberty in terms of the absence of coercion: and in this rather limited sense of the term there is little doubt that there is a trade-off between liberty and the attainment of other aims such as social justice and community (that is, measures designed to achieve the latter will involve some encroachment on the former). Whether this matters will depend on, first, the relative value placed on liberty compared with the other objectives and, second, the extent of the encroachment. Most defenders of the welfare state would place a lower priority on the claims of liberty than would extreme libertarians; they would also argue that the welfare state's effects on liberty are often less dramatic than libertarians allege. For instance, whether it is parents who choose the school to which a child is sent or the state, the liberty of the child is abrogated; there does not seem to be any reason, even on libertarian grounds, necessarily to prefer the tyranny of parents to that of the state.

All in all, therefore, the case for continuing state provision (albeit with improvements in the sensitivity and accountability of the relevant institutions) and for resisting privatisation proposals involving a reduction in that provision is robust. Unfortunately, the same cannot be said of proposals that involve reductions in state subsidy, as we shall now see.

## The case against state subsidy

The offering of services by state-owned agencies at little or no charge to all prospective users is widespread throughout the social services. Obvious examples include most medical care under the National Health Service, almost all forms of state education and social work assistance. Other services are provided at a price which, although not negligible, is substantially below that which would obtain in the absence of subsidy; examples are dental care, residential homes, council housing and public transport. For some services the amount will depend on the user's means or circumstances, but even the maximum charge in such cases is generally well below the cost of the services used.

Not only does the state subsidise its own services but it also subsidises private-sector activities in the same areas. There are direct grants to house owners for the purpose of improving their property; various subsidies to first-time house buyers, such as the option mortgage scheme; and assistance to local authorities who wish to place children in private schools.

More important, there is a variety of tax reliefs and exemptions which have exactly the same impact on the public budget as direct grants to the individuals concerned. Of these, by far the most important are the tax exemptions available to owner-occupiers, including mortgage interest tax relief and the exemption of the proceeds of the sale of owner-occupied houses from capital gains tax. The first has been estimated as costing £2,030 million in 1981/2 and the second as costing £2,800 million (*Government's Expenditure Plans*, 1982, vol. II, p. 98) – costs that together amount to nearly 50 per cent more than total *direct* expenditure on housing in that year (£3,320 million: ibid., vol. I, p. 13). Indeed, the total involved is even larger if, as many argue, the relevant tax expenditure is not mortgage interest tax relief but the non-taxation of imputed income (roughly, the rent that owner-occupiers would have to pay if they did not own their own houses);[3] for this has recently been estimated as £6,000 million (Shelter, 1982, p. 10).

Less significant in terms of absolute amounts but equally important in terms of symbolic value are the tax reliefs that accrue to private education. Private schools, by virtue of their charitable status, are exempt from income tax, corporation tax and capital gains tax on any of their income or profits. Gifts to private schools are partly exempt from capital transfer tax; and they are entitled to a 50 per cent reduction in rates. A Labour Party publication (1980, p. 29) has estimated the tax loss from all these sources as £38.5 million in 1980/1.

Subsidies in one form or another are thus endemic to the social services. But is subsidisation – on this scale and in this form – consistent with the principles underlying the welfare state, as summarised at the beginning of this chapter? It is far from clear that it is.

Subsidy can be justified on the grounds of efficiency or of

social justice. A subsidy to a service can be efficient if the service concerned confers what economists term 'external benefits' or if, in the production of that service, there are economies of scale. External benefits arise when an individual using the service benefits not only himself or herself but also others not directly involved in the decision to use the service. A classic example is vaccination: if I decide to be vaccinated against a particular disease, this not only reduces the chance of my getting the disease but also reduces the chance of your catching it from me. Other oft quoted examples are: commuters using public transport rather than driving to work, thus reducing rush-hour congestion and delays to other travellers; the renovation of slum property, which raises the values of other houses in the neighbourhood; and the increase in political, cultural and social awareness that results from education.

If external benefits exist, then there is a case for some subsidy to the services concerned. For if individuals have to pay the full cost of a service each time they use it, they will not use it as much as would be consistent with social efficiency. For instance, consider the decision concerning whether or not to be vaccinated. In making that decision individuals will take account only of the costs and benefits to themselves; unless they are unusually altruistic they will not consider the benefits that may accrue to others. If they are charged the full cost of the vaccination, for some this private cost/benefit calculation will result in their deciding not to be vaccinated, an outcome that is likely to be inefficient from a *social* cost/benefit point of view that took account of the wider benefits of vaccination. In such cases, one way of ensuring that in making their private decisions individuals also make socially efficient decisions is to subsidise the price of the service concerned, so that the right number of individuals will use the service.

Do the social services create external benefits on such a scale as to justify the existing levels of subsidy? This is extremely doubtful. The only area of health care that confers external benefits of the kind discussed here is that concerned with infectious diseases. This accounts for only 3 per cent of the National Health Service budget, an amount that is hardly sufficient, on its own, to merit providing the whole service free. Education is supposed to create external benefits that legitimate subsidy: its contribution to labour productivity and hence to the nation's wealth, and its encouraging of culture and social stability. But in neither instance is the case strong. The increase in labour productivity is not really an 'external' benefit at all, for if an individual's productivity is increased by education, then this will be reflected in the income that he or she can command. The benefit will thus be internal rather than external; in so far as the nation benefits, it will be through the normal process of exchange (income for skills) rather than as a by-product of other activities. The promotion of social stability is a legitimate externality; as we noted earlier, education does have a role to play in promoting social cohesion. But, as was also noted earlier, this role is better promoted by state ownership and control of schools; simply subsidising people to send their children to privately owned schools is likely to promote social divisiveness rather than social harmony.

There is a slightly better case for subsidising housing and public transport on the grounds of external benefits. A building's state of repair or disrepair undoubtedly affects its immediate neighbourhood. Indeed, the whole process of gentrification on the one hand and of slum creation on the other is a classic example of what happens when markets operate in the presence of external benefits or costs. However, only one of the vast array of housing subsidies is specifically directed at external maintenance: housing improvement grants. These constitute only about 2 per cent of direct housing expenditures; none of the remaining 98 per cent of direct expenditures or the 100 per cent of tax expenditures can seriously be justified in this way.

Public transport too confers external benefits by virtue of its impact on road congestion. However, this benefit arises only because rush-hour road travel itself is subsidised. Motorists travelling during peak hours do not pay the full cost of their activity; in particular, they do not pay for the delays, extra pollution and psychological aggravation that they create. Rather than subsidise public transport as well, the sensible way to deal with this problem would be to levy a charge on rush-hour drivers, as is done in, for instance, Singapore.

In short, therefore, the general case for subsidising the social services on the grounds of external benefit is weak. What of the second efficiency argument: economies of scale? We have already encountered these as part of the arguments justifying state provision. For reasons that are somewhat technical and that are therefore consigned to a note,[4] their existence can also be used to justify state subsidy. However, as noted above, it is likely that within the social services this point is of relevance only to capital expenditure on the railways.

Let us now consider the case for subsidies as a means of promoting social justice. In the context of the social services justice is generally interpreted either in terms of minimum standards or, more broadly, in terms of equality. That is, the aim seems to be to ensure either that the poor make at least a minimum use of the service concerned or that there is greater equality of use right across the social spectrum.[5] However, it is not clear that subsidising services is a useful way of attaining either end. Simply making a service free, or offering it at a low price, is no guarantee that the poor will use it; for instance, despite decades of grants to cover fees and maintenance, today less than 3 per cent of the relevant age range in the working class go to university (Halsey, 1980, p. 108). Nor is there any guarantee that the poor's use of subsidised services will increase in relation to that of the rich. Again, the example of universities is instructive: over the past fifty years the gap between the proportion of the middle class that goes to university and that of the working class has actually widened, both in absolute and in relative terms (ibid.).

Moreover, many social service subsidies offend against another interpretation of social justice: that of distributing resources towards the poor. It has been estimated (Le Grand, 1982) that by comparison with the amounts received by the bottom fifth of the population, the top fifth receives 40 per cent more National Health Service subsidy per person ill, 50 per cent more total education subsidy per person in the relevant age range (including over five times as much more university subsidy), seven times as much tax expenditure on owner-occupiers and nearly ten times as much on rail travel. It is difficult to reconcile such figures with a commitment to social justice, however the latter is defined.

It has to be acknowledged that not all social services subsidies have the characteristic of favouring the better-off. In particular, means-tested benefits, such as rent rebates and allowances, favour the less well-off. However, these raise problems of their own. Because of their relatively low take-up rates, they do not contribute to social justice as much as they might, and the stigma often associated with them by both recipients and non-recipients promotes social divisiveness.

More generally, the widespread subsidy of the social services has a more insidious impact on redistribution. The fact that health care, education, housing and so on are heavily subsidised fuels the widespread belief that Britain is a broadly egalitarian and just society. The poor are supposed to make substantial use of these services; if they do not exploit the opportunities available to them, then this simply illustrates their general feckless-ness and irresponsibility. In particular, given that they receive all these services free, there is no case for trying to ensure that they have higher incomes or own a larger fraction of the nation's wealth. Views such as these can act as a substantial impediment to genuine redistribution, and widespread subsidies to the social services must therefore bear some of the responsibility for the failure to eliminate poverty and deprivation in contemporary Britain.

Overall, therefore, it is difficult to make a case on the grounds of either efficiency or social justice for extensive subsidy of the social services. It is easier to support means-tested sub-sidies on the grounds of justice at least; however, they offend against the third aim of the welfare state, that of the promotion of community.

## Implications for policy

Two principal conclusions emerge from this discussion. On the one hand, the case for state provision of social services remains a powerful one. Because of, among other things, the existence of powerful professional organisations, economies of scale, poorly informed users and the high cost of alternatives, the social ser-vices offer innumerable opportunities for the exploitation of private monopoly power, and private exploitation of such power creates substantial inefficiency and injustice. Further, by encouraging and legitimating self-interested behaviour at the expense of co-operation or altruism, private provision exacerbates social divisions and thereby offends against any spirit of community that the welfare state is trying to promote.

This implies that privatisation proposals involving a reduction in state provision should be strongly resisted. These include the sale of council houses; the closing of local authority residential homes for children and the elderly; and the education voucher scheme, which, in most of its variants, predicates an expansion of private education and a corresponding reduction in state provision. More positively, the role of private provision in the social services, far from being increased, should be actually reduced. In particular the phasing out of private medicine and private education must remain a key element of Labour policy, for both medical care and education offer unparalleled opportunities for the exploitation of monopoly power; moreover, their public provision makes an essential contribution to social cohesion and a sense of community.

On the other hand, the case for state subsidy is, in many cases, significantly weaker than the case for state provision. Public subsidies to the social services can rarely be justified in terms of social efficiency. Further, such subsidies often contribute to, rather than reduce, social injustice, for by and large they benefit the better-off to a greater extent than the poor; moreover, their existence contributes to the (mistaken) belief that Britain is a highly egalitarian society and thereby impedes genuine redistribution. Means-tested services are a partial exception to this; however, they are widely considered to exacerbate social division.

Thus privatisation proposals that involve a reduction in state subsidy should generally be welcomed. In particular, the following deserve serious consideration.

First, subsidies to higher education are among the worst offenders in terms of promoting social injustice; moreover, they are difficult to justify in terms of efficiency. Hence they should be substantially reduced, if not eliminated altogether. Institutions of higher and further education should be required to charge fees that accurately reflect the cost of educating their students. Simultaneously, the student grant scheme should be replaced by some form of government-provided loans. Alternatively, the grant could be increased to cover the increased fees, the means test dropped and a special tax introduced on the earnings of graduates to retrieve the money spent. Second, all tax subsidies to owner-occupiers should be withdrawn. Again, it is impossible to justify their continuation on the grounds of efficiency and justice. Similarly, the tax advantages of private education should be removed (thus, it is to be hoped, contributing to its demise). Third, charges on road travel in cities at peak hours should be introduced. This would promote the more efficient use of road space and would have desirable distributional consequences as well. Moreover, it would permit operating subsidies to public transport (perhaps the most inegalitarian of all subsidies within the social services) to be phased out.

Public expenditure savings that result from any of these proposals could be channelled into those areas of the welfare state that benefit the less well-off. These include subsidies to council houses and most of the social security system (particularly pensions and supplementary benefit). As a result, some measure of genuine redistribution would be achieved.

Although many of these proposals are in line with official Party policy, others will be more controversial – particularly, I suspect, those that involve the withdrawal of subsidy from such cherished institutions of the welfare state as universities and public transport. But if an instrument has failed to achieve its ends, that instrument, however hallowed, must eventually be discarded. While state provision has been an effective tool for promoting efficiency, social justice and community, the same cannot be said of state subsidy; hence while the former has to be defended, the latter must be curtailed.

## Notes

1   The idea behind education vouchers is that a child's parents are given a voucher equal in value to the cost of educating that child. They can present this voucher to any school of their choice; the school then redeems the voucher for cash from the Department of Education. Most of the proposed schemes permit parents also to supplement the voucher with cash payments if necessary.

2   Although it is not a necessary feature of education voucher schemes, it is generally assumed that a large proportion of schools would be privately owned and operated.

3   For a fuller explanation of the issues involved, see Le Grand (1982, pp. 90–1).

4   If there are economies of scale, then the marginal cost of production will fall below the average cost. In that case, pricing according to marginal cost, as required by efficiency, will generate insufficient revenue to cover the full costs of production: hence a subsidy will be needed.

5   This is only one of the possible interpretations of equality in the context of the social services. For a fuller discussion, see Le Grand (1982, ch. 2).

# References

Blaug, M. (1970) *An Introduction to the Economics of Education* (Harmondsworth: Penguin)

*The Government's Expenditure Plans 1982/3 to 1984/5* (1982) Cmnd 8494/I and II (London: HMSO)

Halsey, A. H., Heath, A. F., and Ridge, J. M. (1980) *Origins and Destinations* (Oxford: OUP)

Labour Party (1980) *Private Schools* (London: Labour Party)

Le Grand, J. (1982) *The Strategy of Equality* (London: Allen & Unwin)

Millward, R. (1982) 'The comparative performance of public and private ownership', in Lord Roll (ed.), *The Mixed Economy* (London: Macmillan)

Shelter (1982) *Housing and the Economy* (London: Shelter)

Titmuss, R. (1970) *The Gift Relationship* (London: Allen & Unwin)

# 6

# Income Maintenance
Mike Reddin

## Private sweats and public chills

While the sensitivity of our political and economic thermo-
meters is always suspect, times are indeed cold for some and
decidedly frosty for many more. Those who believe that cold is a
Good Thing see expenditure cuts chilling us back to consciousness: we will stir ourselves to survive rather than lazily adjusting
the Welfare State thermostat.

In contrast, real people behave in different ways when temp-
eratures fall. Some have no options: they are too old, poor, confused or weary and they shiver away with hypothermia. Some,
younger or more vigorous than the rest, exercise themselves and
generate some personal warmth. Others, more passive or more
affluent, put on more clothes or order extra fuel. Yet others find
it pays to congregate around a common fire heating many
hands: each individual then spends less time gathering sticks
and more keeping warm. What all may realise is that colder
climates demand more thought, time and energy — just to keep
warm: what each may start to realise is that savings on the
public fuel bill may be offset by private costs.

## Clearing the ground

Income maintenance policies have to combine credibility with
flexibility: they must be reliable whilst being changeable (US
Dept HEW, 1979). They must be credible to those who are
taxed or save today and to those who may be beneficiaries
tomorrow. Yet this future, its resources and their distribution,
can never be fully guaranteed under *any* social or economic sys-

tem. There will always be dependencies. They will hinge on our future capacity to generate resources, on our ability to maintain purchasing power and on the future acceptability of our credentials when we claim our personal resource share. Finally, inedible cash has to be convertible into goods and services: we are all dependent on somebody's future will to produce them.

This last dependency does not require a work force of a particular size. Current anxieties focus on the contributor/dependency ratio, a fear that too few worker-taxpayers must support more and longer-living beneficiaries. But we do not need *individual* contributors. We can tax anything we like, just as future incomes can buy goods and services from a tiny work force, possibly in another country: one fat oil well (ours) may be sufficient to finance our future. Our concern must be with the resource/dependency ratio. Since that resource future (and the will to share it) cannot be guaranteed, the credibility of future promises is always limited.

Income-maintenance policies must also incorporate the capacity to change. Our society will change, and we will change our expectations. Fixed and inflexible systems become increasingly ill-fitting; they lose their compatibility with the people they are designed to serve. Thus we must have policy structures which can be modified, dismantled or reconstructed. Our ideal policy-maker had best be a pre-fab builder and demolition worker rather than a monumental mason.

## Premises

In the longer term I assume that a more equal society is most likely to be achieved when both the target and the route to it are openly declared: rather than pursue social goals by stealth, we need to 'come out' for our social objectives. Further, whenever possible, this openness should be expressed in the fabric of our social programmes and not just in their rhetorical preambles.

Such an explicit, visible approach may be highly vulnerable — especially in cold times. It is argued that the welfare states which prosper (in terms of spending on public programmes), and with least popular resistance, are those which rely upon indirect 'invisible' taxes: the nations in welfare decline are those with high visible rates of direct taxation. If this thesis is correct, then my plea for high visibility may be strategically dangerous (Wilensky, 1974).

Much may rest on our level of 'civic literacy' — do we understand the workings of our social programmes, or what assumptions do we carry about the ways in which they work? (Harris and Seldon, 1979). It is not inconceivable that if we understood our social and economic world better and appreciated both the efficacy and efficiency of some public actions, we would support them more positively (Preston, 1973).

It is hardly surprising that we are reluctant tax-payers when Governments of all persuasions view public spending so negatively or apologetically. However, this antagonism exists at a time when individuals are persuaded to part with more and more of their earnings to finance 'private' benefits. The private tax bill (for company pensions or health insurance) has been growing dramatically, often to exceed the public claim (*Lloyds Bank Economic Bulletin*, 1980).

We seem willing to pay, at least, for things which we view as offering us some advantage. It is crucial to recoup this private welfare spending into the fabric of our society, for the benefit of all. Affirming the advantages which flow from our *public* taxes will be a necessary part of any rehabilitation of public action and public policy: visible tax systems will not hinder the growth of welfare in a world which views its welfare positively or sees private advantages in public acts.

The world of income maintenance is large, and this discussion is necessarily limited. A comprehensive review of income-support schemes would range from the individual self-helper through the collectives of private insurance to the occupationally based collective response; from the workings of local authority income benefits, and the court's role in compelling income transfers, to the major state social security systems and the tax treatment of them all. Increasingly, income support schemes must accommodate job (income) creation programmes and 'industrial subsidy' in its many shapes and forms. I deal with but a few of these components. My primary focus will be how we are to pay for our current and future benefits assuming that the future continues cold.

This analysis does not assume that all is rotten in the state of UK income maintenance. The complex ways in which schemes interact with the society in which they operate make it hard to know just *how* they work or *why* they work as they do. Hesitancy in crying 'Success' or 'Disaster' stems from this recognition of uncertainty, which is far from saying that nothing can be said. There *are* major weaknesses in our current income maintenance policies and practices which require redress. First, many schemes are too restrained in their financial techniques, and this limits their capacity to cope with future needs. Second, many of these techniques are *invisible* to the social eye and this has major negative social consequences; the widespread use of *employer's contributions* creates a false sense of dependency, of something for nothing, and extends the studied servility which characterises British industrial relations. Third, our systems are far too closely associated with employment. It is particularly foolish to link work and welfare in an age of uncertain job futures, and especially cynical to pursue non-transferable, job-based 'occupational welfare'. Fourth, we have too long tolerated the juxtaposition of choice and welfare. There is no reason why choice should be expropriated by the private sector of the mixed economy: choice can and must find a positive place *within* the public welfare agenda. Fifth, as 'public minimalists' we have privatised generosity. The curse of the subsistence minimum hangs over our state benefits: we must raise most of them dramatically.

We operate a generally efficient social security system, cheaply run and 'ripe for development': it is to the neglect of this potential that we shall turn. State provisions both could and should be setting the pace with creative redistributions rather than apologetically letting the private tail wag the public policy dog.

## False scents and false equations

Income maintenance is rife with false scents and false equations. For instance, we observe one component of a system (e.g. its contributions), designate it as progressive or regressive in character and assume that all that flows from the component will reflect the trait. Yet progressive benefits can be derived from regressive tax bases and vice versa: we have to observe our income support schemes in the round. Redistributive effects are a product of six main dimensions in three matching sets. The input side describes who pays for a benefit, how much they pay towards it and for how long they go on paying. Outcomes are juxtaposed with these inputs, asking who receives the benefit, how much they receive and for how long they receive it. Alter any one of these six variables and we alter the redistributive consequences: we need a complete equation before we can describe a system's impact.

Again, we falsely equate some *techniques* for income support, like funding (schemes based on savings) with certain kinds of *agency* (like 'private' or 'occupational' agencies), when the technique could be operated by any kind of agency — the state, trade unions or local communities. Likewise, we falsely equate a *technique* (e.g. funding) with a particular *attribute* (security) as if it were innately true that a funded scheme is safe from depredation. We have too frequently been confused by such juxtapositions or, more seriously, have damned strategies because of an ideological association of technique, agency and attribute. I shall try to distinguish the components from their assumed qualities.

## Paying for today and tomorrow

We have to pay for the benefits we promise ourselves and others, but we have a wide range of options as to methods. I concentrate here on who now pays for benefits and on some assertions as to who should do so. I then turn to consider whether these payments should be made *specifically* or *generally* (that is, through contributory or non-contributory systems) and only then consider the *techniques* (such as savings or taxes) that we might use to realise our aspirations. Throughout I try to point out that these are *separable* dimensions which we can further distinguish from choices about the *agencies* which might be used for their implementation. Different approaches may suit different benefits, and no particular approach is inherently progressive or inherently egalitarian. Our guidelines must be: how does this approach work out? Who is advantaged by it? And at whose expense?

## Who pays now?

In the UK three characters are currently viewed as paying for benefits – employees, employers and the Exchequer. I want to look briefly behind the façade of these persona and suggest some additions to the cast.

Any discussion of who pays or should pay must begin with the question of *incidence*: does a tax or contribution rest where it is first placed? A tax levied on a car at the point of sale is forwarded to the tax collector by the person who sells the car. But since the tax is part of the purchase price of the car, the tax is actually *paid* by the car buyer. Less visibly, if the car is bought for a company, then the tax is incorporated in company costs and moved forward (via the price of its products) to be met from consumers' pockets. Thus *all* taxes end up as levied on consumers: only individuals pay taxes (Sandford *et al.*, 1980). So what of the venerable tripartite contributory system?

The employer's contribution is best recognised as an employee contribution at one remove – the employer holds back part of the employee's wage. The employee in turn pays contributions from wages. Employer and employee contributions combine as labour costs which must then be accommodated in prices: again, it is the consumer who stands at the bottom line. (Thus, we cannot make employers pay taxes. Individuals alone, in Wendell Holmes' phrase, can pay taxes, 'the price of a civilised society'.)

In the same vein we can consider the Exchequer contribution to UK social insurance (now reduced to 15 per cent of contribution income). It is derived from the multitude of taxes upon which the Exchequer calls, and its distributive 'input' characteristics are thus in direct proportion to the composition and incidence of these various revenue sources. (In 1980/1 some 42 per cent of Exchequer revenues came from income taxes, some 8 per cent from corporation taxes and some 39 per cent from taxes on expenditure.) The character of this Exchequer contribution thus changes over time as the balance of taxes changes.

Taxes and contributions are not, however, the only ways in which we pay for benefits. Some people die young: the life-long contributor who dies at the retirement party makes a generous donation to survivors. Men generally die earlier than women and thus make transfers to women's benefit costs. Some people leave the country: those of us who remain enjoy some benefit from their departure and former taxes. Society may gain financially as a result of divorce: whereas formerly we were collectively liable to pay benefit to a dependent spouse (with no extra contribution from the person upon whom he or she was dependent), we now have two single people each responsible for taxes and contributions to buy his or her own single benefits. We gain substantially if a married woman works in paid employment for a period of up to fifteen years. If she did not work, then she could enjoy benefit 'free of charge' as a dependent of her husband. Typically, she will need to work and contribute for about fifteen years before earning enough pension benefit in her own right to equal that dependent's addition. Again, in funded pension schemes (the occupational funds) those of us who have been immobile, who have stayed in our jobs, have long benefited from the bequests of the mobile — those pension and benefit assets which were left behind as they moved to other jobs: this has resulted in substantial transfers from manual to non-manual workers and from women to men. Similarly, the pension-fund beneficiary (apart from the benevolence of tax relief on a grand scale) enjoys income from the fund's investment earnings: those earnings were someone else's loan costs — transfers into the fund from those debtors. And so on, and so on.

In brief, many people help to pay for benefits. Many are hard to identify and we are often simultaneously contributors and beneficiaries. We cannot talk simplistically of three contributory parties nor assume too easily who 'finally' pays for benefits. If it is only individuals who *can* pay, the relevant questions now become: which individuals should these be? And how should they pay, through savings or taxes, by contributory or non-contributory means?

*How should we pay: funding, Pay-As-You-Go or hybrids?*

Revenue from any *source* (a tax on workers' incomes or on video tape purchases) can be used in conjunction with any *technique* to help fund (through savings) or to provide current income (Pay As You Go: PAYG) to finance current benefits. PAYG gives us immediate flexibility – the capacity to respond quickly or to make changes when desired rather than wait for funds to accrue. It is also, of course, a technique which can be exercised only by continuing institutions, of which perhaps the state is the sole living example. PAYG ties us to the immediate capacity of the contemporary economy to deliver the cash we need, so that it may make sense to have some level of reserve to cushion us against sudden changes and to give us further flexibility, an approach (PAYG plus Reserve) which is worth distinguishing from active funding.

As a technique funding is hard to square with my earlier appeal for visibility, since it is the most *covert* of resource-collecting techniques. The whole magic of fund accrual (when it works) offers a delightful sense that the future is being costlessly financed: a small input today, and the passage of time allows money to ripen and expand. But, accrual can occur only at the expense of others (those who pay the interest). Our visibility test suggests it be avoided, yet deliberately visible 'costings' could allow its retention. Funding may well be suited to playing a larger role in the *personalisation* of benefits; it offers a contractual type of equity within which *my* personal contributions can lead on to *my* personal benefit returns.

We could thus propose a different mix of PAYG/funding within a three-tier benefit system. A basic flat-rate benefit could derive from a predominantly PAYG system (while we steadily built up a working reserve). A second tier of compulsory earnings-related benefits (associated more with personal income replacement) could offer a different balance, perhaps leaning more heavily on funding. A third voluntary tier (which I discuss below) could offer a 'personal benefit account', funded exclusively with its benefits on a 'money-purchase' basis. Each tier could operate with a different floor or ceiling on contributions and could, if desired, enjoy different fiscal treatment from the others. As a *complementary* rather than as an *alternative* technique, funding can offer us further flexibility. It never makes our future more secure, nor does it necessarily generate a *bigger* future (Barr, 1979).

Funds do, however, present us with the dilemmas of capital management: they have to be controlled and invested, and we have to decide by whom, at what level of the economy and on what criteria. It is important to confront these responsibilities as citizens, rather than leaving them in 'irresponsible' hands (Titmuss, 1963).

What we may best commend is a hybrid response – in state hands. PAYG is a valuable macro-technique, which cannot safely be practised by individual companies (Lynes, 1967). Conversely, funding is a technique which, on its own, is severely limited: funds cannot handle changes which have any retrospective implications, they can cope best with predictable futures. Used by 'surviving' macro-units (like the UK Ltd) funds can provide a useful long-term cushion to complement the PAYG approach. The combined dynamism of PAYG and the cushion of the reserve fund offer us greater security and greater flexibility.


## A contributory or non-contributory approach?

In contributory schemes relations between contributions and benefits are not pre-ordained. They range from the nominal (in which a minimal contribution earns a lifetime of benefit) to those in which benefits closely reflect personal contribution inputs. The term 'non-contributory' describes schemes in which there is either no directly identifiable individual contribution (e.g. the employer alone finances the company pension) or benefits are financed from general, non-specific taxes – such as the UK child benefit or supplementary benefit schemes.

I have equated contributory schemes with visibility and specificity, and each concept merits distinct attention. Despite frequent assertions (in connection with both state and private benefits) about the British love for contributory schemes, I know of no direct evidence for this longing. Indirect evidence contradicts the popularity of visible worker-borne contributions, since 'making the employer pay' is the favoured technique for both state and private schemes. Any state preference for contributory systems usually equates contributions with benefit security.

Contributory specificity and benefit reliability are linked in several ways. Payment into a specific 'benefit account' (whether funded or PAYG) is assumed to offer a better benefit guarantee than schemes in which benefits are to be financed from future general taxes. Empirical evidence of this relative reliability is hard to divorce from the many other variables which determine the survival of benefit programmes. In the UK some non-contributory benefits such as family allowances/child benefit have indeed fallen in value over the years, but newer additions to the non-contributory field, like mobility allowance, have broadly maintained their worth.

On the other hand, most contributory records have loose links with current benefits. Many people receive decidedly *more* than they are contractually bound to receive. Each pension reform since 1926, when state pensions became contributory, has given some advantage to current pensioners and not just to future beneficiaries. Conversely, past contributions have not protected anybody from the recent abolition of earnings-related schemes or the de-rating of basic benefits for the sick and unemployed. Nor have contributions protected people from inflation or falling tax thresholds (so that more of their 'earned' benefits have been returned to the Inland Revenue). What might be argued is that the state programme financed from *specific* tax revenues is least vulnerable to the consequences of *other* governmental decisions.

From the perspective of the agency paying out benefits, one attraction of specific tax revenues must be that the money has been distinctly appropriated: there need be no Cabinet battle against the claims of defence or road-building, nurses' pay or foreign aid. While specific tax systems cannot behave as if they were financial worlds unto themselves (a raised contribution lessens the potential for other tax rises), they may be more resistant than most to contraction.

The strength of a specific hypothecated tax lies perhaps in the continuing popular equation of contributions with 'contracts'.

Contributions may be viewed, more or less realistically, as earning very personal rights. (My contribution entitles me to some future benefit even if its level will largely be decided by a future generation.) But, contracts tend to be *exclusive*: some people have limited opportunities to contribute. If contributions are viewed as inherently good, then we must either enable non-contributors to join in or offer alternative membership plans. We might, for instance, consider a wider conception of the 'contribution'.

Contributions have been restricted typically to those in the formal economy, although caring for children (in the domestic economy) is now viewed as a contribution-equivalent known as 'home responsibility' and can earn basic benefit rights. Such contribution units could be awarded on wider criteria and, if we wished, given different weightings. If such an approach offers many opportunities for dispute, we should not shrink from the challenge. By extending the contributory options we enable more people to become members: if we insist on being contractual in our income maintenance thinking, then this approach offers a wider base for such contracts.

Such intricate attempts to extend the contributory approach do multiply our moral agonies. Wouldn't it make more sense to drop the expense and exclusivity of contributions and opt for non-contributory alternatives? Generally financed schemes, which recognise us as citizens rather than as 'worker-citizens' in the formal economy, can much better embrace the informal and domestic economies (and the movements we may make between the three). The more emphasis we can put on the non-specific tax base, the greater our potential membership. Similarly, the more emphasis we put on the individual contributor rather than the employer, the more equitable we shall be as between employed and self-employed. The less closely linked the contribution and benefit sides of our social equations, the greater our freedom for positive redistributive manoeuvre. The non-contributory approach fits in with our expressed concern about the real incidence of contributions. If all bucks stop at the consumer, then perhaps we should settle for the indirect taxation of expenditure rather than the dubiously direct taxes we now favour (Meade, 1978; Kay and King, 1978). Our benefits will have to be more overtly progressive to compensate for the incidence of this indirect tax base.

The question of who does and who should pay therefore focuses increasingly on who should be *seen* to pay or who *feels* that s/he is paying. If it can be demonstrated that we are most prepared to pay for better benefits through specific contributions, then it is foolish to reject this technique. But we don't have to be technically exclusive. I suggest that we should finance all basic benefits from the most comprehensive and progressive revenues we can find — we can still have a specific social security (expenditure) tax or even designate particular tax sources to finance particular benefits. Only when people wish to differentiate their benefits from one another (for reasons of earnings-relation, dependencies, 'benefit personalisation') would we offer specific *contributory* opportunities — with contributions solely from individuals and the employer's contribution banned! I turn now to consider further specific propositions.

## Policy proposals

### Loosening the chains of work and welfare

I have had to make many assumptions about the economy within which these proposals are set. I have assumed a mixed market economy and a continuing wage system; I have also assumed that wages will continue to be heavily differentiated — and that trade unions will continue to devote their efforts to sustaining these differentials. Thus, we will move into the foreseeable future with highly diverse wage packets and a varied capacity to buy, to pay taxes and to save. We will also enter the future with varied powers to retain jobs, or to find new ones, or to negotiate work-related benefits — if we have any work.

Currently, jobs provide our major legitimation for giving one another income rewards. Yet as long as we can generate sufficient resources, there is no *a priori* economic reason why we should be concerned about the level of employment. I have assumed that the need for a large-scale labour force is diminishing (more positively, we may *wish* for its diminution). It is the social consequences that are problematic. My guess is that in the short run we will make the worst of this situation. We will have a continuing shortage of 'whole' jobs while Government and trade unions settle for unemployment rather than work-sharing; we will prefer to see people on the dole rather than redistribute employment. In this light, the relationship of occupation to income maintenance acquires a new prominence (Reddin, 1981).

It seems crucial that we *minimise* this work/benefit linkage: the possession of jobs, their remuneration and duration should not determine (directly) our benefit futures. Jobs and the rewards they offer are too unpredictable, and too unevenly and irrationally distributed, to provide a legitimate base for allocating incomes or benefits. While a job gives access to many state social insurance schemes, I need a *particular* job if I am to enjoy an occupational benefit. I must work for the right employer, be in a particular grade and work long enough to be eligible for scheme membership. Further, as those with occupational benefits recognise the advantage of their tax-relieved and employer-sponsored position, I would guess that their interest in the sustenance of universal public provisions will be dispersed. Since the cost of sustaining these sectional advantages are high, it seems likely that the occupational beneficiary will seek constraints on contributions to the public purse – in order to be able to afford the 'occupational' taxes: thus, the state scheme will lose both tax revenue and the high aspirations of these better-organised worker/consumers. Add to this sectionalism the policy of 'contracting-out' (which has allowed the majority of occupational pension scheme members to step aside from state provision into yet another tax-payer-protected haven) and it is hard to think of a more divisive system (Reddin, 1982a). Occupational welfare is divisive between those in paid employment and the non-employed, between those in 'covered' employment (members of a scheme) and those who work beside them in 'non-covered' jobs, between the well covered in the public sector and the badly covered in the private sector, between full- and part-time workers and between women and men (Cunningham, 1981). These are systems which drive yet more wedges between members of a well divided society. Any comprehensive income-maintenance policy has to recognise them in order to complement, accommodate or countermand their effects. We move closest toward countermanding their divisive qualities if we extend national systems on a universal basis (Reddin, 1982b).

### Abolishing the 'employer's contribution'

To diminish the link with work and simultaneously to bring into the open what is now concealed, we need to abolish the employer's contribution. We should revive the Truck Acts and demand a cash wage economy! Employers' payments to public or private benefit schemes should be converted into real wages: any specific contribution should derive explicitly from individuals. If people want to subsidise their canteen lunches, the company cricket pitch or their pensions, they can contribute accordingly. Individuals have been buying these benefits at one remove. It is time they stopped being grateful and realised that it is *their* money that buys them.

The immediate effect for many would be a significant rise in visible wages. Allowing for some related tax adjustments, they would then be faced with increased personal tax/contribution demands, from Government or employer, if they wished to sustain their current benefit packages. In these circumstances people might be more jealous of the benefits they were procuring. Millions of potential occupational beneficiaries have lost dramatically year by year as they have left employment: in modern times I know of no expropriation of property to have gone so shamelessly ignored for so long (HMSO, 1981).

One other consequence of this move is that the 'other half' of the work force, which now enjoys few (if any) occupational benefits, will become much more aware of the remunerative disparities between itself and its 'covered' brothers and sisters (often in the same place of work). More of our work inequalities will then be apparent: from such a position we will perhaps each be able better to judge our preferences and assess the appropriate mix of solutions.

### Pooling risks and the fixed-term contribution

Among the social strategies which we have neglected are the redistributions made possible by altering the time spans of taxes and benefits. We might, for instance, achieve many more effective outcomes by paying more generous benefits for shorter periods. We can moderate redistributions by limiting or extending the period over which individuals pay for and receive their benefits, a dimension which has added relevance when it comes to pooled insurance systems. The pooling of risks is not invariably positively redistributive (in the sense of directing more resources towards the poor): the redistributions of pooling depend on what you pool (Reddin, 1977, 1983). Pooling longevity (as in pension schemes) has different consequences from pooling the risks of unemployment or of sickness. If we insist on *positive* income redistributions from all schemes, then we require different formulae in each case. It also follows that our formulae must be adaptable; they will not be right for ever, even if we get them right at the outset.

For example, we can consider paying pensions after forty contribution years — the number could be reduced or increased depending on our resources and generosity. (Conventionally, this would mean that pensions would be payable after forty years' work, although with the wider contributory concept suggested earlier, it could be shorter.) The 'forty and out' approach offers more equitable outcomes than many current schemes. Thirty-six per cent of unskilled male manual workers are dead before pension age, and they probably joined the labour market in their mid-teens. If the remaining 64 per cent reach pension age, they will have done so after fifty years of contribution (both as specific National Insurance contributors and as tax-payers — aiding the Exchequer contribution). This can be contrasted with the more typical forty- to forty-five-year 'membership' of the further-educated middle class with greater life expectancy. Thus the short-lived poor get a worse deal from pensions than their longer-living, shorter-contributing, better-off neighbours: a 'forty and out' approach offers some redress.

## Single and married: ending the dependent subsidy

Why should the single continue to subsidise the married? Currently, there is a common contribution towards social insurance benefits, regardless of whether a person is married or single.

Meanwhile, those with dependent spouses enjoy a higher benefit than their single neighbours. There is a transfer from the single to the married. I suggest we redress this balance, with higher contributions from those who choose to have a dependent spouse, and that we move increasingly towards individual benefit systems. This becomes increasingly important as we recognise the impermanence of many personal relationships (Rimmer, 1981).

Marital status cannot be considered a *fixed* variable in our lives. If people choose to live singly, to cohabit, to marry, to divorce or to find partners of their own sex, there is no reason why we should assume any associated dependency. There is no *a priori* reason why we should assume collective responsibility for the formation or change of such relations. If we want our benefits to cover adult dependants, why shouldn't they be bought? Conclusion: if you take on 'dependants', expect to pay for the privilege.

## Choice, savings and taxation

Most wage-earning individuals now face two obligations to save, publicly through National Insurance and occupationally through a contributory pension scheme. Only after these obligations have been met can individual savings choices begin. I have assumed that we are likely to see continuing (and considerable) disparities in our ability and desire to save and that people may seek a variety of savings media. These choices and needs are best met in two ways, the first by reforming our tax treatment of savings and the second by offering 'savings choices' within the mainstream of social insurance.

Our income tax system now discriminates substantially in favour of certain kinds of savings: funded pension schemes enjoy exceptional tax exemptions and entail staggering (and rising) tax expenditures (Reddin, 1980). While the number of people who stand to win or lose by fiscal change is greater than ever, reform is essential: we have, however, many options as to the pace of change.

The interests of equity and choice would seem to be served best by the withdrawal of tax relief from all forms of saving. In the first case, this would diminish the inequalities of treatment as between those who can and those who cannot afford to save. For instance, pension savers now reduce their tax liability; the Exchequer presumably makes up the revenue loss by imposing other taxes, and some of these 'replacement' taxes fall on those who cannot afford to save in the first place. Secondly, the withdrawal of tax relief would mean that choices between savings media – a building society, a pension fund, a Post Office savings account – could be made without the current 'pension bias'. It would also help to resolve the disparities between public and private choices. A contribution to National Insurance is not tax-deductible, something most evident to someone faced with the choice of contracting in (taxably) or out (deductibly) of the state pension scheme. Such choices do not offer the most positive framework for public/private decisions: the state has loaded the dice heavily against itself. Extending the structural inequalities of tax relief to the public domain would merely double these inequalities rather than balance them out.

A demand for greater compatability of public and private schemes leads me to argue for a radical shift in our thinking about savings and benefit systems generally. Individual contributory/benefit opportunities should be provided *within* the mainstream of social insurance. The Additional Voluntary Contribution to the occupational scheme could equally be grafted on to the individual National Insurance benefit record, a voluntary layer of contributions beyond those compulsorily required.

We are unfamiliar with this notion of choice *within* the welfare state, but it is essential that it be developed. Pragmatically, government is extremely efficient in this cash-benefit field. More generally, social policy should be seen as enabling and enlarging choices rather than as restricting them or hiving them off to the market place.

### The equities of protection

The statutory indexation of taxes and benefits is a novelty in Britain. There are still substantial benefit sectors (both public and private) in which it does not occur at all or arises only spasmodically. Private welfare benefits have been particularly devoid of benefit guarantees, as many individuals have found, belatedly, to their cost. While we undoubtedly give credibility to benefits by protecting their future value, we should first look hard at who benefits from, and who pays for, such protection (Scott Report, 1981).

Protection is going to occupy a large part of future benefit budgets (Doron *et al.*, 1982). As more resources are demanded to shore up the value of benefits already in payment, the less there will be to extend to more people. It is crucial, therefore, that we note the distribution of benefits among citizens when we *start* to protect them (just as we must be concerned with the source of this protection money). We may view the inflation-proofing of earnings-related and 'voluntary' pensions differently from our basic benefits: more resources must go into benefit equalisation before we undertake the protection of the already well endowed.

## Ending public penury

Substantial improvements are needed in the levels of all our main income maintenance benefits. As one example, there is no reason why we should not aim for a 100 per cent wage-replacement rate in state retirement income. There is nothing dramatic about this proposal, since most occupational pension schemes already make such promises (albeit irresponsibly) to half of the work force (Government Actuary, 1981). Added to full benefits under the new state scheme, a future pension at 140 per cent of previous take-home pay is easily foreseen and is, indeed, already being achieved by some. I judge it unkind to foster this excess for some while leaving the majority to languish on pensions representing less than one-third of average take-home pay. In total (including public, occupational and private schemes), many of us already put more than sufficient resources into our pension futures and are wildly over-pensioned. We must withdraw the contracting-out option and lay claim to the contributions that these combined systems now consume in order to offer decent and reliable benefits to all. The complementary schemes can then accommodate themselves accordingly – rather than determining the lines within which the state is permitted to operate.

# Conclusion

The intentions of the preceding proposals were:

- to look at the financial options and to favour a mixed financial base in state hands
- to maximise the part played by generous flat-rate benefits available to all citizens
- to erect an adequate and attractive second tier of earnings-related benefits for all
- to create an area of 'choice within welfare' — a third tier of benefits of which membership could be voluntary
- to end 'contracting-out' at any level
- to end the subsidisation of the married by the single
- to increase the likelihood that poor people will receive pensions, by way of a 'forty and out' formula
- to abolish all employer contributions
- to minimise the need to be in the labour market to achieve any benefit entitlement

Each proposal, I believe, has some merit in its own right, but they do not all have to be swallowed whole or *en masse*. Indeed, my point is to emphasise the diversity of possibilities open to us: we are trapped only by the limits of our imaginations. Several of the proposals are, quite coincidentally, of a 'no-cost' nature: it is hoped that they will be operable in the coldest of climates. They constitute changes in themselves and offer the prospect of new views of the world. They variously seek to get things out of the closet — to let us, as workers and consumers, see that it is we who both generate and (ought to) dispose of the nation's wealth. These are proposals which are designed to raise or revive our consciousness. Social policies can be more than tired responses to society's distress signals; they can be social initiatives designed to solve problems and also to provoke, promote and make aware. In a cold climate they are necessities rather than luxuries.

## 100   *Socialism in a Cold Climate*
# References

Barr, N. (1979) 'Myths my Grandpa taught me', in *Three Banks Review*, no. 124, December

Cunningham, M. (1981) *Non-Wage Benefits* (London: Pluto Press)

Doron, A., Shamai, N., and Tamir, Y. (1982) 'Maintaining the standard of living of families in Israel under conditions of inflation', *International Social Security Review*, no. 1 (International Social Security Association)

Field, F. (1981) *Inequality in Britain: Freedom, Welfare and the State* (London: Fontana)

Government Actuary (1981) *Occupational Pension Schemes 1979: Sixth Report of the Government Actuary* (London: HMSO)

Harris, R., and Seldon, A. (1979) *Over-Ruled on Welfare* (London: Institute of Economic Affairs)

HMSO (1981) Cmnd 8271 *Improved Protection for the Occupational Pension Rights and Expectations of Early Leavers* (London: HMSO)

International Labour Organisation (1977) *Pensions and Inflation* (Geneva: ILO)

Kay, J., and King, M. (1978) *The British Tax System* (Oxford: Oxford University Press)

*Lloyds Bank Economic Bulletin* (1980) no. 19 (London: Lloyds Bank)

Lynes, T. (1976) *French Pensions* (London: Bedford Square Press)

Meade, J. E. (1978) *The Structure and Reform of direct taxation* (London: Institute of Fiscal Studies)

Preston, M. (1973) 'Incentives' Distortion, and the System of Taxation', in B. Crick and W. A. Robson (eds.), *The Future of the Social Services* (Harmondsworth: Penguin)

Reddin, M. (1977) 'National insurance and private pensions: who gets what from whom?', in K. Jones, M. Brown and S. Baldwin (eds.) *The Year Book of Social Policy in Britain 1976* (London: Routledge & Kegan Paul)

Reddin, M. (1980) 'Taxation and pensions', in C. Sandford, C. Pond and R. Walker (eds.), *Taxation and Social Policy* (London: Heinemann)

Reddin, M. (1981) 'Universality and selectivity: another formulation' in D. Nevin (ed.), *Trade Union Priorities in Social Policy* (Dublin: Federated Workers Union of Ireland)

Reddin, M. (1982a) 'Occupation, welfare and social division', in C. Jones and J. Stevenson (eds.), *The Year Book of Social Policy in Britain 1980–81* (London: Routledge & Kegan Paul)

Reddin, M. (1982b) 'The future of occupational pension provision in Britain: comments', in M. Fogarty (ed.), *Retirement Policy: The Next Fifty Years* (London: Heinemann).

Reddin, M. (1983) 'Pensions, wealth and the extension of inequality', in F. Field (ed.), *The Wealth Report*, vol. 2 (London: Routledge & Kegan Paul)

Rimmer, L. (1981) *Focus on Families* (London: Study Commission on the Family)

Sandford, C., Pond, C., and Walker, R. (eds.) (1980) *Taxation and Social Policy* (London: Heinemann)

Scott Report (1981) *Inquiry into the Value of Pensions*, Cmnd 8147 (London: HMSO)

Titmuss, R. M. (1963) *Essays on the Welfare State*, 2nd ed. (London: Allen & Unwin)

US Department of Health, Education and Welfare (1979) *Social Security in a Changing World* (Washington, DC: US Government Printing Office)

Wilensky, H. L. (1976) *The 'New Corporatism', Centralization, and the Welfare State* (Beverley Hills: Sage)

# 7

# Conceptualising Equality for Women

Jane Lewis

Nineteenth-century feminists expected that they would have to choose between motherhood and a career. All they demanded was a 'fair field and no favour' if they chose the latter. Thus they deplored the idea of protective legislation for women wage-earners and what they regarded as 'special privileges', such as maternity leave. Either women were equal to men or they were not. Many early twentieth-century feminists — mostly Fabian and socialist women — objected to defining equality on male terms and began to demand that greater recognition be given to the work that women did in the home. But this set of feminist arguments still presumed that women would have to choose between motherhood and a career and was grounded on the assumption that women were equal but different.

Today's feminist analysis rejects both these earlier concepts of equality. Equality cannot be achieved on men's terms because women start unequal. Nor can women be treated as equal but different because this will only reinforce sexual divisions. The feminist movement of the 1970s and 1980s has developed a more complex analysis of sex inequality, which recognises the way in which women's work as mothers, housewives and carers of both children and otherwise dependent relatives structures their experience as waged workers. In this analysis, the domestic division of labour and the segregation of male and female paid work are seen as mutually reinforcing. Where there is no large-scale provision of care for either children or the elderly and infirm, a majority of women are caught in what may be described as a vicious circle of inequality. Because it is assumed that women will 'naturally' undertake the work of child-rearing and caring, it follows that their paid employment will be considered by them, as well as by society, to be of secondary importance (Chiplin and Sloane, 1976). Family responsibilities mean that women will tend to seek work that is nearer home and part-time, and their periodic absence from the labour force means that they will tend to be found in lower-paying, lower-status jobs and in the lower grades of any particular occupation. This, in turn, serves to reinforce the idea that their primary duty is to home and children.

The equal opportunities legislation of the 1970s – the Equal Pay Act (1970) and the Sex Discrimination Act (1975) – assumed that women were in a position to compete on equal terms when they patently are not, chiefly because they bear a disproportionate burden of family responsibilities and because of the strong socialisation into familial roles and female jobs that girls experience via parents, schools and the media. Moreover, because the relationship between sexual divisions in the home and women's position in the labour market has not been confronted by policy-makers, it has often been the case that policies have tried to effect greater equality in one area of women's lives while actually reinforcing traditional sexual divisions in another. A classic example comes from the legislation passed by the last Labour Government in 1975. It delivered anti-sex discrimination legislation on the one hand and on the other two new insurance benefits which perpetuated assumptions regarding 'the normal household duties of married women' and hence their unequal treatment. These were the invalid care allowance, which may be claimed by all persons other than married women giving up paid employment to care for sick relatives, and the non-contributory invalidity pension, which is payable to married women only if they are able to prove their inability to do housework. No other category of claimant has to meet this condition. This illustrates the ready assumption that women will take primary responsibility for household and children. A real equality between the sexes will prove impossible while such continues to be the case.

Conceptualising equality for women thus entails evolving strategies designed to break down sexual divisions. This is a deliberately more complex formulation than the proposition that equality will be achieved when sex difference is no more important than hair colour. Such an idea of equality is derived from a focus on the public sphere alone and the need to treat women who enter it on the same terms as men. But as a matter of course it will be men who define those terms. This won't do, because in large part women's subordination rests on the way in which their work in the home and the skills that they have traditionally brought to the workplace — as nurses or typists, for example — have been grossly undervalued. Breaking down sexual divisions in the public and private sphere thus implies a fundamental change in the way work is defined and hence in the degree of esteem and pay that is derived from particular jobs. Until both public and private spheres belong equally to women and men, we will not succeed in widening women's choices.

It is very difficult to work out a coherent programme for change. For example, at the political level it appears paradoxical that feminists wishing to break down sexual divisions also insist on women-only meetings. Yet this is a necessary and logical strategy. While our sights may be set on a society that will enlarge the opportunities of women and men, this is not to deny the fact that men are the stumbling block and that women must organise themselves, whether in women's groups or within the labour movement. Similar tensions are encountered in devising policy prescriptions. It is easy to criticise the notion of equality embodied in the equal opportunities legislation, yet the Acts are vastly better than nothing. But where and how can the circle of inequality be *effectively* broken? This chapter considers policy options affecting women's position in two crucial areas: the labour force and the family.[1] The elimination of sex segregation in the labour market and unequal pay depends in large part on the degree to which men are prepared to share household tasks and the work of parenting and caring within the family. While more direct intervention by the state is undoubtedly necessary to secure equal pay and job opportunities, few people would want to see a similar strategy in regard to the private sphere, as the feminist struggle for control over all aspects of reproduction shows. Rather, change is needed in the assumptions regarding traditional sexual divisions which underlie policies affecting the family — as in the insurance example quoted above – and which at present serve to reproduce these divisions. What this chapter stresses is the need to concentrate on the structures that give rise to sex inequalities rather than on the eradication of the manifestations of inequality in the lives of individuals.

## Women and paid employment[2]

The material results of the equal opportunities legislation have been meagre. In the case of pay there was a convergence between male and female average pay until 1977, but the improvement has not been maintained. In 1980 full-time women workers earned only 71 per cent as much as men, less than in 1977 and only a few percentage points more than in 1975, when the Equal Pay Act (EPA) was fully implemented (Routh, 1980). When it is also remembered that a large and increasing proportion of women (40 per cent in 1977) work part-time and that part-time workers earn less hour for hour than full-time workers, then the position of women workers in 1980 was in all probability no better than in 1975. Similarly, the latest assessment of trends in job segregation shows that the degree of sex segregation in the labour force diminished between 1975 and 1977, only to rise again to the 1973 level by 1979 (Hakim, 1981). Despite the Sex Discrimination Act (SDA), women remain concentrated in a small number of low-status, low-paying jobs.

Equal opportunities legislation defines inequality narrowly as an individual problem that can be dealt with in a separate compartment, to one side of the mainstream economic and industrial concerns and in isolation from women's other concerns and responsibilities. But women are trapped as a *group*, as well as individuals, within certain grades and kinds of work.

The concept of discrimination under such legislation is problematic. In the case of the EPA, a woman has to prove that she is being paid less than a man doing 'the same or broadly similar' work. The chance of being able to do this when male and female work is so highly segregated is obviously remote. Moreover, during the five years that employers were given to implement equal pay, many circumvented the Act's provisions by reclassifying the work done by their female employees. A job-evaluation exercise may establish the value of a women's job as equal to that of a man working in the same establishment, but no obligation is imposed on employers to carry out job-evaluation exercises. Moreover, because it is necessary to prove direct discrimination, there is little possibility of remedying the gross undervaluation of female skills in the all-female jobs of secretarial work or nursing.

Even when it is accepted that men and women are doing 'the same or broadly similar' work, the Act allows pay to vary between them for reasons of 'material difference' other than sex, as, for example, when men have greater seniority or work more unsocial shifts or more overtime. The Act does stipulate that overtime *rates* and annual increments must be the same for men and women; however, differences in overtime or seniority *payments* are substantial. Overtime payments raised male manual workers' pay by £15 a week in 1981 and manual women's by only £2, yet it is probable that the better overtime rates do not reflect fair productivity differentials. As each individual works more hours, so the value of productivity in each additional hour falls. It should also be noted that it is women's responsibility for their families that inhibits their capacity to work overtime. There are also circumstances in which no justification for additional payment is attempted, and higher pay for men rests on precedent. Many collective agreements make changes in wage structures subject to the provision that no individual finds himself (*sic*) worse-off as a result. Thus if a man (or, in theory, a woman) has his job downgraded or is moved into a woman's job, he may retain his existing pay level as a 'red-circled' (protected) employee. At Trico in 1976 an Industrial Tribunal ruled that men were entitled to higher pay because in the past they had worked on night shifts, and their wage still included the 'red-circled' night shift bonus. The women at Trico struck successfully for equal pay, thus underlining the point that relative pay reflects levels of organisation as much as, or more than, relative productivity.

The SDA prohibits discrimination in appointments, promotions, dismissals, redundancies and access to training and education, to credit and to other services. However, it does not cover pension rights, taxation, social security or family law – areas in which policies often reinforce sexual divisions within the home. The concept of discrimination is wider than that covered by the EPA and includes indirect as well as direct discrimination. Indirect discrimination occurs where a condition or requirement imposed on a group, while it does not appear to have anything to do with sex, effectively means that more of one sex than of the other can comply with it. The concept does not cover instances in which employers can claim sex as a 'genuine occupational qualification' for all or part of a job – as in the case of a woman shop assistant made redundant from a tailoring business in preference to her less experienced male colleague on the grounds that the male assistant was needed to take inside-leg measurements.

Both the Acts have become at best occasional safety nets for but a few individuals. In the case of the SDA, fewer than a tenth of the applications made under the Act are upheld. In 1980 only fifteen cases were successful.

Under the Acts the onus is put on the woman to prove discrimination. An individual woman has a lot at stake should she lose and is likely to face considerable sexist bias on the part of trade union officials, Arbitration, Conciliation and Advisory Service officers (who measure their success in terms of the number of cases that do not need to go forward to a Tribunal) and Industrial Tribunal officials, who are predominantly male (Gregory, 1982; Coussins, 1976). Women who take action under the Acts may well be exceptional in recognising that they are experiencing discrimination. Female socialisation encourages women to be submissive, and women have long been expected to subordinate their employment aspirations to the needs of family and household. In this context equal opportunities legislation has served a valuable purpose in raising the consciousness of workers (Coussins, 1980).

In the debate on the Second Reading of the Sex Discrimination Act Roy Jenkins stressed that the legislation was intended only to provide 'a basic floor of rights and powers' (Snell *et al.*, 1981). In these terms the legislation has been relatively successful. The EPA aimed to provide women in jobs comparable with men's with equal pay, not equal earnings, and the SDA aimed to promote the equal treatment of women without touching the basic division of labour between the sexes in the allocation of household duties. However, amendments to both the Acts have long been proposed by the National Council for Civil Liberties, The Equal Opportunities Commission and the Trades Union Congress, which would undoubtedly improve their effectiveness.[3] Chief among them are a broader definition of equal pay, the placing of the onus of proof on the employer in all cases, the extension of the concept of indirect discrimination to cases involving a claim for equal pay and the merging of the two Acts. The latter would put an end to cases such as that of Mrs Meeks, who as a part-time secretary earned a lower hourly rate than the full-time workers. Her claim to an equal hourly rate failed under the EPA because there were no male secretaries with whom she could compare herself (Sedley, 1980). It is perhaps a measure of the indifference of both major political parties, and especially of the present Government, that the pace of reform in employment and family policies has been set by rulings in the European Court and directives from the European Community.

Strengthening the equal opportunities legislation should be seen as a preliminary step, for the material effects of the legislation have not been very encouraging. Some feminists have suggested that the narrowing of male/female pay differentials until 1976–7 coincided with periods during which flat-rate incomes policies were in effect, but it is arguable that the greatest problem facing the majority of women workers is a wage so low that it is little affected by any redistributory effects of such policies (Weir and McIntosh, 1982).

Both the setting up of trades boards (later wages councils) in 1909 and the passing of an Equal Pay Act amounted to bypassing the traditional processes of wage-bargaining. In the event, the state proved no more successful than the trade union movement in reaching the low-paid, and it may well be that the considerable rise in unionisation and militancy among low-paid women workers during the period 1970–7 was crucial in raising the wages of certain groups of women workers and thereby causing some congruence between male and female pay. The Low

Pay Unit and the Equal Opportunities Commission have recommended a moving minimum-wage target of two-thirds of the (median) average male earnings for low-paid women workers, to be achieved in three to five years (Low Pay Unit and EOC, 1980). Certain trade unionists also advocate a minimum wage, to be negotiated as part of the collective bargaining process (Fisher and Dix, 1974). A firm policy on low pay, accompanied by adequate job guarantees, is desperately needed.

The particularly low status of women workers is closely related to the segregation of male and female jobs, which the SDA has had little success in combating. It is perhaps significant that the latest Department of Employment survey of sex segregation in the labour force found that only women in professional occupations made some headway between 1973 and 1979 (Hakim, 1981). Women who have managed to obtain the necessary education and training for a professional career are likely to be better able to make use of equal opportunities legislation because there will always be men doing the same jobs with whom they can compare themselves in regard to possible discrimination in hiring, pay, promotion, etc. The SDA has done more to promote awareness of discrimination in appointments to better paid male jobs than in some of the other areas it covers, (for example, redundancy). Similarly, a study of the maternity rights granted under the 1975 Employment Protection Act also indicates that in the main it has been women in better-paying jobs who have benefited. Only 6 per cent of manual workers who took maternity leave and stated their desire to return to work were able to do so (Daniel, 1981). This is undoubtedly related to the lack of provision and cost of childcare facilities.

Thus for many women equal opportunities legislation merely provides formal rights of which they cannot take advantage. In order to combat sex segregation in the labour market, what is needed is a policy that focuses less on individual instances of discrimination and more on changing the structures that give rise to it. Feminists and other pressure groups are therefore in favour of initiating positive action programmes (Roberts, 1981), which have so far been strongly rejected in this country for both women and blacks. There are many types of positive or affirmative action programmes and apparently little understanding on the part of employers as to the differences between them; not all involve a quota system or reverse discrimination (Fogarty *et al.*, 1981). Affirmative action programmes need the backing of unions and of government, directly through schools and through monitoring via the SDA (which at present allows for limited positive discrimination in training, but not at the point of hiring) and indirectly through requirements built into government contracts.

The most thoroughgoing form of positive action – the quota system – raises the fear that the implementation of social goals will be allowed to override the rights of individuals. The dilemma arises from pitting the rights of individuals against the rights of minority groups and women, with the burden of adjustment falling on individuals who may not themselves have been guilty of discriminatory practices (Raphael, 1980). But, as one feminist philosopher has argued, men as a group have historically expected and received more than their fair share, and it is on this basis that affirmative action may be justified (Richards, 1980).

Nor is it merely a case of ensuring that both sexes are more equally distributed across the occupational structure. All women experience acute tensions at certain stages in the life cycle between the burden of their family responsibilities on the one hand and of their paid employment on the other (Ginsberg, 1976). Very little has been done to ease the sources of this tension. Indeed, the important right to maternity leave granted by the 1975 Employment Protection Act has been seriously eroded by the present Government's 1980 Employment Protection Act. All Governments have shown but a weak commitment to day care and nursery education in peacetime. The numbers of children receiving nursery education did rise between 1974 and 1977 from 140,000 to 210,000, but this total fell far short of the Plowden Committee's recommendations (Blackstone, 1980). Under the present Government the 1980 Education Act actually removed the legal responsibility of local education authorities to provide nursery education for 3–5-year-olds. In addition, it has encouraged the use of child-minders rather than day-care centres, a strategy that is cheap and accords both with the emphasis that the Government has placed on community care and with the maternal deprivation theorists' preference for care on a one-to-one rather than collective basis (Coulter, 1981). Any programme for positive action *must* be adequately supported by ready access to day care and nursery education. However, it is true that historically women have 'preferred' to make their own arrangements for day care (Hewitt, 1975). This 'preference' may well often be dictated by lack of suitable alternatives (Tizard, 1976), but private arrangements — often with a relative or neighbour — may be genuinely preferred for their greater flexibility and closeness. The history of the personal health services, such as that provided by home helps, should sound a warning against over-eagerness to professionalise day care. What is crucial is that those wanting to employ a child-minder should be able to pay enough to secure good care and to give the child-minder a decent wage. Child-minders should not be the favoured solution because they are cheap.

Many married women reconcile their conflicting obligations to family and to paid employment by working part-time. In 1956 12 per cent of women workers were part-timers; by 1977 this figure had risen to 40 per cent. Indeed, the expansion of the total female labour force from 7.4 million in 1951 to 9.1 million in 1971 was accounted for almost entirely by the expansion in part-time work (Hurstfield, 1978). The most pressing need of this group of workers is for the same rights as those enjoyed by full-time workers: protection against redundancy, the right to reinstatement after maternity leave, equal pay and promotion opportunities and access to state insurance benefits. In 1977 22 per cent of female part-time employees were earning less than £15 a week, which at the time defined the boundary of non-employment for social insurance purposes. By 1979 this percentage had more than doubled. During the late 1970s the boundaries of the formal labour market became increasingly tightly drawn, and it was largely women who were excluded. The prospect of rapid technological change and its effects on working time, as well as the existence of mass unemployment, makes action more urgent on the issue of part-time workers and the parallel problem of those who incur penalties under the social security system because they work for only short periods.

The campaign on behalf of part-timers must be seen as a step along the road to eliminating the division between full- and part-time work and to achieving a shorter working day for all workers. This is crucial to the sharing of parenting and household tasks. To the same end, maternity leave must become – as in Sweden – parental leave, so that the legislation no longer reinforces the assumption that women bear the whole responsibility for child care. Whether such a provision is successful will, of course, depend on how far women's position in the work force improves. At present, few couples could afford to rely on the woman's wage while the man cared for the child.

Real, substantive equality for women means that there has to be a change in the idea that women take primary responsibility for home and children and that men are the breadwinners. Thus a solution to the problems facing women in paid employment is bound to have serious implications for employment and industry as a whole. Factors affecting the position of women must be seriously considered in any strategy for industrial regeneration. What kinds of new jobs are to be created (Gardiner and Smith, 1981)? Will their creation be accompanied by positive action programmes for women? Will more material incentives be given by both Government and unions to people wishing to work part-time or to job-share? Or will women continue to be marginal members of the labour force and have to wait yet again for full employment?

## Women and the family[4]

The second essential focus for an attack on sex inequality is policies affecting women's position in the family. During the late 1970s the campaign for Women's Financial and Legal Independence adopted the slogan 'Disaggregation now!' (Rights of Women, 1979). Like the fight for equal pay and employment opportunity, this demand that social policies stop aggregating the income or needs of husband and wife for the purpose of assessing their tax or welfare rights is designed as an attack on the concept of the breadwinner family model which is fundamental to the maintenance of women's subordination. Lower pay for women, whether married or single, is still usually justified in terms of men's greater financial responsibilities as breadwinners. Since 1975 legislation in areas such as pensions and social security has given greater recognition to women's claim to financial independence, but the aggregation of income is only one of the assumptions underlying policies affecting the family. Unless financial independence for women is accompanied, first, by greater equality in the workplace and, second, by an equal division of labour and resources within the family, women run the risk of being treated equally when they start unequal.

The idea of the family wage has historically appealed to both right and left on the political spectrum. In 1909 Ramsay Mac-Donald described family allowances as an 'insane outburst of individualism' and declared that 'under socialism mothers' and children's right to maintenance will be honoured by the family not by the state' (Land, 1980). It has been argued that the encouragement given by husbands and trade unionists to working-class married women to stay at home should be seen as a legitimate wage-bargaining strategy to raise the standard of living of the working-class family (Humphries, 1980). But apart from any consideration due to the female desire for autonomy, it remains true that such a strategy was devised by men and increased the male wage. Evidence has shown repeatedly that resources are rarely shared equally within the family. Housekeeping frequently does not keep up with rises in the husband's pay, family size or, more recently, inflation (EOC, 1977; Pahl, 1980). This is but one aspect of the larger truth that different family members do not experience the institution of the family in the same way.

Commentators on the right have perceived the breadwinner family model as securing male work incentives and hence social stability. The marriage contract has a different meaning for men and women: men assume the obligation to maintain their wives and children, and refusal to do so can lead in the last instance to imprisonment; women take on an obligation to care for children, sick and elderly relatives and husbands. It is significant that under social security law an equal obligation to maintain is laid on both husband and wife, but prosecution is confined to men who are considered work-shy. Notions of female economic dependency and the family wage have persisted despite evidence that has existed since the late nineteenth century showing both the crucial contribution made by married women to the family economy and the inability of a majority of working-class husbands to earn a wage that would enable their wives to be completely dependent. In 1975 four times as many families with children would have had incomes below the supplementary benefit level if the wives had not been employed as well as the husbands (CPRS, 1980).

From the beginning the social security system has catered to the male breadwinner family model. Women workers have never been easy to fit into the system because of their low pay, part-time hours and tendency to have interrupted work careers. Despite Beveridge's concern to avoid labelling wives as dependants and his reference to marriage as a 'partnership', his 1942 Report made women completely economically dependent on their husbands for insurance purposes and this principle was carried through into the legislation of the later 1940s (Beveridge, 1942). At the time feminists criticised Beveridge for 'denying the married woman, rich or poor, housewife or paid worker, an individual personal status' (Abbott and Bompass, 1943). What were being expressed were different notions of equality. Beveridge talked of marriage as a partnership of 'equals', obviously in the sense of 'equal but different'. The feminists were aware that the recognition Beveridge sought to give women in their role of housewife and mother could easily turn into prescription.

The social security legislation of the mid-1970s began to break down the assumptions of female dependency. Under the Social Security (Pensions) Act of 1975, married women's rights to pensions were improved, and the married woman's option (not to pay full contributions and to rely instead on her husband's contribution record) was phased out. During the debate Conservatives argued that married women should retain the option of relying on their husbands' pensions, maintaining that 'what is involved is not the concept of the dependence of the woman on her husband, but family insurance' (Groves, 1982). Labour's pensions legislation went considerably further in women's favour than had previous Conservative proposals.

Nevertheless, the improvements in widow's pension rights served to reinforce women's position as dependants. It is possible to favour increases in pensions while also deploring the grounds on which better pensions were made available to this group of women. Similarly, while the changes in the administration of supplementary benefits and family income supplement demanded by the EEC and scheduled for 1983 will allow either partner (rather than the man alone, as at present) to claim benefit as long as s/he has been engaged in full-time work for a specified period, this means that the concept of *a* breadwinner is still retained. The changes do nothing to recognise the fact that the majority of families depend on the earnings of both husband and wife.

Severe difficulties are involved in the implementation of policies that give women financial autonomy. It is much easier in the case of pension reform to give widows better pensions and institute a scheme of 'home responsibility credits', to take account of the years spent out of the work force caring for children and relatives, than it is to improve the position of women as members of pension schemes in their own right. In other words, it is hard to push through full disaggregation when women occupy an inferior position in the labour force. The 1975 legislation gave women equal access to occupational pensions, but occupational pension schemes are rarely the same for all categories of worker within an organisation, and women often find themselves offered an inferior pension plan by virtue of their lower job status rather than on grounds of sex *per se*. Thus women's unequal position in the labour market will tend to be reflected in their unequal position in old age (Groves, 1982).

Disaggregation in the case of social security law would mean that married women who could not get a job could claim supplementary benefit in their own right, regardless of their husband's income. This raises a problem of conflicting policy priorities which must be squarely confronted. Families in which women happen to be married to men with high incomes would stand to benefit most, providing they were willing to make themselves available for work and thus to become eligible for benefits (Fairbairns, 1979). Hitherto the argument that this would represent a waste of state resources has automatically prevailed over the equally valid consideration of sex equality. Disaggregation would also mean that the married man would no longer get an allowance for his wife, who, presuming that the work test is retained, would thus be forced into the labour market. This may well disadvantage many women, especially older ones who have had little or no work experience since marriage. It may be argued that this is necessary to break the ties between married women's dependence and their inferior position in the labour market (McIntosh, 1981). But there are certainly means of easing this transition which should be adopted first — for example, the provision of training programmes for older women and the liberalisation of the conditions for drawing unemployment benefit (Lister and Finister, 1981). The rules for unemployment benefit have always operated to restrict claims from married women and, of course, a married woman has never been able to claim supplementary benefit in her own right. Policies must work consistently towards full disaggregation. This does not mean that women who chose the socially approved role of housewife and mother should be subjected to sudden and painful change, which could be interpreted as further depreciation of work that is already undervalued. What is needed is a reassessment of the value of both paid and unpaid work.

The early feminist campaigners for family allowances recognised the relationship between women's position in the labour force and their economic dependence in the family and called for an allowance that would meet the full costs of supporting a child, in order that men would no longer have to bargain for a family wage. They argued that this would remove the only reasonable impediment to equal pay. Their analysis still holds, which is why feminists today desire that basic family support should come not from the individual but from the state, in the form of a substantial increase in child benefit (Coussins and Coote, 1981). They believe that this would reconcile the two functions of the wage, which at one level provides a reward for effort and skill and at another must meet the costs of reproducing labour power. In the case of the latter, it conspicuously fails where the family is large and/or the breadwinner is low-paid.

The labour movement has always feared that the removal of dependants from the wage-bargaining process would put labour at a disadvantage. On the other hand, if unions no longer faced family hardship as a result of a strike it could be argued that their position would be strengthened. Any shift to making the state the main source of child support would have to be very carefully negotiated. In the interests of sex role equality and disaggregation, the new benefit would also have to be attached to the child rather than to a parent.

This is to talk in terms of long-range goals. In fact, the Conservative Party has performed an about-face on the issue of child benefit because any increase in it pushes up public expenditure, and while the Labour Party was responsible for introducing the scheme, it implemented it reluctantly. In large part this was because both political parties have been reluctant to disturb the distribution of resources within the family; the measure almost foundered on the issue of the transfer from 'wallet to purse' (Land, 1977).

It is also true that a policy of substantial increases in child benefit, necessarily backed up by collective day-care provision, is expensive. The simplifications of the medium-range alternative of an extended parental grant system are therefore worth exploring. This would involve paying a substantial sum (perhaps three times the present child benefit) to families in which there are children under school age by way of compensating for loss of earnings or meeting the costs of day care (envisaged as a private rather than as a collective provision) in cases in which both parents prefer to work. Substantial redistributive effects might be expected because the poorest families are those in which there are children under 5 years old. The underlying assumption of such a scheme is that both parents are normally employed. This is consistent with a disaggregation strategy, but its success depends on the improvement of women's opportunities and rewards in the labour market and either the adequate provision of care for children during working hours by schools or a shorter working day for both sexes. The major sticking-point in such a strategy is likely to be the relative levels of payment and the question of whether these would not in practice encourage women to stay at home. In view of this and the fact that extended parental grants would not tackle the fundamental problem of reconciling the two functions of the wage, most feminists would still favour working towards a policy of free child care, with a small stipend for parents preferring to look after their own children in addition to a child benefit for all children to cover the basic costs of child-rearing.

To dismantle policies that reproduce women's economic dependency is perhaps the most obvious means of attacking the male breadwinner family model. As crucial is the development of policies to encourage the sharing of work within the family. Indeed, to move towards treating couples as autonomous individuals for economic purposes, without equalising the burden of parenting and caring, would be as harmful as to ignore the problems posed by women's position in the labour force and provision for dependent children. This is illustrated by the changes recently proposed in family law and in the tax system. The Family Law Commission has recommended that because indissoluble marriage no longer exists in English law, the courts should pay more attention to the wife's capacity to earn when assessing her claim to maintenance. But this overlooks the fact that the work of caring for the young, the old and husbands effectively reduces women's leverage on the labour market and that the obligation to care for young and old often continues after divorce (HMSO, 1980a).

In the case of the tax system, discussion has centred on the aggregation rule under which a wife's income is deemed to be that of her husband for tax purposes, and on proposals to abolish the married man's allowance, paid to all men regardless of whether or not their wives actually stay at home. The Government favours a solution which would establish formal equality by giving a transferable tax allowance to each partner (HMSO, 1980b). Thus a wife who stays at home could transfer her personal allowance to her husband to set against his income, which would give husbands an incentive to discourage their wives from re-entering the labour force. Moreover, there is no differentiation between childless families in which one spouse (in almost all cases the wife) is a full-time housewife out of preference and families in which the wife performs the socially useful work of parenting and caring. In other words, the Government's proposals protect the position of the childless, single-earner couple and the family in which the wife stays at home rather than that of families in which both spouses work. Critics of the proposal have strongly advocated using the money saved by abolishing the married man's tax allowance to increase child benefit (Lister, 1981).

The question of the division of resources and work within the family is crucial in view of arguments in favour of equalising the capacity to buy services. While valid in terms of a class analysis, these proposals tend to ignore the greater importance that services may have for women because of their inferior economic position and because of the work they do. For example, it has been suggested that women use the health service more than men because of their reproductive roles and because of the tensions they experience in reconciling their conflicting responsibilities as housewives, mothers and workers (married women suffer considerably more mental illness than married men) (Oakley, 1982). Women also have greater need of social services because of the work of caring they do within the family. Indeed, any run-down of the personal social services, such as we are presently witnessing, serves only to reinforce women's role as carers. Community care for various categories of sick and disabled people was promoted during the 1960s as a more humane alternative to institutional care, but the concept has been colonised by successive Governments whose primary motive has been to cut costs. Without the provision of necessary ancillary services, the burden borne by women in the community has become greater. Moreover, it is a burden that is bound to increase. Between now and the end of the century the total number of people over retirement age will remain fairly constant. However, the number over 75 will increase by nearly one-third, from 2.6 to 3.5 million. At present, only 2 per cent of the elderly population is in residential accommodation (Finch and Groves, 1980; Land, 1981).

## The politics of equality

During the 1970s both parties talked of the importance of policies to support the family as if such policies were politically neutral (Steiner, 1981). In fact, there is little doubt that the Conservatives intended to strengthen the male breadwinner family model and traditional sexual divisions, as their recent policies have demonstrated. Policy documents issued by the Department of Education and Science have stressed the importance of including education in morals and preparation for parenthood, with the emphasis on sexual differentiation rather than on sexual equality (David, 1982), and nursery education and maternity rights have been eroded. The proposed changes in the tax system and in family law may thus be seen to be part of a series of measures that will result in greater pressure on women to choose either the role of wife/mother/carer or that of childless career woman.

The Labour Party of the 1970s showed greater responsiveness to the demands of the feminist movement on the question of women's position in the labour market and on the issue of disaggregation. Yet in 1978 James Callaghan advocated changes in industrial organisation that would enable working women to perform their work in the home more efficiently (Coussins and Coote, 1981). Such proposals show a lack of appreciation of the interrelation between the pursuit of equality in all areas of women's lives; equal opportunity in the workplace is impossible as long as it is assumed that women will continue to take responsibility for housework, parenting and caring.

In the long term the logic of policy initiatives will have to be radically rethought. For example, Anne Coote has suggested recently that we might begin with a question like 'How shall we care for and support our children?' rather than 'How can we regenerate industry to create full employment?' (Coote, 1981). I agree that it is exactly this kind of shift in thinking that is necessary; pursuit of substantive rather than formal sex equality raises fundamental questions regarding the way in which work is defined – within the family as well as at the workplace – and the function and source of the wage. To demand changes in the structures upholding sex inequality is not at odds with the pressing concerns outlined in other chapters in this book. Indeed, it is because equality for women involves fundamental changes in the organisation of the labour process and the family that it is impossible to compartmentalise 'women's issues' and add them to a list of policy priorities – usually at the bottom. What the Labour Party must demonstrate is a firm understanding and commitment to working towards a substantive sex equality, such that important goals, like job creation, are pursued in a way that actively considers and improves the position of women.

## Notes

1  This inevitably omits consideration of other important aspects of women's lives, in particular female access to education and women's struggle to control all aspects of biological reproduction.
2  I am grateful to Irene Bruegel for discussing many of the ideas in this section with me. The whole section relies heavily on her paper 'Women's employment, legislation and the labour markets' (Bruegel, 1982).
3  I am indebted to Ann Sedley, Women's Rights Officer, National Council for Civil Liberties, for information on these proposed amendments.
4  I am indebted to Hilary Land for many of the ideas expressed in this section and in particular to her paper 'Who still supports the family: an examination of recent developments in income maintenance, taxation and family law' (Land, 1982).

## References

Abbott, E., and Bompass, K. (1943) *The Woman Citizen and Social Security* (London)

Beveridge, Sir William (1942) *Social Insurance and Allied Services*, Cmd 6404 (London: HMSO)

Blackstone, Tessa (1980) 'Education', in N. Bosanquet and P. Townsend (eds.), *Labour and Inequality* (London: Heinemann), pp. 226–43

Bruegel, I. (1982) 'Women's employment, legislation and the labour market', in J. Lewis (ed.), *Women's Welfare/Women's Rights* (London: Croom Helm)

Chiplin, B., and Sloane, P. (1976) *Sex Discrimination in the Labour Market* (London: Macmillan)

Coote, Anna (1981) 'The AES: a new starting point', *New Socialist*, Nov./Dec., pp. 4–7

Coulter, Angela (1981) *Who Minds the Minders?* (London: Low Pay Unit)

Coussins, Jean (1976) *The Equality Report* (London: NCCL)

Coussins, Jean (1980) 'Equality for women. Have the laws worked?', *Marxism Today*, Jan., pp. 6–11

Coussins, J., and Coote, A. (1981) *The Family in the Firing Line* (London: NCCL/CPAG)

CPRS (1980) *People and their Families* (London: HMSO)

Daniel, W. W. (1981) *Maternity Rights* (London: PSI)

David, Miriam E. (1982) 'The New Right, sex, education and social policy: towards a new moral economy in Britain and the USA', in J. Lewis (ed.), *Women's Welfare/Women's Rights* (London: Croom Helm)

EOC (1977) *Women and Low Incomes*, evidence to the Royal Commission on the Distribution of Income and Wealth (London: HMSO)

Fairbairns, Zoë (1979) 'The cohabitation rule – why it makes sense', *Women's Studies International Quarterly*, vol. 2, pp. 319–27

Finch, J., and Groves, D. (1980) 'Community care and the family. A case for equal opportunity?', *Journal of Social Policy*, vol. 9, pp. 487–511

Fisher, Alan, and Dix, Bernard (1974) *Low Pay and How to End it* (London: Pitman)

Fogarty, Michael P., *et al*. (1981) *Women in Top Jobs 1968–1979* (London: Heinemann)

Gardiner, J., and Smith, S. (1981) 'Feminism and the AES', *Marxism Today*, Oct., pp. 24–30

Ginsberg, S. (1976) 'Women work and conflict', in N. Fonda and P. Moss (eds.), *Mothers and Employment* (Uxbridge: Brunel University), pp. 75–88

Gregory, Jeanne (1982) 'Some cases that never reached the tribunal', *Feminist Review*, no. 10, pp. 75–90

Groves, Dulcie (1982) 'Members or survivors? Women and retirement pensions legislation', in J. Lewis (ed.), *Women's Welfare/Women's Rights* (London: Croom Helm)

Hakim, C. (1981) 'Job segregation trends in the 1970s', |*Department of Employment Gazette*, Dec., pp. 521–9

Hewitt, Margaret (1975) *Wives and Mothers in Victorian Industry* (Westport: Greenwood Press)

HMSO (1980a) *The Fiscal Consequences of Divorce: The Basic Policy*, Cmnd 8041 (London: HMSO)

HMSO (1980b) *The Taxation of Husband and Wife*, Cmnd 8093 (London: HMSO)

Humphries, J. (1980) 'Class struggle and the persistence of the working-class family', in A. Amsden (ed.), *The Economics of Women's Work* (Harmondsworth: Penguin), pp. 140–65

Hurstfield, Jennifer (1978) *The Part-Time Trap* (London: Low Pay Unit)

Land, Hilary (1977) 'The child benefit fiasco', in K. Jones (ed.), *The Year Book of Social Policy in Britain, 1976* (London: Routledge & Kegan Paul), pp. 116–31

Land, H. (1980) 'The family wage', *Feminist Review*, no. 6, pp. 55–76

Land, H. (1981) *Parity Begins at Home. Women's and Men's Work in the Home and its Effects on their Paid Employment* (London: EOC)

Land, H. (1982) 'Who still supports the family? An examination of recent developments in income maintenance, taxation and family law', in J. Lewis (ed.), *Women's Welfare/Women's Rights* (London: Croom Helm)

Lister, R. (1981) *Social Priorities in Taxation* (London: CPAG)

Lister, R., and Finister, G. (1981) *The Case Against Contribution Tests* (London: CPAG)

Low Pay Unit and EOC (1980) *Minimum Wages for Women* (London: Low Pay Unit)

McIntosh, Mary (1981) 'Feminism and social policy', *Critical Social Policy*, vol. 1, pp. 32–43

Oakley, Ann (1982) 'Women and health policy', in J. Lewis (ed.), *Women's Welfare/Women's Rights* (London: Croom Helm)

Pahl, Jan (1980) 'Patterns of money management within marriage', *Journal of Social Policy*, vol. 9, pp. 313–30

Raphael, D. D. (1980) *Justice and Liberty* (London: Athlone Press)

Richards, Janet Radcliffe (1980) *The Sceptical Feminist* (London: Routledge & Kegan Paul)

Rights of Women and Women's Legal and Financial Independence Campaign (1979) 'Disaggregation now', *Feminist Review*, no. 2, pp. 19–31

Roberts, Sadie *et al.* (1981) *Positive Action for Women. The Next Step* (London: NCCL)

Routh, G. (1980) *Occupation and Pay in Great Britain, 1906–79* (London: Macmillan)

Sedley, Ann (1980) *Part-Time Workers Need Full-Time Rights* (London: NCCL)

Snell, M. *et al.* (1981) *Equal Pay and Opportunity*, Dept. of Employment Research Paper No. 20 (London: HMSO)

Steiner, Gilbert (1981) *The Futility of Family Policy* (Washington, DC: Brookings Institute)

Tizard, Jack (1976) 'Effects of day care on young children', in N. Fonda and P. Moss (eds.), *Mothers and Employment* (Uxbridge: Brunel University), pp. 54–74

Weir, Angela, and McIntosh, Mary (1982) 'Towards a wages strategy for Women', *Feminist Review*, no. 10, pp. 5–20

# 8

# Industrial Relations

Colin Crouch

A sharp decline in membership and income, a heavy loss of political power, a deteriorating capacity to mobilise members for conflict but continuing enormous public hostility: the reversal of the position of British trade unions since they reached the peak of their power in the years around 1974 has been extraordinary but should not be surprising. The right, both in Britain and elsewhere in the industrialised West, did not take kindly to the intensified social conflict and associated rise of left-wing forces that occurred generally from the late 1960s onwards. Across a whole range of policy areas the right equipped itself for a counter-attack, with the aim of reversing the full employment and tolerant social climate which had prevailed since the 1960s and which had done so much to strengthen the confidence of organised labour and other forces of the left. Monetarism, an attack on the welfare state, the mobilisation of popular right-wing values and a more aggressive role for the forces of civil order are among the main products of this reorientation. The policies have been put into action both when right-wing parties have come to power and, irrespective of Governments, through such agencies as central banks and multinational enterprises.

The left was ill prepared for this counter-attack, partly because it had not realised how exposed its position had become. The power of unions to disrupt (through strikes, inflation and inefficient working practices) has been far in excess of their power to make positive gains for ordinary workers. This negative aspect of much union power has created many enemies among ordinary people, for whom union action means disruption and inconvenience to their daily lives. The agonising paradox of this has been that the right has been able to add to its already formidable array the one resource that had been assumed to be labour's main source of power: the sentiments of the mass of the working population. Increasingly, the labour movement has fallen back on the strength vested in its formal organisations – organisations which, once bereft of mass support, become empty bureaucracies.

The lessons of this experience must be learned by the labour movement and its strategy reorganised in that light. If not, the defeat, which could extend far further than it has so far done, will be severe and prolonged. The most important lessons are the following.

First, nothing can dislodge full employment as the prime goal of a trade union movement. This is true not only because of the misery and anxiety produced directly by worklessness but also because of the diminution of the rights and dignity of every employed person that takes place when the employer can easily dispense with his or her labour. Because full employment seemed to have been so easily achieved by postwar capitalism, many left-wing commentators (though very few people in the union movement itself) dismissed it as no great gain for the left, as something which capitalism itself needed for its own continuation (e.g. O'Connor, 1973; Miliband, 1969). It is true that full employment did not secure social and economic equality or abolish the power of capital, but it did considerably improve the position of workers in their continuing struggle with employers, both as a movement of organised labour and as individual workers seeking security and the right to be treated with respect. As capitalism is again moving into a period when it either cannot or does not need to provide full employment, the period of Keynesian economics appears increasingly to have been labour's golden age. Full employment is a prize worth having at considerable cost.

Second, the apparently impressive strength of the shop-floor movement that spread so widely in Britain between about 1950 and 1979 was far more dependent on the basic stance of Government economic policy than was generally realised. Governments did not like the shop-floor movement, Labour little less than Tories, but for a long time they maintained macro-economic and industrial relations policies which enabled that movement to flourish. True, shop-floor strength was established by workers themselves without help from the Government legislation on which unions in most other societies have relied for extensions of their rights; but it was dependent on Keynesian economics and on a basic acceptance of the role of unions within industry.

Third, a right-wing Government can whittle away the labour movement's hard-won rights without provoking popular outrage and with no automatic recovery for the party of labour. Indeed, the evidence is very strong that trade-union power remains highly unpopular among the class on whose behalf it is supposed to be exercised. However dismissive one is of superficial polls of public opinion, findings that over 90 per cent of the population, including over 90 per cent of Labour voters, favour legislative action to limit various union powers (Crewe, 1981, 1982) cannot be glossed over. The argument that this public opinion is the result of appalling bias in the daily newspapers and even on television and radio is true but in some respects irrelevant. It is that state of opinion, however derived, with which Labour now has to come to terms.

These are the lessons of the current spell of reactionary government. Behind them lie some more fundamental and even more disturbing facts concerning the modern international economy. Two major forces are moving like pincers towards the labour force of the Western industrialised countries: microprocessor technology and the shift of production to the newly industrialising nations. These both threaten traditional patterns of employment in countries like Britain. The former process is gradually removing the need for many jobs, spanning divisions of skill and divisions between manual and non-manual work. The process can, of course, be resisted by organised workers, who can either prevent the use of the new technology or insist that its use should have no effect on manning levels. This has been done by several groups in Britain. However, even if labour can retain sufficient strength to enforce this resistance, its consequence will only be to make British goods more expensive than those from countries in which the new technology is operating, reducing demand for them and hence reducing both employment and production. In other words, the long-term consequence of resistance is worse than that of acceptance. In some sectors of the British economy we have already reached that long term.

The shift of production to a number of Third World countries which have begun to industrialise successfully (Froebel *et al.*, 1979) cannot be stopped even temporarily by ordinary union action. In some respects, of course, this was something that had to happen one day if the poorer countries of the world were to extricate themselves from dependence on subsistence agricultural production, but the way in which development has occurred has an ugly twist. Those countries which have developed as rivals to Western industrial nations are those with large surplus populations (and hence labour which is in a very weak bargaining position) and with dictatorial right-wing Governments which resist demands for the extension of civil and union rights. Even where these conditions are less dramatically evident, labour conditions in newly industrialising countries with a history of poverty will almost inevitably be worse than in Western nations.

In these circumstances international companies choosing new sites for development have a major lever to use against labour movements and, if necessary, Governments; if union rights in a particular country are too strong, or health and safety standards too stringent, or taxes on profits too high, then there are many other countries which will be only too happy to oblige these companies. This is sometimes a bluff that can be called; the geographical locations of the old industrialised nations and the pattern of skills and work disciplines available within them frequently offer crucial advantages. However, as time passes these advantages are becoming less significant, especially the latter; here the simplified working methods and increased scope for the control and surveillance of a work force offered by new technology combine with the new international division of labour to produce the same result: the weakening of the power of organised labour.

As Michael Mann shows elsewhere in this volume, the new internationalisation of the economy makes even political action, if it remains at the national level, inappropriate and impotent. In Britain for well over a century, elsewhere in the industrial

world for shorter periods, we have been accustomed to societies
in which the production of goods and services has depended on
the employment of the majority of at least the adult male population in large concentrations and under highly organised conditions. These circumstances have been favourable to the organisation of that population, both industrially and at the political
level of the nation state, so that it might struggle for its own
interests. We are now in the early stages of an economy which
no longer needs that concentrated working population and to
which the level of the nation state is not a very important political unit. The problems which such an economy will raise for the
politics of labour are immense.


## Reconstructing labour politics

It is within this hostile context that the future industrial relations policy of the labour movement has to be constructed. I
shall deal first with issues that assume the continuing relevance
of the nation state; it should not be written off yet, and in any
case it provides the major springboard for international action.
Later I shall devote some attention to the new international context.

All the developments discussed in the opening section of this
chapter strike with particular force at a movement with the
background of British unions, which have relied predominantly
on their own industrial strength rather than on the political
strength of their associated party. Other northern European
labour movements have sought advances in their power primarily through legally established rights. They have often envied
British unions their independence from politics and law; an
autonomously bargained right is often better suited to workers'
interests than one that has been processed through the parliamentary and legal systems. However, it could be argued that
legal rights are less easily disbanded during a recession than
those which depend essentially on the organised exploitation of
full employment.

This assertion is not entirely true. It is easier for employers to
ride roughshod over workers' legal rights during a recession, as

German unions have been complaining recently; and legal rights can be repealed by hostile Governments. However, it is notable that the present Conservative Government has been far more reluctant to take away the rights won by labour in the legislation of the mid-1970s than it has been to encourage the wrecking of informal shop-floor power in industry after industry.

Further, it is difficult to find a Western country in which the unions are so widely held to blame for economic problems but in which unions seem to care so little about that fact. One recalls Italian unions avoiding prolonged strikes in public services that might be considered to hurt the working class in its daily life. Of course, it has been *weakness* and past experience of how Fascist regimes can manipulate public opinion against organised labour which makes Italians, Germans and others so squeamish about causing public hardship, but British unions' toughmindedness can also be seen as disturbingly complacent in the current Western political climate. There is also something more than mere rhetoric in the claim of many European unions that they represent the class, not just an occupational group, and must therefore think about the wider effect of their actions; this can be read as meaning 'Think of the voters as well as the members'! Only a union movement like the British one, which believes that its achievements owe relatively little to the identity of the party in power, can afford to ignore that advice.

Taken together with the more general collapse of the Labour Party, the current decline in the strength of the unions suggests an alarmingly rapid dissolution of the place which, over many decades, the labour movement established in British political and economic life. Since no historical achievements can be assumed to be permanent, we have as yet no idea how far this process will extend. Such a crisis should provoke a general willingness to reorient and reform, but this is hindered by the false comfort of prevailing Party orthodoxy, which is to insulate the British economy from foreign competition and to suppress all unwelcome domestic developments by state regulation, so that, within the haven thereby created, full employment can be re-established with no threat to existing manning levels or working practices. Free collective bargaining would also return, made possible by, first, state borrowing and the mobilisation of resources to reduce the dependence of investment levels on profit margins; second, a rise in the price that British labour could demand following the exclusion of foreign competition; and, third, the inability of British consumers to shop elsewhere. Many of the problems of such an economic strategy are discussed in Meghnad Desai's chapter in this volume; for present purposes the most important one is the impossibility of having a totally regulated economy in which wages alone follow *laissez-faire*.

The usual riposte to this argument (e.g. Benn, 1980, pp. 153–5) is that some kind of understanding over income growth would be acceptable once there was a socialist economic policy. But this misses the point that the forces of decentralised shop-floor bargaining which have been the main opposition to union co-operation with incomes restraint in the past have to do not with a socialist or any other economic policy but with groups of workers who would like more money and have the organisational means to secure it. National questions of economic policy are not relevant at the level of shop-floor groups because of the logic of their position. Although the existence of many groups maximising their immediate interests has major macro-economic consequences, no individual group can take that into account. The effect of a particular wage rise for a small group on the overall level of prices in the economy, which its members will eventually have to face as consumers, is infinitesimally small; in no way can it be expected to worry about the ramifications. Indeed, if the group expects a rise in the general price level, it must put in a very high wage claim or its members will lose out. The group that says it will restrain its wage claim in order to help combat inflation will simply be overwhelmed by the inflation caused by everybody else, while its own abstention will make no perceptible impact on the general price level. This will be true both for unofficial shop-floor groupings and for small unions or sections of unions able to isolate their bargaining from that of other unions.

Since the *initial* effects of the Labour Party's Alternative Economic Strategy would be to reduce the supply of cheap goods through import controls, prices would rise, and it must be expected that workers would respond by making large pay claims. Given the logic of unco-ordinated bargaining spelled out above, it would take something a good deal more powerful than appeals to support a socialist economic policy to prevent this logic from being acted out.

It is impossible any longer to avoid the conclusion that the contradiction within the British labour movement – that between a liberal collective bargaining strategy and a socialist political strategy – has reached the limits of tolerance. That there is such a contradiction has long been recognised, but it has been possible to postpone its implications by means of a variety of devices: the acceptance of rather high levels of inflation, a stop-go economic policy, reliance on the general postwar growth of the Western economy and, in the background, the declining legacy of Britain's former economic world domination. Virtually all of these have now reached the end of the line.

To point out this contradiction is not to make a fundamental attack on the Labour Party's historical base. All major political movements embody contradictions; the question is whether the implications of the contradictions can be kept from realisation. And the fact that Labour's contradiction has been realised is not necessarily a gain to British society. A combination of liberal, decentralised bargaining and socialist politics has much to recommend it; the reliance on industrial rather than state strength that has been so important to British unions is part of that highly attractive feature of British life, the autonomy of civil society. The problem is that the use of that kind of strength in the straitened economic circumstances of modern Britain can have only two consequences: the wrecking of any attempt at a planned return to full employment, and the triumph of a reactionary policy which treats the permanent ending of full employment as the only counter to union power.

The conclusion to be drawn from this predicament is the opposite of that advocated by the Social Democratic Party, which seeks the depoliticisation of the unions. Instead the unions need to become far more political, in the sense that they must accept a share in responsibility for macro-economic policy, for efficiency and manning levels and for the effect on electoral opinion of their own conduct. How is this to be achieved?

First, the Government has to deserve the confidence of effective decision-makers within the unions in its determination to follow a path of economic growth and recovery of employment, and it has to involve union leaders closely in the pursuit of that policy. This aspect of the argument is, of course, accepted Party orthodoxy; it constitutes a justified criticism of the last Labour Government and a *sine qua non* for future policy. As such, it needs little further discussion here; it is more important to address issues which the Party is less willing to consider. The major one is the balance between central and localised power within the unions, in the light of the above observations that it is only a national leadership which can act in relation to national political goals.

## Elements of a new policy

It is an unusually helpful irony that certain current problems of the labour movement may contribute to a solution. First, the current recession has drastically eroded shop-floor strength. This gives national leaderships a chance to seize the initiative during a reconstruction of the movement's position under a Labour Government, as happened during the wartime coalition following the interwar depression. Second, the long-term difficulties that will be experienced during the re-establishment of full employment will entail the dependence of the unions on political (that is, Government) action. Only Government will be in a position to encourage the generation of worthwhile employment in new sectors following the now inevitable decline of traditional areas of employment. British unions will therefore be much more aware than in the past of their dependence on Government and therefore of the need to avoid destroying the support base of Governments that are friendly to them. Third, in the wake of the current Conservative Government the unions will also be dependent on Government for instituting major changes in the law, partly to repeal Conservative legislation and partly to remedy the serious gaps in workers' rights which the recession has revealed.

In other words, there may soon be the chance that a British Labour Government could have associated with it the kind of union movement typically found alongside northern European socialist Governments: a movement equipped with a strong central leadership that is deeply concerned with pursuing policies compatible with full employment and a successful, efficient economy in support of its Government. The question remains of how this initially advantageous situation can be turned into something more permanent than the similar but extremely fragile situation under the social contract of the mid-1970s. This involves discussion of four areas: incomes, labour law, manpower and industrial democracy.

*Incomes policy*

As Lord McCarthy has argued (1981), 'there is a necessary link between incomes policy and socialism', not because it is a means of securing equality or because within a socialist economy there should be no need for bargaining, but because for a long time to come we shall be in conditions of considerable scarcity. I would add: under conditions of scarcity no Government can both allow unrestrained collective bargaining and guarantee full employment. Given the priority which socialists must accord to full employment, unrestrained collective bargaining is an excessively expensive luxury; indeed, since unemployment destroys free collective bargaining, there is not really a choice.

However, as McCarthy goes on to argue, there is no point in an excessively ambitious policy which creates both labour-market rigidities and resentment. The main need is simply to ensure that overall bargaining strength is being deployed in a manner compatible with both high employment levels and stable prices. This suggests that the rough general targeting of the social contract is a better guide to future policy than the detailed norms and exceptions of the Heath Government's Pay Board or the preceding Wilson Government's National Board for Prices and Incomes. On the other hand, there was something impressive about the detailed investigations of efficiency carried out by the latter; the British economy still needs considerable probing of this kind. Again, the 1974 Government provides a better guide; the job of the detailed investigation of individual firms was given to the Price Commission, abolished by the Conservatives in 1979 just as it was beginning to gain a powerful place in questioning firms' pricing procedures. A similar commission charged with investigating both prices and productivity would have a major part to play under a future Labour Government, and clearly its activities would be relevant to incomes. However, income restraint itself is best left to voluntary understandings between Government and unions.

The main need is to ensure that aggregate rises in labour costs do not strain competitiveness. There is little point in Governments|trying to ensure that every wage rise is compatible with the policy; there must be sufficient flexibility both to allow responses to labour-market developments and to make possible occasional breaches of policy when individual unions have an internal political need to break rank. Provided restraint is working adequately most of the time, such occasions need cause no crises. The problems that breaches of the general norm create for comparability are best dealt with by being thrown back on the internal organisation of the movement; it is not an appropriate field for state action.

There are two requirements for a policy that would meet this need. The first, which would be popular, easy to establish but utterly useless if not accompanied by the second, is some kind of national forum within which unions, Government and employers would try to agree on basic economic desiderata, including a prediction of the wages developments which would be compatible with an optimal growth path: the National Economic Assessment which has become Party policy. Whether new institutions would be needed to do this or whether the National Economic Development Council could take on this task is a secondary issue.

The prior and far more essential need is for a union structure that is sufficiently centralised in its main decision-making on wages questions to be able to make effective the national-level decisions which its leaders recognise as necessary. At the time when the social contract was collapsing in early 1979, there was much discussion in Britain of the German system of Concerted Action, which was seen to provide a national forum for setting income and other economic targets; it was widely advocated that the establishment of a similar forum here would help to achieve effective income restraint. Observers failed to note that at that time Concerted Action had been boycotted for two years by the German unions and that few German commentators had credited it with much influence on events since the early 1970s (Hardes, 1974). What was, and remains, a significant feature of German wage developments is the centralised structure of German unions and the ability of the leadership to accept particular policies as compatible with national economic development, whether these are agreed through Concerted Action procedures or less formally (Clark *et al.*, 1980; Crouch, forthcoming).

It would be both foolish and politically impossible for a Government to try to impose a different structure on the union movement by law. Changes have to be brought about by the unions themselves. But Government is entitled to put maximum pressure on the unions to persuade them to try to do this. Two kinds of sanction are available.

First, Government can make active use of the value to organised interests, including unions, of access to its own decision-making machinery. We have in this country on the one hand an elaborate system of consultative contacts between Government and private interests but on the other hand a marked reluctance to use this system as a sanction. Trade unions, firms and others who do not co-operate should be frozen out of detailed consultation, appointments to official bodies and so forth. In the case of unions, this sanction would be invoked against those doing nothing to amend their internal bargaining structure. A liberal, gentlemanly norm rather than a socialist one of mobilisation for full employment and an efficient economy has too long dominated relations between Governments and organised interests.

Second, use should be made of political exchange between Government and unions. Many of the substantive gains which unions expect to receive from a Labour Government could be made dependent on co-operation. A curious feature of the social contract was that the Government conceded to the unions virtually all their demands for industrial relations law reform before they began to co-operate on wage restraint. In future the response to union demands should be more extended and gradual, conditional on co-operation. The objective should be to make the political exchange continuous, with a permanent flow of demands and responses on both sides. This would serve the further purpose of reducing the strain and importance of any individual exchange.

## Industrial relations law reform

It would be wrong to consider law reform purely from the perspective of the political use which might be made of it. What are the main issues which should, in their own right, be addressed by a Labour Government? The diminution of union rights embodied in the 1980 and 1982 Employment Acts will demand immediate attention. Limitations on secondary industrial action, restrictions on picketing and the social security handicap on strikers' families are all intended to shift the balance of industrial power away from workers. Given the economic outlook established at the outset, the industrial balance of power in the coming years will be bad enough from labour's point of view without these additional legal aids to employers. Prohibitions on secondary action are particularly unacceptable. Many labour struggles concern workers who are in a weak position to fight their employers alone. It is central to trade unionism that the weak should be able to borrow the strength of the strong. These issues merit immediate attention.

The closed shop, which generates far more political energy on both sides than it merits, should receive a less instinctive response. Far worse obligations and indignities are imposed on workers in the employment relationship than the requirement to join an organisation devoted to defending their own rights. On the other hand, it is doubtful whether union strength would be materially affected by the trickle of awkward individuals who insist on not being members. The arguments for and against the closed shop are finely balanced: put simply, the problem is that of the free rider who enjoys union benefits but will not pay the dues *versus* the unhealthiness of a union's dependence not on its own ability to attract members but on co-opting the employer's power to force workers to do things.

At a time when unions are becoming increasingly out of touch with working people, substituting organisational shells in the place of real, vibrant popular strength, the latter arguments are becoming more powerful. The movement should reconsider the idea that workers in closed shops should have the right to opt instead for payment, to a nominated charity, of a sum equal to their union subscription. This would solve the free-rider problem while preserving the status of the movement as voluntary and independent of employer power.

In addition to repealing Conservative measures, Labour will want further to improve workers' and unions' legal rights. The legislation of the mid-1970s marked a significant shift towards putting labour rights on a statutory basis, breaking with the voluntarist tradition more than is admitted. In particular, the establishment of the Advisory, Conciliation and Arbitration Service and the Central Arbitration Committee has been a notable success. In a hostile economic climate in which shop stewards' power has been revealed to be more fragile than was earlier assumed, this tendency to legal protection should be extended. There should be a continuous monitoring of the kinds of grievance which workers are pursuing through conflict action, with the aim of embodying many of these in formal codes of rights.

It is in this context that the rights removed by the 1980 Employment Act through its repeal of Schedule 11 of the Employment Protection Act 1975 should be considered. Two in particular merit attention. First is the right to have extended to all members of a given category of workers the terms of an agreement negotiated generally for them. As provision of this kind first appeared during the Second World War, but its retention has been a matter of dispute between employers and unions since the late 1950s. It would be reasonable for a union movement which had demonstrated its ability to co-ordinate general restraint to demand the restitution of a right to general benefit. Second, the 'right' to union recognition provided under Schedule 11 had been, at the unions' insistence, one that was subject to a good deal of voluntary action. As the Grunwick case showed (Rogaly, 1977, ch. 11), this made it very difficult to operate. It also ran into great problems when the issue of union recognition became in many cases a dispute over which of two or more competing union organisations was to represent the workers in question, not over the principle of recognition. Clearly, a good deal of thinking remains to be done within the unions over this question before a demand for future action can be made.

## Manpower policy

Manpower policy is becoming as important to workers' rights as legal protection and to the economy as wage restraint. On the one hand, it will only be through carefully planned programmes that this country will be able to move from current patterns of employment to those more suited to the new technologies of the future. People will have to change jobs and occupations, and many of these transitions will be painful; but the degree of pain and, in particular, of insecurity could be a good deal less than under current policies, which 'squeeze employment out of the system' and hope some new entrepreneurial future will emerge into the vacuum thereby created. On the other hand, unions will have to accept that many of their stances on craft training, manning levels and job definitions are hopeless attempts to preserve a lost past.

The Manpower Services Commission, independent of Government and under tripartite administration, has proved to be a valuable forum for making progress on these questions. Under the Conservative Government its role has been hamstrung by budget reductions and by Ministers who have devised short-term and *ad hoc* schemes which interfere with the Commission's longer-term policy-making and which are often designed to create the impression that 'something is being done' about unemployment rather than to make a serious assault on long-term manpower problems. Despite this, the Manpower Services Commission has held together. Union representatives on it have appreciated the possibilities it offers for eventually developing something like Swedish active manpower policy; and employers have occasionally taken up a common front with the unions within the Commission against Government. This augurs very well for its future under a Government genuinely sympathetic to its aims and willing both to allocate it adequate funds for its work and to grant it policy autonomy within its field.

*Industrial democracy*

Agreed income restraint, law reform and manpower policy all involve union leaderships rather than shop-floor groupings and enhance their power within the union movement. To the extent that one of the movement's problems has been its unco-ordinated nature, this is a necessary development. Two objections must, however, be considered. First, shop-floor strength is a valuable democratic achievement that should not be lightly cast aside. Second, the power of the shop-floor movement has historically been such that, whatever its temporary reversals during a recession, it just will not be cast aside. This question must therefore be faced: what will be the role of the shop-floor movement if wages policy is more tightly co-ordinated at a national level and if many of the working practices which it is the business of shop-floor groups to defend are either negotiated away or forced to disappear by the bankruptcy of the companies which maintain them?

The answer lies in schemes for industrial democracy which would give elected workplace representatives the power to contribute to the development of management policy at several different levels of the firm. An opportunity was dreadfully wasted when the right and left wings of the labour movement gave either a lukewarm or a downright hostile response to the Bullock Report on industrial democracy (Bullock, 1977). Much of the debate within the movement over both Bullock and other schemes for worker participation has centred on the issue of whether they are means of extending workers' power or means by which workers' representatives will be forced to take account of economic forces wider than those of their immediate bargaining interests. The correct answer is that *both* aspects of the question are involved, and that both are desirable. Workers do need more power, but they do need to exercise it under the constraint of what makes sense for efficiency and growth.

It is very welcome that the Party has revived industrial democracy, properly setting it in the context of economic planning, in its joint document on the question with the Trades Union Congress (Labour Party, 1982). Meanwhile, the recession has generated the growth of a number of schemes for worker participation, aimed primarily at the problems associated with labour-shedding and changing working practices and usually instigated by employers (*Department of Employment Gazette*, 1981). These schemes will not all die on the election of a Labour Government, and many shop-floor organisations will have found them to be useful channels of influence or at least information. Industrial democracy has not disappeared from the agenda to the extent that the practice of the present Government suggests.

But in constructing policy Labour and the unions must confront one prickly issue: is industrial democracy to relate closely to workers' lives, or is it to be an external imposition of machinery automatically dominated by union functionaries? If it is the latter, it will serve the purposes neither of channelling shop-floor militancy nor of bringing unions closer to the workers. Anxiety over the Party's intentions is not allayed by references in the new policy document to 'joint *union* boards' (my italics) as the form to be taken by representation. This follows Bullock's insistence on union channels of representation. Why not risk genuine elections for worker representatives among the entire work force of a company, elections in which unions would run their own slates of candidates and put their organisational weight behind their campaigns but which would give workers a chance to express their current attitudes to union representation? West German unions have to do this in the triennial elections of works councils; and despite the lower level of unionisation of the German economy, nearly 80 per cent of works councillors are union candidates, and overall turnout for the elections is higher than that for British general elections. This system gives the unions powerful votes of confidence.

There was also considerable substance to one of the objections of employers' representatives on the Bullock Committee to the Committee's majority recommendations. This was that schemes for industrial democracy should not start from the top with the sudden imposition of board-level representation but should grow up gradually from participative machinery at lower levels. Employers had their own reasons for arguing this point, but it is also relevant to the continuing problem faced by the labour movement of providing institutions that are meaningful to workers and not simply to union functionaries, whether these are paid officials or shop stewards. Mechanisms for participation which grow out of actual experience are likely to command wider assent and to be used more effectively by workers if they start from points accessible and comprehensible to the workers themselves. This suggests a gradual policy, based on experiment and with a good deal of internal flexibility but guided by the aim of providing a strong constitutional place for union representation in company decision-making.

## Conclusion: the international context

At one level the strategy outlined above is defensive, pessimistic; it represents a drawing in of horns, a suggestion that the labour movement must sacrifice many of its accustomed ways in the interests of survival in the cold climate of the last quarter of the twentieth century. But it is also the kind of strategy that has been pursued for a much longer period in those countries which have the best records of labour-movement political success: the Scandinavian countries, Austria, to a certain extent the Federal Republic of Germany. There is no need to regard that route as less congenial to socialist politics than free collective bargaining.

There remains the looming problem, discussed at the outset of this chapter, of the changed international economic situation which enables employers to pick and choose between countries and currently threatens all the powerful social democracies. Here there are just two lines of potential optimism. First, there remain many advantages to production within the older advanced industrial nations: access to markets, political stability, the availability of an educated and experienced work force. When to these is added a union movement which, while strong in defending its members' rights, is prepared to co-operate in the service of future efficiency, there is less need to fear the flight of capital.

Second, there is scope for action at the international political level to restrict capital's freedom. In principle, for example, there is nothing to prevent groups of countries from imposing special tariffs on goods from countries which do not permit free trade unions or which do not meet minimum standards of industrial health and safety. A recent study (Hanson, 1983) argues that, under certain circumstances, such as incorporation of 'social clauses' into international trade negotiations could afford some help to workers and unions in the exporting as well as importing countries. It is certainly of more benefit to workers in exporting countries than other forms of trade protection exercised by importers. The obstacles to the realisation of policies of this kind are severe. Pressure for action would come only from countries in which labour interests were strong; international trade agreements are hard enough without these added complications. Action against producers with poor labour conditions entails reductions in the supply of cheap goods for domestic consumers. Even before one considers the political pressure that would be imposed by multinationals to prevent such action, the problems are daunting.

However, demands for action will mount as the challenge becomes more severe. And the issue carries with it two clear lessons for organised labour. First, all necessary action would have to be carried out at political level, as only Governments have the capacity to act internationally, even though union pressure will be crucial in persuading them to act; collective bargaining will not be an effective instrument here. Second, nothing will be achieved by a labour movement which tries to reduce all its problems to those which can be resolved by itself alone within closed national borders.

These lessons will be as unwelcome to current thinking within the Labour Party as the rest of this chapter. There are, however, important stirrings of realism among those directly confronting the current impasse of British trade unionism. For example, since the bulk of this chapter was drafted, David Basnett, General Secretary of the General and Municipal Workers Union, has published his Fabian pamphlet *The Future of Collective Bargaining* (1982). Not only does he accept the need for change in the unions' approach to the role of Government in wage bargaining, but also three of his major proposals are very similar to those made here on incomes policy: the establishment of a national forum for an annual economic assessment; a shift in the structure of bargaining to allow more central co-ordination; and the revival of the Price Commission, with acknowledged implications for wage levels. The national economic and political climate may remain frozen, but there are signs of a thaw in attitudes within the labour movement itself.

# References

Basnett, D. (1982) *The Future of Collective Bargaining*, Fabian Tract 481 (London: Fabian Society)

Benn, A. (1980) *Arguments for Socialism* (London: Cape)

Bullock, Lord (1977) *Report of Committee of Inquiry into Industrial Democracy* (London: HMSO)

Clark, J., Hartmann, H., Lau, C., and Winchester, D. (1980) *Trade Unions, National Politics and Economic Management* (London and Bonn: Anglo-German Foundation for the Study of Industrial Society)

Crew, I. (1981), 'Why the Conservatives won', in H. R. Penniman (ed.), *Britain at the Polls, 1979* (Washington, DC: American Enterprise Institute for Public Policy Research)

Crewe, I. (1982) 'The Labour Party and the electorate', in D. Kavanagh (ed.), *The Politics of the Labour Party* (London: Allen & Unwin)

Crouch, C. (forthcoming) 'The conditions for trade-union wage restraint', in L. N. Lindberg and C. S. Maier (eds.), *The Politics and Sociology of Global Inflation* (Washington, DC: Brookings Institution)

*Department of Employment Gazette* (1981) 'Developments in employee involvement', February–June, September

Froebel, F., Heinrichs, J., and Kreye, O. (1979) *The New International Division of Labour*, English edn. (New York: Cambridge University Press)

Hanson, G. (1983) *Social Clauses and International Trade* (London: Croom Helm)

Hardes, H.-D. (1974) *Einkommenspolitik in der Bundesrepublik* (Frankfurt: Herder & Herder)

McCarthy, Lord (1981) 'Socialism and incomes policy', in D. Lipsey and D. Leonard (eds.), *The Socialist Agenda: Crosland's Legacy* (London: Cape)

Miliband, R. (1969) *The State in Capitalist Society* (London: Weidenfeld & Nicolson)

O'Connor, J. (1973) *The Fiscal Crisis of the State* (New York: St Martin's Press)

Rogaly, J. (1977) *Grunwick* (Harmondsworth: Penguin)

# 9

# A Politics of Location

Doreen Massey

## The problem

Different stages in the economic and political development of a society have different implications for its economic and social geography. In the UK the birth of industrial capitalism saw the rapid growth of towns, especially in the north and west, and the impoverishment of agricultural areas and of agricultural labour in the south and east. The decline of Empire was marked by the decline of the major industries on which British world dominance had been built, and that in turn brought with it the collapse of the economies of particular regions. By the 1930s the areas on the labour of whose workers British capital ruled the world were suffering the highest unemployment and the most abject levels of poverty. Capital had moved on. At the same period, and over subsequent decades, investment in new industries was concentrated in the south-east and the Midlands of England. That latest burst of growth too is now slackening. Manufacturing employment grew in Britain until the mid-1960s but since then has been declining. Britain's deindustrialisation has been faster, so far, than that of other industrialised capitalist countries. Another reorientation of the world economy is under way, and the UK is losing out as a manufacturing economy. And, once again, a shift in the international economy, of Britain's place within it and of its own economic and political development, has brought with it a change in the national geography.

To simplify greatly an immensely complicated process, what is happening this time is that, with the decline of manufacturing, including many of those industries which have arisen only in the last fifty years, has come the collapse of the manufacturing heartlands of the country. The West Midlands has been particularly badly affected and has slumped in the space of little more than a decade from a booming central region to one with an unemployment rate well above the national average. The inner cities too have been hit, especially because much of the manufacturing investment there was older and often less profitable – and therefore most vulnerable when that wave of capitalist growth in its turn ran out of steam.

National economic and social development, and national economic and social geography, are thus closely linked. And for socialists, therefore, national economic and social policies should be closely linked with considerations of geography, of geographical distribution and of geographical equity. This is not to argue that spatial distribution supersedes social distribution, that all would be well if each region had its fair share of each class and social group. Nor is it to argue that 'spatial' policies are any solution – indeed our conclusion is if anything the opposite. But it *is* to argue that geographical distribution is important, both economically and politically, and it *is* to argue that whole areas – and the people within them – should not simply be developed, exploited and then just as suddenly abandoned as greater profits can be made in pastures new. It *is* to argue that one of the rights of capital which must be challenged is its right to locate where it will. There must be social control, with socially and democratically determined priorities, over the geographical organisation of the economy. We need a politics of location.

There is not much positive experience to go on. There has been a long history of spatial policy in the UK. Most obviously, there has been a 'regional policy', changing in form and intermittent in operation, since the 1930s. And in the last decade there has been the newly urgent concern to 'do something' about the plight of the inner cities. But almost all these policies have had a number of characteristics, shared underlying assumptions, which it is important to challenge.

Perhaps most significant, these policies have almost always been reactive. As an area or region has gone into crisis, some spatially specific response has been devised. In the 1930s the

Special Areas Act and associated measures were too late to cope with the appalling conditions in the Welsh valleys and the north-east of England. In the late 1950s the renewed decline of ship-building provoked visits by Lord Hailsham to the unemployed of Tyneside, and regional development strategies were hastily concocted. In the 1960s the colliery closures were pushed through with the promise of Special Development Area status for affected areas and, in the 1980s, the closures of steelworks with the consolation of an Enterprise Zone. Most recently, the political threat posed by serious rioting in inner-city areas saw another Conservative Minister (this time Michael Heseltine) making another trip north (this time to Merseyside) with more promises and policies.

The history so far, then, has been very much a question of stimulus and response: the stimulus – the threat of trouble from an area suffering the effects of the withdrawal of capital; the response – elastoplast for the particular area in question. Two things should be noted. First, the stimulus has only rarely been the fact of inequality itself; generally, it has been the fact that inequality might provoke political and social unrest. During the long postwar boom in the 1950s the inequality in unemployment rates between the regions of the UK was actually greater, in a simple statistical sense, than in the 1960s. But the low absolute levels of unemployment meant that even the regions where the rate was highest were quiescent. The lack of political pressure enabled nothing to be done. And so the 1950s, the decade which in economic terms offered the greatest opportunity for an attack on geographical inequality and the regional problem, passed with scarcely any action being taken.

Second, though, and to return to the central argument, policies which are as simply reactive as this, which are so clearly post hoc responses, do not amount to planning or social control at all. Apart from a few honourable exceptions, mostly embodied in Commission Reports rather than in actual policies, we have never really attempted in Britain to take positively planned social control over the general geographical distribution of jobs.

There are other criticisms too. Emergency measures for 'problem areas' (note how, in a nice turn of phrase, it is the area that is seen to be the problem rather than its desertion by industry) are rarely related to other policies, in other fields, being pursued at the same time. Often in the past they have been undermined by programmes with which they have been in contradiction. The cut-backs in public services, for instance, have had especially serious effects (in terms of jobs as well as services) in many areas supposedly benefiting from special state aid. Policy towards nationalised industries has conflicted with that towards inner cities and peripheral regions. Further, these spatially specific emergency responses have for the most part taken the form of boosting the competitiveness of certain areas. The workers in one region are still left competing against those in another: all that has happened is that the relative advantages of these competing places has been altered. Once again, this is hardly planning or social control. Moreover, the solution has always been seen in terms of the private sector, in attempts to turn the area, through improvement or subsidy, into one in which private profits can be made. The role of the public sector has been indirect, confined to creating the conditions for renewed exploitation by private industry. The only exceptions to this rule have been occasional decentralisations of central government functions. All these things put together point to a final, and politically most important, characteristic. Policies so far have been fundamentally undemocratic. They have not grown out of the work experience and the requirements of the people of the areas in question. They have been run, very often, by central government or by special, unelected, bodies. There has been very little understanding, at grass-roots level, of what the issues are and therefore very little coherent strategic political pressure. The emergency has already arrived before the issue is placed on the political agenda, and all too often anything has looked better than nothing. And the whole process has remained subject to the dictates of private industry.

## A new approach

A number of general principles, then, can be defined for a socialist policy on industrial location and the geography of economy and society. First, it must be positive planning built around long-term strategic objectives. Spatial policy must stop being simply a response to already existing problems. It must also be about long-term balanced growth. This in turn means that location policy towards industry, and spatial policy in general, must be fully co-ordinated with other arms of policy and, in particular, with national economic strategy. Spatial policy must not be a cosmetic afterthought. It is not a question of first making plans for national economic recovery and then thinking about the geographical implications of that strategy. The two must go hand in hand. And spatial planning must be co-ordinated with other aspects of policy too. There are very few areas of politics which do not have geographical implications.

A socialist policy on location must also abandon the method of forcing areas to compete against each other. At the best of times this is politically unacceptable because it simply plays one group of workers off against another to the benefit of capital. But in the cold climate which we face today it is simply absurd as advertisements, inducements and enticements – and (public) expenditure – are piled on top of each other in the competition for the few crumbs of new investment which are around. Abandonment of that approach will mean different things in different cases. In general, it will mean greater social control. For those companies which in the past have been able to sit back while the competing incentives mounted it must mean some degree of public control over their location strategies. There must not be a repeat, for instance, of the humiliating Nissan episode, when local communities and work forces were forced to bid against each other in an attempt to sell themselves to this multinational which had (or might have had) a few thousand jobs on offer. Further, one conclusion which the competitive approach has always neatly avoided is that some areas must lose. Instead of a race of leapfrogging bribes, this fact must be faced politically. Instead of handing out vain hopes, it must be recognised that there are many areas in the UK to which private capital will not soon return, even with the most massive 'inducements' and even with considerable public and state pressure (it will either not invest, or it will go abroad, thus holding back national employment growth). In these areas it is quite unrealistic to rely on private investment to promote economic recovery. Public investment, directly, must take the lead, combining the aims of improving the environment, rebuilding dilapidated infrastructure, providing much needed social and public services and creating employment. Here again, then, spatial policy links directly with the overall framework of a national Alternative Economic Strategy (AES).

Finally, a socialist politics of location must be democratic. Indeed, regional and locational policies can themselves be a *means* for decentralising and democratising control over national economic policy. Already we are beginning to see, for instance, a hierarchy of alternative economic strategies, from the national AES, through metropolitan-level strategies, to mini-AESs in local boroughs. Such spatially defined strategies can also be an arena for linking industrial and community issues in the process of drawing up local plans and proposals. There are some obvious opportunities: power workers and local communities on plans for district heating; public-sector workers and local service provision. The present habit of tacking 'democracy' on to the end of economic policies will not do. Democratic forms and local and grass-roots organisations must be the basic building blocks of policy. And that applies to regional and inner-city policies as much as any other. Without that, we will simply perpetuate that unhappy legacy of the Labour Governments of the 1960s and 1970s, disillusionment with all forms of public intervention and social control.

These general principles imply also a very different organisational framework for spatial policy. Instead of just defining areas for different levels of subsidy or with different powers of economic policy-making, a range of varied structures needs to be devised to intervene in, and control, the different processes through which geographical inequality is produced and to provide a co-ordinated subnational basis for local economic planning.

At national level there should be at least two strands to this. First, there should be some mechanism for the scrutiny of major national policies which are not in themselves explicitly spatial. Their urban and regional implications should be evaluated against wider geographical policy. This evaluation should, of course, include in its remit the AES, especially in relation to strategic policies – for instance, in connection with broad decisions about which industries to promote and support and which industries might be restructured and how. Second, there will have to be a specifically spatial policy to deal with inter-regionally mobile jobs and investment and the internal organisation of multiregional and multinational companies. At sub-regional level a kind of geographical hierarchy of AESs is developing. The best-known examples are those built around the Enterprise Boards of the Greater London Council and the West Midlands. Attention must now be given both to the extension of these experiments and also to the development of methods of 'horizontal' and 'vertical' co-ordination so as to avoid the problems of competition between areas. It must also be recognised that different local and regional areas have very different advantages and problems, and that it is likely that the problems will demand very different solutions in different places. The same formula will not work everywhere.

The next two sections of this chapter cover two aspects of this structure. The first looks at the question of how to assume some control over interregionally mobile investment. The second looks at inner-city policy. Inner cities are good examples of areas likely to lose out in any competition for private investment in the near future, no matter how much that competition is 'fixed'. In both areas of policy it is shown how past political initiatives have suffered, each in specific ways, from the general problems outlined above, and in each the beginnings of an alternative strategy is presented.

## Interregionally mobile investment

One of the political results of the current high regional unemployment is nostalgia for the regional policy of the 1960s. Although not its only function, it was this policy which was mainly responsible for Government influence over the location of interregionally mobile jobs and investment. The argument here is that it would be quite wrong to resuscitate that form of regional policy.

In its specific ways, the regional policy of the 1960s and 1970s suffered from all the general problems of past spatial policies which have already been mentioned. Although at some periods backed by negative controls in central, congested regions, it was in general a policy based on a range of different sized carrots. Hence it was impossible for there to be any social control over industry, and areas were reduced to competing with each other. Nor, given the levels of information, the nature of the incentives and the nature of the advertising, was it a competitive system which led to a 'rational' distribution, even in industry's profit-oriented terms. The policy, then, was not one which could easily be squared with socialist political objectives.

But, anyway, did it work? The arguments over this have been long and complex, but some things are clear. First, obviously, it did not 'solve' the regional problem; differentials in rates of unemployment persist. Second, although its impact has been overestimated (some of the movement to peripheral regions might have happened anyway), none the less there is no doubt that regional policy did influence the location of some investment. Third, however, the conditions no longer exist for even that degree of success. The impact of the regional policy of the 1960s and 1970s was dependent upon the economic and political conditions of the 1960s and 1970s. In particular, it depended on a high level of spatially mobile investment and employment in the private sector. At present, under a monetarist national Government, such investment is not available. And if economic growth were once again to be promoted, but through an AES, the mix between public and private would change. This would present enormous opportunities for a different sort of regional policy.

Not only did past regional policy not solve the old problems, however, but it was also instrumental in encouraging the emergence of new ones. Levels of unemployment are not the only possible index of spatial inequality, and during the 1960s and 1970s other indices emerged as increasingly important. Differences between regions in the types of jobs available changed and in some ways were exacerbated. The new high-status jobs in management, services, technology and R & D created over this period remained unaffected by regional policy and were located in the south-eastern parts of England. In complete contrast, most of the jobs moving to the old peripheral regions were of low skill requirements, low-paid, often part-time and of very low status. The north/south divide was being recreated in a changed form. Further, because the policy relied above all on attracting inter-regionally mobile investment, and because this in turn was mainly in large, multiplant firms, most of the jobs created in peripheral regions over this period were in branch plants controlled by headquarters elsewhere – often in the south-east. Any policy which operates by competition between areas, which focuses only on numbers of jobs rather than also on their quality and which ignores completely the internal organisation of multiplant firms will reinforce these increasingly important aspects of the regional problem.

What, then, should be done about this level of policy where interregional location decisions are made by major companies?

First, competition between areas must be ended. This aspect of policy should be brought within the scope of enforceable planning agreements. What this should not mean, however, is that management and 'someone from Whitehall' should sit down together drawing up plans in the manner of French indicative planning in the 1960s. Rather even than the tripartite structures of many forms of the AES, we should move towards a situation in which the Labour Party and government, at local and at national levels, support workers' plans. This way the rhetoric of democratising the AES can be given some real meaning. In other words, planning agreements should be linked with work-force plans for industries, where such exist. In most cases, of course, they will not exist. Such plans can be built up only over time. What will be important from the beginning will be to create a climate of possibility and of confidence in the fact both that plans can be drawn up and that the effort will be worth it. Apart from political support, a wide range of open and accessible resource centres would be an essential part of any democratically organised industrial strategy. This all relates, so far, to existing firms and sectors. In a case like Nissan there is no existing work-force. How, then, would a decision be made about the location of new investment? How, then, would the competing claims of London's docklands, Merseyside, South Wales be resolved? This is not only a question of criteria; it is a question also of thinking about the mechanisms through which such a decision should be made. Three things are clear. The criteria for making the decision should be public and should concern social issues as well as considerations of profitability. The procedures themselves must be entirely open; the space for behind-the-scenes deals and for clandestine competitive bargaining must be cut back as much as possible (and to say that these can never be entirely eliminated is no argument for abandoning the attempt to curtail them). Wherever possible, decisions should be linked with existing, wider sectoral plans – decisions about location should be part and parcel of decisions about production.

Second, there is the issue of ownership and control. At present, in discussions of spatial policy this is seen largely as a matter of the geographical location of control. The problem, it is argued, is that ownership and control lie outside the area in question. Now, the geographical location of ownership certainly does have its effects – it can make things far more difficult for trade union negotiators, for instance. But the answer is not to encourage 'local entrepreneurship' or to hark back longingly to the days when most regions had their 'own' capitalist class. Put like this (and such an attitude is, in fact, implicit in much recent policy that is supposed to generate 'indigenous growth'), it is anyway a strange demand for the labour movement to make. What is at issue, rather, is not only the geographical location of control but also its social location. It is not capitalists and top managers we want to restore to the regions but control over production. Once again, the geographical issue is bound up with the organisation of production itself. For socialists, bringing ownership and control back to the local level must therefore mean two things (at least). In connection with ownership it must mean a change in class location, establishing new forms of public and common owner- ship; with control it must mean the at least partial removal of such production from market forces and its evaluation by wider social criteria, including a plant's relation to the community in which it is located. (But here we move into the more local plan- ning concerns of the next section.)

Third, what might be done about the vast variation in the kinds and quality of job available to people in different regions? Here again, previous policy prescriptions have completely missed the point; by focusing entirely on geography without seeing the link between that and the organisation of production, they have ignored the essential problem and their prescriptions have, from the start, been doomed to failure. To see the policy in simply spatial terms is to regard the aim as being to recreate Slough in Sunderland, Silicon Valley in Scotland. What such an approach fails to appreciate is that with the present organisation of capitalist industry, with the present form of technological development and division of labour within production, there will always be places where people do only boring production work if there are to be places where people do all the management and all the R & D. Not everywhere can be Silicon Valley. Nor would simply spreading the high-status jobs around the country do much to help those who anyway get stuck in the low-paid tedium and futurelessness of assembly. And this raises the real point. For it is the kind of technological development that we are pursuing, the kind of division of labour within production which this promotes and which we are allowing, that enables the new spatial division of labour between different areas. More equal, democratic and progressive ways of organising production itself must of necessity lead to less of that kind of geographical differentiation between areas.

The kind of science and technology implicit in the White Heat policies of the 1960s, combined with the lack of control over job quality in the regional policy of the same period, together enabled the emergence of the new form of regional problem. Only when we have a policy on production which recognises that technology is not neutral will we stand any chance of overcoming geographical inequality in employment. It is the Lucas Aerospace shop stewards' plan, which combines the advantages of high technology with an attempt to undermine the divisive hierarchy of skills within production, that points the way forward.

## Inner cities[1]

The inner-city policies of previous Labour Governments (embodied in the continuing Urban Programme and the Inner Urban Areas Act) shared many of the same assumptions and were subject to many of the same criticisms.

First, they were committed fundamentally to a private-sector solution. The role of the public sector was essentially to be one of providing the preconditions for private industry to make a profit, whether this was to be done by building advance factories, by loans and grants or by leasing land to private house-builders.

Second, the inner cities were simply set up as yet more 'assisted areas', in competition with others.

Third, there was a lack of co-ordination between measures specifically directed at inner cities and wider national policies. One of the most obvious cases was that of landownership; inner-city policy failed even to make use of existing legislation. Given its weak formulation, the Community Land Act was never going to be a serious aid in reducing the high price of derelict urban land. But the inner cities legislation failed to take advantage even of the possibilities the Act did offer of enabling local authorities to buy land at 'current use value' rather than at a price based on some potential higher-value use (such as offices). Instead, such was the desperation to attract industry that 90 per cent loans were offered to companies to buy land on the open market – a policy which could only keep land prices up.

Finally, it was a 'top-down' policy. Initiatives and decisions came from senior national and local government officials. Local involvement and control was concentrated in local government – members of the public were excluded from Partnership Area Committee meetings, for example.

This approach can be criticised on two different grounds. To begin with, it can be criticised 'technically': it is most unlikely to work. In the present cold economic climate it would take enormous injections of cash, and major reconstruction, to make these areas attractive again to the private capital which produced the present dereliction. And, given the way that policies have so far been formulated, to the extent that investment and jobs *were* attracted back to inner cities it would only be at a cost to other areas. Jobs for Liverpool at the expense of South Wales – and with private industry calling the tune.

But the more important criticism is political. It is not just that such policies won't work, even in their own terms, but that the approach on which they are based should be challenged politically.

First, in what sense is this an inner-city problem anyway? Past policies have tended implicitly to 'blame' the cities for their unsuitability for private-sector development and have therefore concentrated on area-based policies to 'improve' them. But the loss of jobs in urban areas is part of a much wider process. As we have seen, the present crisis of the British economy is bringing with it also a major geographical reorganisation, and some of the worst effects of that reorganisation are evident in the cities. Many of the major underlying causes of urban decline lie outside the cities themselves. Once again, area-based policies alone will not do.

But, second, that does not mean that employment will simply return to the inner cities with national economic recovery. Geographical characteristics *are* important; even were there to be an up-turn in the economy, new investment would not, first off and undirected, go to inner urban areas. There is, then, a need to pay specific attention to inner cities — a need for a politics of location. What must be faced politically is that without ridiculous levels of subsidy, in one form or another, to private industry, inner cities are the areas most likely to lose in the competitive approach to spatial policy.

But the central political question is: what — or who — is all this policy-making for? The revitalisation of what? Regeneration for whom? The restoration of whose confidence? What, in other words, would it mean to say that an inner-city policy had 'worked'? Both Tory and Labour policies have in the past given the issue what has been called a 'property definition' rather than a 'people definition'. It is simply assumed that if profits *could* once again be made in the cities, the problems would go away. It is important to look at who gains from present policies.

- The incentives approach to location means subsidies to private companies but with no *quid pro quo* in connection with the types of jobs, conditions of employment, or even, indeed, the numbers of jobs created.
- The rates and tax provisions of the Conservatives' Enterprise Zones and the loans for land purchase under Labour provide a potential bonanza for landowners.

● The more way-out schemes are just the same. Marinas are frequently proposed for London's docks. But then, as the schoolkid's poem asked: 'How many East Enders have yachts?'

Urban local government, like other forms of local government, has been bending over backwards to attract investment — development at any price and any kind of development. But this means that the city is thought of in terms of its function as land and location from the point of view of the market. To the extent that there is any real connection between such development and social need, it is usually coincidental. What is required is a rethinking of the whole issue, a redefinition of the problem.

To begin with, any strategy for the inner cities which is both to be socialist and to stand a chance of success needs to have the following characteristics.

● It should be public-sector-led. Instead of the public sector 'creating the conditions' for private capital, it must itself play the leading role in investment.
● It should be integrated with wider socialist aims, including initiatives in new forms of ownership and control; it should demand a real *quid pro quo* for any aid given to the private sector; it should stem from, and seek to build, a strong local base, with much of the local-level initiative being taken by local workers, tenants groups, trades councils, etc., a number of which have already produced local studies and plans.
● It should, in other words, shape itself around social needs rather than the requirements of private profit. We must begin to think what a socially useful city would look like.
● There must be real co-ordination of national and local policies.
● There should be co-ordination between employment and other policies. For example, there must be control over urban land markets (we need something much stronger than the Community Land Act); direct labour organisations must be rebuilt and expanded, and this in turn should be related to extended housing programmes, etc.

● This will require a far greater financial commitment than there has ever been in the past; it will require the use of funds at present controlled by financial institutions.

All this may sound ambitious. In one sense it is. But it is also what is necessary. Tinkering with local-area policies has been tried for over a decade, and virtually no impression has been made on the problem. But it is also a framework in which policies and action can be constructed now. We don't have to wait for the millennium before anything can be done.

Take an example: small clothing firms in inner London, where economic pressures are causing both loss of jobs and a worsening of working conditions. The need is to improve the conditions of workers while not at the same time adding to costs so much that jobs are lost altogether. This can be done through precisely the kind of co-ordination of policies suggested above. Thus at national level government could:

● give (temporary) trade protection to the worst-hit sections of the industry;
● reinforce, and implement, legislation relating to working conditions — such as health and safety provisions.

At the same time, at local level it could:

● provide cheap premises with better working conditions;
● in return, operate a good employer code.

Such an approach would not be competitive with other UK areas; it would both keep jobs and improve conditions; and it would ensure a return for aid to private companies. It could, moreover, be adapted and extended, depending on local political conditions. It could be combined with workers' plans for the industry (including, it is to be hoped, attacks on the entrenched sexual division of labour) — indeed, it would give such plans the space to operate realistically. The degree of control taken by workers or the local authority could vary from 0 to 100 per cent. It could be combined with local campaigns about home-working — as is going on in London now.

In some areas a start on the 'local end' of such policies has already been made. The initiative is being grasped in some cities where the left now has significant influence. In the West Midlands and Greater London it is hoped that money from local authority and other pension funds will enable the public sector to play a larger and more positive role. Moreover, in both areas the principle of *quid pro quo* is being firmly established. In the West Midlands existing companies will be assisted only on the condition that some combination of local enterprise board control, workers' control or a planning agreement is accepted. It is important to realise that this scheme depends on the workers' agreement and initiative; such 'economic' policies are part of a wider politics.

This is what is most significant about these new ventures at local level: the initiative is coming from a wide variety of sources. In London, decisions on where the local authority should put its money are to be made in consultation with shop stewards, trade unions and trades councils. Sectoral planning is to be undertaken by workers in the industry together with the local authority. New forms of organisation are to be experimented with – and proposals are coming in from boroughs, from co-operatives, from trade unions. Mini-AESs are being devised even at the level of individual London boroughs. The importance of all this as a complete rethinking of the 'inner-city problem' was symbolised by a river trip down the Thames. At each stage of the journey local groups argued how they thought their area should be revived. The trip was laid on by the GLC, but the idea came from a local group. The last time such a voyage took place it was so that the GLC could point out to the property sector the 'potential development sites' along the river!

On their own, obviously, these initiatives cannot reconstruct an employment base for the inner cities. Compared with the scale of the problem, they are tiny. Even with the pension funds, their cash resources are small. Moreover, most production today is organised on a basis which goes far beyond the remit of the local authority, so there are severe constraints on the kinds of company and industry over which individual local areas can have effective control or which they can sensibly organise.

And this, of course, is where the link must be made with a

wider framework of spatial policies. Obviously, there must be co-ordination with national investment planning and with other levels of spatial policy. There must also be closer links than in the past with the development of other areas of politics. In the inner-city case the link with policies directed at the financial sector, and at pension funds in particular, is obvious. Inner-city policies based in the inner city must be just a part of a broader politics of location.

It is important these issues are addressed. If they are not, the AES could be as divisive as were previous spatial policies. If they *are* addressed, new areas of political expression will be opened up, potentially linking industrial and community politics.

## Note

1   This section draws on an article by the authors entitled 'Going to town on the jobs crisis', *New Socialist*, no. 4, 1982.

# 10

## Race and Immigration

Christopher T. Husbands

Talking to a group of foreign Jews who had arrived in London at the end of the nineteenth century, Ben Tillett, pillar of the 'new unionism' of the 1880s and 1890s, is reputed to have extended what must count as one of history's most reluctant formal welcomes: 'Yes, you are our brothers and we will do our duty by you. . .but we wish you had not come to this country' (Russell and Lewis, 1900, p. 198). The remark neatly captures the ambivalence with which the indigenous British labour movement has usually reacted to the arrival of any significant number of foreign immigrants. It certainly summarises the pre-dominant attitude of the Labour Party during the past fifteen or more years, after nervousness about white backlash among its supposed traditional supporters and about its reputation for being 'soft' on immigration and on race relations generally moved it sharply away from what one might call the 'brotherhood-of-man' attitude that had been current in the 1950s and early 1960s.[1]

## The Labour Party and the immigration issue

Continuously since 1965 – since 1963 if one is prepared to con-sider as evidence the desultory nature of the Party's parliamen-tary opposition to the extension of the 1962 Commonwealth Immigrants Act – an uneasy synthesis has governed Labour Party policy on immigration and race relations. On the one hand there has been the emphasis upon tightly controlling all new immigration, while on the other there has been an urging of the full integration, on terms of equality, of black settlers already in the country. From several perspectives, of course, these two aims are mutually inconsistent.

Richard Crossman (1979, p. 73) was an unequivocal champion of this dual approach, and by 1965 Harold Wilson also felt strongly that the problems surrounding immigration had worsened (Wilson, 1971, p. 84). Later, speaking in Birmingham in May 1968 in a studied riposte to Enoch Powell's 'rivers-of-blood' speech delivered in that city on 20 April 1968, Wilson did choose to emphasise the 'brotherhood-of-man' aspect of the Party's stance, but he was also careful to make clear to his listeners, as well as to the wider public that was really his intended audience, the demographic and restrictionist realities of the subject (Wilson, 1971, pp. 525–8). It is ironic and unfortunate for Wilson's argument and for his emphasis on equality and brotherhood that his speech was delivered so soon after the passage of the 1968 Commonwealth Immigrants Act.

Even some of the more recent publications of the Labour Party on race and immigration continue the 'steel fist–velvet glove' contradiction of the 1960s (e.g. Labour Party, 1978a, p. 8). Moreover, the Party's campaign literature on the subject has always been anxious to reassure those reading it about such matters as the strictness of present immigration controls, the low number of entrants and the trivial scale of illegal entry (e.g. Labour Party, 1976). This emphasis fits ill with the alternative, 'brotherhood-of-man' tradition within the Party.

What, however, has been the evidence for the impact of immigration and race relations as political issues upon Labour's electoral fortunes and popularity? To what extent have fears such as those expressed so forcefully by Crossman and others in the 1960s been borne out by subsequent events and by what is known about the character of public opinion on the subject?

My argument in the central part of this chapter – based on econometric models of party popularity, analysed month-by-month, which measure the size of the effects for and against Labour and/or the Conservatives of immigration- and race-related events – is that Labour may in fact have had less to fear from this issue than it supposed. The available evidence about the relatively short-term negative effects upon Labour's popularity of various race-related events in the 1960s and 1970s would suggest that the Party can afford to purge itself of its legacy of equivocation on this subject and can actively and without embarrassment, apology or ambivalence pursue policies designed to improve the social and economic circumstances of black Britons.

The theoretical basis for analysing the electoral impact of a political issue has been set out concisely by Butler and Stokes (1974, pp. 287–95). If an issue is to have such an impact upon the balance of support between two parties, each of three conditions must be fulfilled. (1) It has to have more than a minimum level of salience in the minds of electors. (2) There has to be a decided skew in the distribution of the opinions of the electorate on that issue, with a large majority favouring one option. (3) There has to be a universally or widely perceived difference on the issue between the orientations of the two parties.

In one sense at least the first condition has been adequately fulfilled during the past twenty-five years, although a qualification must be made to the view that the electorate has been continuously and explicitly concerned with race and immigration to the frequent exclusion of other issues. The percentage of the national electorate that believes 'immigrants' are 'the most urgent problem facing the country at the present time' in response to the Gallup Poll's inquiries on this matter has usually been quite small – less than 5 per cent during the 1960s and falling to 1 per cent or less during most of the mid-1970s. Yet there is sufficient evidence from the Gallup Poll's series to show that the issue of immigration is certainly one with high latent, if short-term, potential.

Although the percentage spontaneously mentioning 'immigrants' as the country's most urgent problem has usually been well below that mentioning economic issues such as prices, the cost of living or unemployment, or referring to the state of industrial relations or the number of strikes in the country, there have been short periods when the former percentage rose alarmingly in response to some specific race- or immigration-related issue. In May 1968, shortly after Powell's 'rivers-of-blood' outburst, the figure was 27 per cent, and in September of the same year it was still as high as 20 per cent. In September 1972, at the height of the public debate about the appropriate reception to be given to expelled Ugandan Asians, the equivalent figure was 23 per cent. In June 1976, after the publicity given to the plight of displaced Malawi Asians, it was 10 per cent, and it rose from almost nothing to 9 per cent in February and March 1978 after Mrs Thatcher's notorious outburst about 'swamping' made in a *World in Action* broadcast on 30 January of that year.

It is worth noting that this percentage level of concern in response to immigration-sensitised political circumstances has been rather lower in the middle and later 1970s than it was a decade or so earlier. On the other hand, in surveys that allow respondents to mention as many problems as they feel are important in Britain today, immigration is mentioned by a substantial percentage of all ethnic groups in the country. In the survey commissioned by the *Daily Mail* and conducted by National Opinion Polls into attitudes on these subjects in the immediate aftermath of Thatcher's statement (in fact, from 3 to 7 February 1978) 50 per cent of a national sample mentioned 'immigration/race relations' as important problems at that time (NOP, 1978, p. 6). Even allowing for the ambiguity in this context attaching to the term 'race relations', it would be naive to deny the probable restrictionist dimension behind this figure.

The second of the above three conditions is also fulfilled, for numerous surveys have shown a large exclusionist majority on the immigration issue, when exclusionism is defined in the sense of Tillett's remark, 'we wish you had not come. . .'. For example, Butler and Stokes (1974, pp. 303–8) report a percentage agreeing that 'too many immigrants have been let into this country' that (excluding 'don't know' responses from the calculation) was at a minimum of 86 per cent in the autumn of 1964 and rose to 90 per cent in the summer of 1969. Majorities of respondents who gave these exclusionist responses claimed to feel 'very strongly' on the subject. Even conceding the existence of possible wording effects springing from the manner in which the question is phrased, there is no doubt that there is a marked skew in the distribution of public attitudes on this subject.

On the other hand, the third condition is a more uncertain one; the opinion-poll evidence is that the Tories have not invariably been seen as more suitably 'tough' on the subject, even if this orientation has been dominant in recent years. The relative favour with which they have been viewed concerning immigration policy has not been constant but has varied over time and according to location. It is true, however, that two occasions when the Tories' stance on immigration was clearly preferred by the electorate were at the 1970 and 1979 general elections!

Back in November 1961, when the first Commonwealth Immigrants Act was being prepared for the Statute Book, a Gallup Poll reported that 76 per cent of the electorate approved of the measures which the Government intended to take in controlling immigration. Even so, only 31 per cent of the same sample reported disagreement with the attacks that the Labour and Liberal Parties were mounting on the proposed legislation. There was no suggestion at the time that the Conservative Government gained significantly in popularity because of its proposals – in fact, it was the fortunes of the Liberal Party that improved at the beginning of the 'Liberal revival' of 1962 and 1963. Yet it is improbable that immigration and the Liberal Party's position on the subject were related to its increased electoral popularity (*GPI*, November 1961, p. 37). The new legislation came into force on 1 July 1962, and by September 1963 70 per cent of the electorate reported their approval of the new Act, compared with 19 per cent who disapproved and 11 per cent who did not know their views (*GPI*, September 1963, p. 164). In June 1964, four months before Labour's victory in the subsequent general election, only 26 per cent of the electorate were reported by Gallup as believing that there was a difference on the subject between the policies of Labour and the Conservatives. Thirty-four per cent saw no difference, and the balance of 40 per cent did not know (*GPI*, June 1964, p. 63). However, even as early as 1964 there were some systematic differences in the public's perception of the two parties according to the local presence of black people. That minority of the electorate which lived in proximity to black settlers was significantly more likely to regard the Conservative Party as the more restrictionist. Forty-three per cent of people in this situation regarded the Conservative Party as more likely to 'keep immigrants out', as opposed to 22 per cent of respondents in areas without black settlement who felt this to be the case. The percentage that saw no difference on the matter between the two major parties was lowest in the former type of area (Butler and Stokes, 1974, p. 305).

By 1965 exclusionist feeling was widespread and deeply entrenched. In August 87 per cent of Gallup's national sample said that they approved of the 'strict limitation on the number of immigrants allowed from the Commonwealth', and 52 per cent thought that, 'on the whole, the country had been harmed through immigrants coming to settle here from the Commonwealth'; only 16 per cent believed there to have been a net benefit from this source (*GPI*, August 1965, p. 123). Shortly before the 1966 general election 31 per cent of the electorate rated the 'immigration of coloured people' as among the most important items that would influence their decision about the party for which to vote (*GPI*, April 1966, p. 35). By October 1967 the percentage believing that immigrants had done net damage to the country had risen to 60 per cent; a belief in net benefit was held by only 9 per cent of those polled (*GPI*, October 1967, p. 164). In December 1967 over a quarter of the nation — asked to give an affective assessment of black people — rated them as 'poor' or 'very poor' (*GPI*, December 1967, p. 196).

The introduction of the Commonwealth Immigrants Act of 1968 scarcely earned the Labour Government of the time any public gratitude or popularity. It was a panic response to a perception of electoral pressure, and it seems rather to have evoked an 'About time too' reaction from the majority of the electorate. The existing restrictionist legislation of 1962 was seen by many as unacceptably liberal, and the nature of the Labour Government's response meant that it too came to be seen in a similar light. Ninety per cent of Gallup's April 1968 sample felt that the Government had been obliged to bring in the measures concerned, but 63 per cent said that the proposals were insufficiently stringent, and 48 per cent thought that the issue had been badly handled by the Government, as opposed to only 35 per cent who were prepared to allow that it had behaved well on the matter (*GPI*, April 1968, p. 37). Exclusionist sentiments at this time continued to harden. In May 1968 74 per cent of the electorate expressed agreement with Powell's views as formulated in the Birmingham 'rivers-of-blood' speech, and only 30 per cent approved the principles of the 1968 Race Relations Bill, published on 9 April (five days after the assassination in Memphis of Dr Martin Luther King and the consequent riots in many American cities), as opposed to 46 per cent who disapproved and 24 per cent who did not know (*GPI*, May 1968, pp. 51–2). By the beginning of 1969 Labour was well established throughout the electorate as a whole as the party that was 'softer' on the immigration issue; the practical – though not necessarily logical – complement of this was that the Conservatives were increasingly seen as 'better' than Labour on the issue. In February 1969, 44 per cent of the electorate thought that the former was the 'best' party for a policy on the 'immigration of coloured people', as opposed to only 16 per cent who thought this of Labour and 20 per cent who saw no interparty difference (*GPI*, February 1969, p. 27). Of course, sentiments such as these set the stage for the notoriously racism-laden 1970 general election, when the Tories played the race card explicitly and unashamedly in numerous local campaigns. For example, that run by Nigel Lawson, since 1981 Secretary of State for Energy, in his unsuccessful attempt to defeat Joan Lestor in Eton and Slough must rank with more infamous examples (such as Smethwick in 1964) of the use of race as an electoral tactic.[2] Two studies have sought to calculate the size of the net electoral benefit gained by the Conservatives in 1970 from the race and immigration issue; Miller (1980) offers a figure of net pro-Conservative swing of about 1.5 per cent and Studlar (1978), using a different method of assessment, presents data from which one can infer a similarly sized net swing. This figure may not seem large but it would have affected which party won in about twenty-five seats and, in any case, it is certain that the issue significantly helped the Conservatives to win various marginal seats in the West Midlands and elsewhere that were so important for their parliamentary victory (Schoen, 1977, pp. 45–68, esp. 66). The manner in which the issue was used by Enoch Powell was especially important; his pronouncements and the content of his election address were widely reported in both the national and the local West Midlands press.

During the 1970s, of course, race-sensitised political circumstances recurred, particularly around the time of the Ugandan

Asians' arrival in late 1972, in the summer of 1976 and throughout 1978 leading up to the May 1979 general election. As will be seen in the next section, although the Conservatives suffered relative unpopularity in late 1972 and 1973, it is improbable that the decision by the Heath Government to admit expelled Ugandan Asians into the country resulted in a loss of any more than 1 or 2 percentage points.

Thatcher's 'swamping' statement in early 1978 proved highly important in pushing immigration to the forefront of the political agenda in the run-up to the 1979 general election. In February 1978, 49 per cent of the electorate 'strongly agreed' that 'Britain was in danger of being swamped by people with different cultures', while an additional 21 per cent slightly agreed. Thirty-two per cent strongly agreed that the Labour Party was not controlling coloured immigration, while a further 25 per cent slightly agreed (*GPI*, March 1978, pp. 10–11). As the year progressed, the balance of public opinion seemed to move increasingly to the disadvantage of the Labour Party. In May 1978, 61 per cent felt that controlling immigration was an 'extremely important' issue, a higher percentage than for any of several other issues about which responses were sought, and a further 27 per cent said 'quite important' (*GPI*, June 1978, p. 8). In June 59 per cent disapproved of how the Government was handling immigration, while only 28 per cent reported approval (*GPI*, July 1978, p. 7). During the period immediately preceding the May 1979 election campaign immigration was repeatedly mentioned by a large number of the electorate as one of the subjects about which more should be said in campaign speeches – the implication being that the Labour Party in particular had something to hide on the subject. Even so, only 5 per cent of the electorate actually named immigrants or race relations as among the two most important issues affecting how they would cast their vote (*GPI*, June 1979, p. 10).

As can be seen, it is incontrovertible that a deeply restrictionist strain on this subject exists in large proportion, and almost certainly a majority, of the British electorate. It is also true that many who share this view have been consistent or sometime Labour voters. However, voting intentions are not formed in isolation from other issues – issues both related and also unrelated to race – and it is correspondingly uncertain to what extent aggregate voting trends in both long and short term can be ascribed uniquely to intolerance on the subject of race. Thus, although it can of course be no part of the argument of this article that public opinion is characterised in reality by a latent or repressed liberalism on the subject — such an assertion would be absurd in the light of the evidence from the early 1960s onwards that has been reviewed here — what has been said is not necessarily inconsistent with the conclusion that Labour's electoral losses from this issue, controlling on other factors also influencing voting intention, may not have been as draconian or as permanent as some within the Party have feared. This subject is assessed systematically in the ensuing section of this chapter.

## Party popularity and the race issue

The level of popularity of a Government or an Opposition is not random; it moves more or less predictably in relation to trends over time in various other phenomena. Certain political scientists and econometricians have expended considerable effort on developing models of the 'political business cycle'. The earliest efforts were by American researchers, but Goodhart and Bhansali (1970) broke new ground by producing an innovative model for the popularity of British Governments. The literature on this subject accumulated during the early 1970s, with contributions from writers such as Miller and Mackie (1973), and more recently revisionist perspectives have been put forward, focusing especially upon alleged econometric deficiencies in some of the model specifications of the earlier research. Pissarides (1980), for example, has reformulated Goodhart and Bhansali's work, and a publication edited by Whiteley (1980) contains papers discussing most of the findings and current controversies in this area of research.

Locksley (1980) writes that 'skeletal popularity functions are composed of three elements: unemployment, inflation and growth.' Accordingly, it is logical to construct a model of party popularity that includes variables for these various factors (simultaneous and/or lagged) and to embellish this basic model with variables for other factors and phenomena that have relevance for an understanding of popularity. Such further variables may be economic in nature or may describe other factors. Specifically in the present context, these further variables can be derived from race-related incidents that have occurred at particular times. This section therefore presents and discusses regression models of the popularity of the Conservatives and Labour separately for each of three periods of government; April 1966 to April 1970, July 1970 to December 1973 and November 1974 to March 1979. The race-related variables have been entered as so-called dummy variables (i.e., 1 or 0) uniquely for each month within the period when a highly publicised race-related incident occurred whose effect was to raise awareness of immigration as a 'problem' in the public's consciousness. In fact, those months within each period in which 8 per cent or more of the electorate regarded immigrants as the country's most urgent problem (as reported by the Gallup Poll's inquiries), plus the succeeding month of each such sequence, have been coded as 1 so that the coefficients produced by the regression analyses measure the net effects of the specific incidents in the months concerned as percentage-point gains or losses of party support.[3] In addition, the six models of that table (Conservative and Labour for each of the three periods) contain combinations of further independent variables, whose coefficients have been excluded in the interests of simplicity. These further variables are: a measure of inflation, a measure of growth in monetary wages, a measure of the level of real wages, a measure of unemployment in the immediately preceding quarter, and a variable to assess the so-called 'honeymoon-effect' identified by several researchers (e.g. Goodhart and Bhansali, 1970; Miller and Mackie, 1973) that increases expressions of support for new Governments in the early part of their term of office (this effect has been deemed to last six months and coding used a dummy variable). In addition, specific lagged versions of relevant variables have been incorporated into these models where significant, including in four of the six cases a lagged version of the dependent variable in order to remove an otherwise unacceptably high amount of auto-correlation (Kelejian and Oates, 1974, pp. 190–207). All such lags are on a one-month basis. By contrast with much previous work on this subject, the present analysis has used month-by-month instead of quarter-by-quarter data in order to be able to isolate more accurately the short-term character and extent of any

Table 1　*Percentage-point gains (+) and losses (−) of party support for Conservative and Labour in individual months involving publicised race-related events, net of effects of economic variables, in three periods of time*

|  | Conservative gains and losses (%) | Labour gains and losses (%) |
|---|---|---|
| *Period 1: April 1966 to April 1970* | | |
| May 1968 | +1.4 | −2.1 |
| June 1968 | −2.1 | −1.7 |
| July 1968 | −3.2 | −0.1 |
| August 1968 | −5.7 | +5.0 |
| September 1968 | −4.3 | +1.9 |
| October 1968 | −1.8 | +2.4 |
| *Period 2: July 1970 to December 1973* | | |
| September 1972 | −2.1 | +2.7 |
| October 1972 | −1.0 | +1.8 |
| November 1972 | −2.6 | +0.1 |
| December 1972 | −2.0 | +1.4 |
| January 1973 | −1.2 | −1.8 |
| *Period 3: November 1974 to March 1979* | | |
| June 1976 | −0.5 | −1.2 |
| July 1976 | −4.4 | +0.5 |
| August 1976 | +0.5 | −0.3 |
| February 1978 | +1.4 | −2.2 |
| March 1978 | −0.6 | +2.0 |
| April 1978 | −2.3 | +2.5 |

*Note:* The appendix (pp. 178–80) gives more detail about how these net gains and losses have been calculated, as well as providing a slightly more technical presentation of these same results. It also describes and defines the independent variables that have been included for control purposes in these analyses.

race effects. As can be seen from Table 1, these are often confined to one or two months only. However, one drawback in the use of monthly data is their greater susceptibility to sampling errors.

The data in Table 1 shows the effects of race-related incidents in terms of percentage-point gains or losses of party support. These effects clearly have a quite rapid time decay when calculated net of the large number of other factors that affect voting intentions for Government and Opposition — as expressed in response to the standard Gallup Poll question about voting 'if there were a general election tomorrow'. The findings offer some comfort to those worried about the effects of publicised racial incidents upon the popularity of the Labour Party. Let us discuss each period in turn.

The benefit accruing to the Conservatives that is uniquely attributable to Enoch Powell's 'rivers-of-blood' outburst in late April 1968 was worth less than 1.5 percentage points for no more than a month; thereafter the net effects were, if anything, negative, after taking into account non-race-related factors determining Conservative popularity. By the same token, Labour suffered a loss of about 2 per cent for two months (unhappily, these two months did include a set of local elections in which Labour's loss of seats and councils still haunts the collective memory of the Party). By August 1968 Labour had recovered slightly from the nadir of May and June, and its continuing relative lack of popularity was clearly attributable to other factors. This interpretation is not to deny that Labour was unpopular in the summer of 1968, although it is to doubt whether race was *especially* responsible for this state of affairs; nor is it to deny that Powell's speech had a substantial illiberalising impact upon public attitudes towards race and immigration.

The findings about the second period suggest that the Heath Government may have lost 1 or 2 percentage points in popularity because of its handling of the Ugandan Asians' expulsion in the autumn of 1972. Complementarily, Labour, as the Opposition party, may have received a slight boost from the loss of popularity on this account of the Government. However, respective losses and gains were small in absolute size.

During the third period there were two sequences of race-related incidents: around the summer of 1976, with the arrival of displaced Malawi Asians and the 'four-star-hotel' treatment by much of the national press of the arrival of one family, plus a number of further well-publicised race-related incidents during June and July; and the early part of 1978 after Thatcher's 'swamping' outburst. Ironically enough, the first set of incidents had remarkably little independent effect upon the popularity of Government or Opposition. Labour may have suffered a loss of 1 per cent or so for a month only, but there is no unambiguous evidence of any great Conservative advantage. Even on the second occasion, Conservative gain and Labour loss attributable uniquely to the events of that time were no more than 1 or 2 percentage points, and these changes too had evaporated within a month.

In conclusion, therefore, despite an abundance of evidence for illiberalism on the race issue among a large part of the British electorate, it is much less certain how far this factor has been a major reason for any long-term loss of popularity experienced by the Labour Party. True, if race and immigration could be kept in the forefront of popular awareness for a long period, the Party's popularity might well suffer irretrievably on that account. However, in practice this has not happened, and other factors, such as the performance of various economic indices, have quickly returned to overdetermine any specifically racial influence.

## Policies for Labour on race and immigration

If the Party does indeed have little to fear in terms of vote loss from the issue of race and immigration, it can afford on this pragmatic basis alone – irrespective of the ethical reasons that also favour such a stance – to push more actively than hitherto those policies that seek to redress racial disadvantage and, incidentally, to gain permanently the electoral support of black Britons. There are at least five major areas upon which attention should be focused.[4]

First, there must be a concerted effort to correct racial disadvantage in such spheres as jobs, housing and education, thus recognising the existence of institutional racism, as the Americans learned to do more than a decade ago (Knowles and Prewitt, 1969). Micro- and macro-level approaches will be needed. On the former level a body with statutory powers may be necessary in order to establish quotas, targets and timetables to correct the underrepresentation of black people in individual firms and local authorities. Such a body, if set up, would have the authority to compel compliance and would therefore obviate the ineffectiveness of attempts so far to secure goals of equal representation.[5] The use of explicit quotas would necessitate legislative changes, although an alternative view is that, even without quota-based policies, there is much scope for intervention using the hitherto little-used provisions of the 1976 Race Relations Act. Similar measures should also be taken to monitor the allocation of housing, in both public and private sectors.

On the macro-level research should be conducted to identify the social location and degree of racial disadvantage in various spheres — that is, the increment of such disadvantage that is attributable to ethnic status alone, irrespective of other characteristics of the individual, such as age or sex. Party policy (Labour Party, 1978a, p. 33) has already called for such fact-finding in education. The envisaged research would answer questions such as whether there is a particular level of educational attainment at which the decrement faced by black Britons is particularly acute — for example, among those with GCE O-level passes but no further qualifications. Micro-level policies would then be formulated and adjusted according to the findings of this research.

Second, there should be much more vigorous prosecution of those publishing any material that indulges in racial incitement. This would convince the black community that a Labour Government cared about the derogation of their persons and characters. Prosecutions for incitement have hitherto been bedevilled by weaknesses in existing legislation and an apparent reluctance of juries (or at least London-drawn ones) to convict even for the most outrageous racist abuse.[6] Despite this, exemplary prosecutions against major mainstream institutions such as certain national newspapers, even if initial cases were unsuccessful, would help to convince the black community that a Labour Government was seriously concerned about this issue. There seems little doubt that several national newspapers have been guilty, at least *prima facie*, of racial incitement in view of the manner in which they have reported specific incidents. Evans (1976) reviews a number of suspect instances taken from the summer of 1976; other media researchers have produced similar cases (e.g. Troyna, 1981, pp. 24–6).

Third, strong measures must be taken on all necessary fronts against the perpetrators of the increasing number of physical attacks upon black people. The problem has long been recognised on the left (e.g. Bethnal Green and Stepney Trades Council, 1978) and has even been belatedly admitted and documented by the Home Office (1981). Unfortunately, typical police reactions have been ignorance, deliberate indifference or hostility. Evidence of questionable police attitudes on this matter has accumulated, and the trial of the Bradford Twelve was only one of the more notorious instances in which what may be charitably called police ignorance on this subject was again revealed (*Guardian*, 21 June 1982, p. 11).

Fourth, there must be greater control over the activities of the police, particularly concerning their relationships with black people. *Pace* the views of Lord Scarman (1982, pp. 199–203), there seems little point in pinning hopes upon 'community policing' and similar liberalising exercises for any large-scale improvement of relationships between black people and the police. An abundance of both impressionistic and more systematic evidence from studies of the police (e.g. Reiner, 1978, pp. 220, 226; Colman and Gorman, 1982) shows that, as a group and therefore as an institution, the police are disproportionately inclined to conservatism, authoritarianism and racial intolerance, more so even than the generality of the population, which itself scarcely sets an absolute standard for liberalism on these subjects. True, a minority of individual policemen have tolerant views, and one must respect them for this, but in general authoritarian and intolerant persons select police work precisely because of the opportunities that it provides for the gratification of these psychological dispositions. This is not likely to be changed in any significant way by such practices as longer training periods, courses in sociology, the advocacy of 'community policing' and the like. Any liberalising will be slow and will take place only over the longer term.

In the meantime the issue reduces to one of control over how the police behave and do their work, an implied confrontation from which successive Labour Home Secretaries have drawn back. Even so, greater central control and sanctions against non-compliance are the only short-term methods of liberalising the behaviour, if not the attitudes, of a notoriously enclosed and autonomous institution. Roy Hattersley has already committed the Party to establishing an independent, elected authority responsible for the Metropolitan Police (*Guardian*, 20 February 1982, p. 3), and *Labour's Programme 1982* (Labour Party, 1982,

p. 37), although still to be finally ratified, extends this proposal to all areas of the country. Labour is also committed to the dismissal of individual policemen who can be shown to have engaged in racist behaviour (*Observer*, 18 April 1982, p. 2; *The Times*, 19 April 1982, p. 2), although full control over the police is surely a prerequisite for the honouring of such a commitment.

Fifth, at a minimum, the discriminatory element in immigration and nationality legislation must be removed. Party policy already calls for the repeal of the 1971 Immigration Act, as a result of a motion passed at the 1976 conference (Labour Party, 1978a, p. 54), and for the 1981 British Nationality Act to be replaced by an alternative that is not racially discriminatory (e.g. Labour Party, 1980a, 1981, and 1982, p. 40). In fact, the Party's National Executive Committee has now produced proposals that are intended to make the operation of immigration policy more humane and to remove the consequences of the present Government's obsession with illegal immigration (*The Times*, 28 August 1982, p. 3).

However, it may still be appropriate to suggest that the Labour Party take a long, hard look at what *any* restrictionist immigration policy necessarily implies; it may well be possible to devise a policy that – forgetting for the moment any relevant EEC commitments – is not racially discriminatory. Clearly, the abolition of the questionable criterion of patriality, a term introduced in the 1971 legislation (although the concept was implicit in the 1968 Commonwealth Immigrants Act) would go some way towards removing the racist character of present immigration practice. Even so, given the probably unequal distribution among the Commonwealth countries of demand to enter Britain, it is permissible to doubt whether any immigration policy that is both restrictionist and also genuinely non-discriminatory on racial grounds can be implemented. First, such a policy would perforce have to establish some numerical quota or maximum. Second, the immigration service itself, like the police, is an institution not known for its liberalism, and those entering it are also likely to have selected it because of the nature of its work.

The Party may have to think seriously about whether there should be controls at all, given the difficulties of implementing non-discriminatory practice. Certainly, an argument can be made, although not totally convincingly, that such a step might not encourage the immigration of the large numbers of entrants that many fear. So-called primary immigration to this country, like most of the well-known large-scale migrations of recent history, has been labour migration. The trends in the size of such migration are – except when affected by special considerations, such as suspicions about future closure – intimately related to the buoyancy of the economy of the receiving country. American immigration statistics, for example, fell sharply in the depressions of the 1870s, the 1890s and the 1930s before recovering in each subsequent decade (US Bureau of the Census, 1960, pp. 56–7). Immigration by West Indians to this country during the 1950s has been shown by Foot (1965, pp. 11–15) and by Peach (1968, pp. 39–50) to have been dependent upon the state of the British economy, until the likelihood of closure increased the numbers arriving to the point at which they exceeded those of available job opportunities. True, even in periods of serious depression immigration through an 'open door' would not fall to nothing, and in a collection of 'socialist' essays there is something ironic about invoking an argument based on *laissez-faire* to suggest that consideration be given to the abolition of controls. It is also the case that there are at least some countries in the Commonwealth (e.g. Bangla Desh) where indigenous conditions are so appalling that those suffering them would rather face uncertain welcome and probable unemployment in a depressed British economy than continue living where they are; such a state of affairs raises questions that should determine the content of the Party's overseas development policy.

If, after due consideration, a quota is accepted as a necessary component of a policy that is restrictionist but not racially discriminatory, great care will have to be taken in order to ensure that it is indeed implemented in a non-discriminatory manner.

## Conclusion

The intentions of the first and second major parts of this chapter were to document the Labour Party's response to the issues of race and immigration, to discuss the evidence about popular feelings on the subject and to argue that, despite the undoubted hostility and emotion that these issues have often aroused, Labour's losses in terms of popularity among white voters have been either quite small or, if larger on occasion, only short-term. On that basis, it was argued, Labour can afford to be rather more assertive about its policy intentions in this sphere than has hitherto been the case.

However, against such an argument it may well be said that Labour's losses of popularity have been on this nominal scale only because it has adopted a restrictionist policy and has been less keen to publicise those parts of its policies that are in its 'brotherhood-of-man' tradition. It may also be said that it matters little whether losses from this issue are short-term or not if the timing of those losses coincides, through accident or manipulation by the Party's opponents, with general election campaigns; this happened in 1970 and in 1979, both of which were elections fought by Labour at an ideological disadvantage on this and other issues. One must concede the possible truth of such objections. On the other hand, at a time when Labour's support, as reported by the Gallup Poll, stands at 27.5 per cent of the national electorate (*GPI*, July 1982, p. 2), with little immediate prospect of any substantial recovery, the Party has to realise that the black vote is just about the most certain support that it has. It must be understood, of course, that the scope for the large-scale conversion of black voters to Labour from other parties is small. Instead, the Party's tasks are to prevent any defections, say to the SDP, of those black voters who have already voted Labour, and also to attempt to secure the support of those who have hitherto abstained, a particular characteristic of the West Indian community.[7] Only the vigorous pursuit of a set of policies designed to improve the circumstances in which black Britons live will permanently secure their electoral support for Labour.

# Appendix

The dependent variables used in the time-series regression analyses of party popularity are the month-by-month percentages of those intending or inclining to vote Conservative or Labour as reported by Webb and Wybrow (1981, pp. 168–75).

The basic variables used from the DARTS data-retrieval system (see note 1) were:

1 P, the monthly unadjusted index of retail prices for all items, April 1965 to March 1979 (January 1974 = 100);

2 W, the monthly index of earnings of all employees in all industries and services in Great Britain, April 1965 to March 1979 (January 1970 = 100);

3 U, the monthly total registered number of unemployed in the United Kingdom percentaged upon mid-year estimates of the economically active population, April 1965 to March 1979.

From these variables have been constructed the four independent economic variables used in the analyses:

1 a measure of the rate of inflation over the previous twelve months $(\text{Log}P - \text{Log}P_{-12})$;

2 a measure of growth in monetary wages over the previous twelve months $(\text{Log}W - \text{Log}W_{-12})$;

3 a measure of the level of real wages $(\text{Log}(W/P)_{-12})$;

4 a measure of unemployment in the immediately preceding quarter, constructed as a moving average $((U + U_{-1} + U_{-2})/3)$.

In addition, dummy variables to measure any 'honeymoon-effect' have been constructed as follows:
Period 1, April to September 1966, equals one, otherwise zero;
Period 2, July to December 1970, equals one, otherwise zero;
Period 3, November 1974 to April 1975, equals one, otherwise zero.

Some models also included the four economic independent variables lagged by one month if these variants happened to be statistically significant. However, not all economic independent variables were necessarily included in all models; significance determined inclusion.

Table 2, which shows the relevant results of these time-series regression analyses, is a slightly more technical presentation of the data in Table 1. In the interests of economy and simplicity only the coefficients of variables pertaining to the individual months involving publicised race-related events are given in the table, as well as the $R^2$ of each model; the coefficients of the independent economic variables and those of the 'honeymoon-effect' variables are not shown. The coefficients in the table may be interpreted as gains or losses of percentage support among those intending or inclining to vote in a forthcoming general election. An indication of the statistical significance of the coefficients is given in order to provide a further aid to their evaluation.

Table 2  *Metric coefficients for individual months involving publicised race-related events, dependent variables being Conservative and Labour voting intentions, calculated on month-by-month data separately for three periods of time*

| Dependent variables | Percentage with Conservative voting intentions | Percentage with Labour voting intentions |
|---|---|---|
| *Period 1: April 1966 to April 1970* | | |
| May 1968 | 1.4 | −2.1 |
| June 1968 | −2.1 | −1.7 |
| July 1968 | −3.2* | −0.1 |
| August 1968 | −5.7* | 5.0* |
| September 1968 | −4.3* | 1.9 |
| October 1968 | −1.8 | 2.4 |
| $R^2$ | 0.785 | 0.826 |
| | | |
| *Period 2: July 1970 to December 1973* | | |
| September 1972 | −2.1 | 2.7 |
| October 1972 | −1.0 | 1.8 |
| November 1972 | −2.6 | 0.1 |
| December 1972 | −2.0 | 1.4 |
| January 1973 | −1.2 | −1.8 |
| $R^2$ | 0.590 | 0.686 |
| | | |
| *Period 3: November 1974 to March 1979* | | |
| June 1976 | −0.5 | −1.2 |
| July 1976 | −4.4* | 0.5 |
| August 1976 | 0.5 | −0.3 |
| | | |
| February 1978 | 1.4 | −2.2 |
| March 1978 | −0.6 | 2.0 |
| April 1978 | −2.3 | 2.5 |
| $R^2$ | 0.566 | 0.613 |

*Note:* An asterisk against a coefficient indicates that its value is at least once, though less than twice, that of its standard error.

# Notes

1   I am extremely grateful to Dilia Montes, David Blake and Meghnad Desai for their computing and/or interpretive assistance when developing the time-series regression analyses of party popularity that are included in this chapter. I should also like to

express my appreciation to John Tilley, MP, who commented extensively on an early draft.

The computer program used for estimating the parameters of these various time-series models was GIVE (Hendry and Srba, 1978). This computes general instrumental variable estimates of linear equations with lagged dependent variables, unless this option is repressed, and with autoregressive errors. Many of the data for the independent variables included in the analyses were taken from DARTS, a data-retrieval system developed by Diana Whistler of the London School of Economics. DARTS contains much of the content of the data banks of the Central Statistical Office and the Bank of England (Whistler, 1982).

2　The details of this campaign are fully reported in the appropriate issues of the *Slough Observer*.

3　These coefficients may be regarded as maximum estimates of the size of any race effects, albeit with the assumption that no specific event with countervailing influence occurred in the months concerned. *Ceteris paribus*, a model with a relatively small $R^2$ from the economic independent variables and the 'honeymoon-effect' variable alone is more likely to have exaggerated race effects from the month-by-month dummy variables.

4　Of course, on several of the following subjects the Party has already formulated policies, or else proposals about details are being actively discussed. Moreover, the NEC has already made a call for a more sensitive approach to the black electorate (Labour Party, 1980b).

5　Roy Hattersley and John Tilley, among others, have both already elaborated the ingredients of a policy along these lines. For some details of Hattersley's proposals see *Guardian*, 19 April 1982, p. 4, and *Sunday Times*, 11 July 1982, p. 13.

The Commission for Racial Equality's attempt to establish even a voluntary code of practice to seek equality of opportunity in employment and promotion has been modified by the House of Commons Select Committee on Employment and – at the time of writing (August 1982) – still awaits the approval, even in its amended form, of the Secretary of State for Employment (*The Times*, 28 May 1982, p. 4; *Guardian*, 14 July 1982, p. 7). However, the voluntary character of this intended code says little for its likely effectiveness, even if it is accepted in its present form.

6　The Party has already called for a modification of Section 70 of the 1976 Race Relations Act, which amended Section 5 of the 1936 Public Order Act (Labour Party, 1978b). However, the suggested change – in response to the challenge of the National Front at that time – pertains only to spoken and not to written matter.

7　The scanty evidence which does exist shows that black voters have traditionally voted Labour to a far greater degree than would be predicted on class-based considerations alone. One study (NOP, 1978, p. 18), conducted in early 1978, found that 92 per cent of West Indians with a voting intention chose Labour, as did 86 per cent of Asians. However, although likely turnout among Asians exceeded the national average, electoral non-participation by West Indians was about twice that of the total electorate.

# References

Bethnal Green and Stepney Trades Council (1978) *Blood on the Streets: A Report by Bethnal Green and Stepney Trades Council on Racial Attacks in East London* (London: Bethnal Green and Stepney Trades Council)

Butler, D., and Stokes, D. (1974) *Political Change in Britain: The Evolution of Electoral Choice*, 2nd edn. (London: Macmillan)

Colman, A. M., and Gorman, L. P. (1982) 'Conservatism, dogmatism, and authoritarianism in British police officers', *Sociology*, vol. 16, no. 1, pp. 1–11

Crossman, R. (1979) *The Crossman Diaries: Selections from the Diaries of a Cabinet Minister, 1964–1970*, ed. A. Howard (London: Magnum Books)

Evans, P. (1976) *Publish and Be Damned?* (London: Runnymede Trust)

Foot, P. (1965) *Immigration and Race in British Politics* (Harmondsworth: Penguin)

Goodhart, C. A. E., and Bhansali, R. J. (1970) 'Political economy', *Political Studies*, vol. 18, no. 1, pp. 43–106

*GPI (Gallup Political Index)*, various issues, November 1961–July 1982

Hendry, D. F., and Srba, F. (1978) *Technical Manual for GIVE* (London: London School of Economics and Political Science Computer Unit)

Home Office (1981) *Racial Attacks: Report of a Home Office Study* (London: Home Office)

Kelejian, H. H., and Oates, W. E. (1974) *Introduction to Econometrics: Principles and Applications* (New York: Harper & Row)

Knowles, L. L., and Prewitt, K. (eds.) (1969) *Institutional Racism in America* (Englewood Cliffs, NJ: Prentice-Hall)

Labour Party (1976) *Labour Against Racism* (London: Labour Party)

Labour Party (1978a) *Labour Party Campaign Handbook: Race, Immigration and the Racialists* (London: Labour Party)

Labour Party (1978b) *Response to the National Front*, Statement by the National Executive Committee (London: Labour Party)

Labour Party (1980a) *Citizenship and Immigration* (London: Labour Party)

Labour Party (1980b) *Labour and the Black Electorate*, Advice Notice No. 1 (London: Labour Party National Executive Committee)

Labour Party (1981) *British Nationality Law — Our Alternative to Tory Legislation*, NEC Statement to Annual Conference (London: Labour Party Research Department)

Labour Party (1982) *Labour's Programme, 1982*, Home Policy section printed as a supplement in *Labour Weekly*, 25 June

Locksley, G. (1980) 'The political business cycle: alternative interpretations', in P. Whiteley (ed.), *Models of Political Economy* (London and Beverly Hills: Sage Publications), pp. 177–98

Miller, W. L. (1980) 'What was the profit in following the crowd?: the effectiveness of party strategies on immigration and devolution', *British Journal of Political Science*, vol. 10, no. 1, pp. 15–38

Miller, W. L., and Mackie, M. (1973) 'The electoral cycle and the asymmetry of government and opposition popularity: an alternative model of the relationship between economic conditions and political popularity', *Political Studies*, vol. 21, no. 3, pp. 263–79

NOP (National Opinion Polls) (1978) *Political Social Economic Review*, no. 14, April

Peach, C. (1968) *West Indian Migration to Britain: A Social Geography* (London: OUP)

Pissarides, C. A. (1980) 'British government popularity and economic performance', *Economic Journal*, vol. 90, no. 3, pp. 569–81

Reiner, R. (1978) *The Blue-Coated Worker: A Sociological Study of Police Unionism* (Cambridge: CUP)

Russell, C., and Lewis, H. S. (1900) *The Jew in London: A Study of Racial Character and Present-Day Conditions* (London: Fisher Unwin)

Scarman, Lord (1982) *The Scarman Report: The Brixton Disorders, 10–12 April 1981; Report of an Inquiry by the Right Honourable the Lord Scarman, OBE, Presented to Parliament by the Secretary of State for the Home Department by command of Her Majesty, November 1981* (Harmondsworth: Penguin)

Schoen, D. S. (1977) *Enoch Powell and the Powellites* (London: Macmillan)

Studlar, D. T. (1978) 'Policy voting in Britain: the colored immigration issue in the 1964, 1966, and 1970 general elections', *American Political Science Review*, vol. 72, no. 1, pp. 46–64

Troyna, B. (1981) *Public Awareness and the Media: A Study of Reporting on Race* (London: Commission for Racial Equality)

US Bureau of the Census (1960) *Historical Statistics of the United States, Colonial Times to 1957* (Washington, DC: US Government Printing Office)

Webb, N. L., and Wybrow, R. J. (eds.) (1981) *The Gallup Report* (London: Sphere Books)

Whistler, D. (1982) *User Manual for DARTS (Data Retrieval System)* (London: London School of Economics and Political Science Computer Unit)

Whiteley, P. (ed.) (1980) *Models of Political Economy* (London and Beverly Hills: Sage Publications)

Wilson, H. (1971) *The Labour Government, 1964–1970: A Personal Record* (London: Weidenfeld & Nicolson and Michael Joseph)

# 11

## Nationalism and Internationalism: a Critique of Economic and Defence Policies

Michael Mann

The main argument of this chapter is that the British Labour Party has not yet responded squarely to recent changes in global power relations. The right of the Party (in common with other political parties) continues to cling to a traditional internationalism dominated by the United States and by international capital. The left reasserts traditional nationalism; in economic policy it drifts towards protectionism and autarchy and in defence policy towards unilateralism. Neither can now make a significant contribution to democratic socialism or to peace. A new internationalism is required that is based on alliance with those classes and nations abroad that are threatened by similar forces. This chapter attempts to identify those friends and to argue for a reorientation of basic strategy towards them.

To an extent, the same argument underpins my treatment of economic and defence policy. But there are sufficiently large differences between them to require separate discussion.[1]

### Economic policy: changes in national and international economies

Democracy is rule by the people. To this ancient political aspiration socialism has added the notion of popular *economic* rule. Democracy can be assured only by popular control of the economy, or at least of its 'commanding heights'. All socialists seek greater public control of economic power, no matter how divided they may be about its forms and its limits. But socialists have rarely faced up to the problem of exactly *where* the control is to be exercised.

If socialism were merely a domestic aspiration, the answer would be clear: control the national state! For this state has a near-monopoly of formal rule-making in the modern world. But as socialism includes economic aspirations, another arena becomes relevant: the *international* power relations of capitalism. In this section I argue that democratic socialism requires controls over both national and international arenas, for *they* exercise power over us. Few socialists have faced up to both: they normally neglect the international arena. Conservatives and Liberals also have difficulty in grasping the dual nature of modern power relations. Indeed, this failure of modern political theory, and of democratic socialism in particular, is general through most of the Western world. Nevertheless, as Britain has the most internationalised economy of any of the major nation states, she may have to find the first democratic socialist solution or go under.

Socialists neglect the international arena because virtually all their gains have been obtained within the bounds of the individual nation state. A few have been won at a local level by groups of workers organised in trade unions, co-operatives and local political parties; but most have come through national organisation and state legislation. True, socialists have usually also voiced international sentiments (given organisational forms in the various 'Internationals' of the last hundred years). But the overwhelming mass of socialist achievements have been national.

There are many historical reasons for this. Probably the most important is that the socialist mould was set in times when international trade and direct foreign investment were at comparatively low levels. Thus democratic control over the economy did not objectively require much international policy. By about 1960, however, it was clear to many socialists that the new international economy was introducing stable constraints on the achievement of traditional goals. These constraints were still not severe until the mid-1970s. Until then Western economic growth could apparently pay for further Keynesian welfare statist policies of a mildly reformist kind. It is only in the last decade that crisis has threatened even this achievement.

What has grown up in the postwar period is a novel form of 'dual economy', one national and to a degree planned, the other international and almost entirely unplanned. Increasingly, the power of the latter is undermining planning in the former. Let me explain this at greater length.

The results of a hundred years of socialist struggle within the nation state are discussed elsewhere in this book. Perhaps such welfare statism has redistributed less power than most of us would have liked. But one of its undoubted achievements has been to encourage the development of centralised planning within the national state. This has been fostered also by other forces, particularly Keynesian economics and economic concentration and reliance on state help by capitalist enterprises themselves.

This has resulted, first, in a large state sector. In Britain state expenditures amount to about a quarter of GDP, a proportion which is about average for the OECD countries. Then we could add other economic payments which flow through the state, 'transfer payments', paid by one group of citizens through the state to another group. This adds nearly another 15 per cent, a figure which is again about average in the OECD. The combined figure of 40 per cent is one indication of the extent of state co-ordination of domestic economic life. But then not even the private sector is entirely dominated by the market. For example, the largest 100 companies operating in Britain in 1978 accounted for 44 per cent of total company assets, a considerable concentration of power, and again about average for the OECD countries. Competitive elements are reduced even further by important sectors such as agriculture, in which prices are usually determined by political negotiations. Finally, some trade unions and most professional associations can use near-monopoly powers to settle their wages relatively independently of the market.

In all these respects Britain is not unusual among advanced capitalist nation states. Among countries of comparable size only Japan has a much smaller state sector – and this is largely a difference of form rather than substance (Japan relies upon more discrete, back-stairs state help for its corporations). One other country is distinctly unusual, however, and that is worth emphasising. It is the United States. Mainly because of her continental size and diversity, partly because of her low level of working-class organisation and her federal political system, the United States still contains far more of a competitive market than any of her rivals. Thus she does *not* offer an economic model suitable for other countries, a point to which I will return later.

The United States apart, this politicised economy is the norm. It is generally labelled *corporatism*, and this term serves well enough. Its core is continuous negotiation between the state, large corporations and (in a somewhat more subordinate capacity) union leaders. This often seems to by-pass parliamentary assemblies. Nevertheless, corporatism is not particularly successful. It is often undermined by the independent activities of capitalists and workers (in runs on the pound and in rejection of pay norms, for example). Increasingly, international pressures have been doing the undermining.

In the international arena the market reigns supreme. In the postwar period, while the United States remained hegemonic, her economy and her dollar provided a large measure of international regulation. The US Government is still the most important single actor in the international arena. But since 1971 currencies have generally 'floated' in response to worldwide market forces. The major nation states and the international agencies like the IMF, the World Bank, and GATT have also encouraged free-trade conditions. In any case, they themselves lack control over the other major international actor of the post-1945 world, the multinational corporation. The relations between all these forces are complex, but they are not planned. Though Keynes pretends to rule within the nation state, Adam Smith still rules without — and therefore, to a large degree, within as well.

Because international trade and direct foreign investment have rocketed since 1945, they have made an increasing impact upon the domestic economy. This is less true for the USA than for any other country, for she is the least dependent upon international trade. Britain is fairly typical in the extent of her trade but is unusually blessed with multinational corporations. Britain ranks second behind the United States in the value of multinational corporation assets and second behind Switzerland in the proportion of GDP that they contribute (40 per cent). Adding the overseas role of British banking and insurance through the City, its 'offshore island', Britain is the most dependent on international capitalism and therefore probably the most vulnerable to its unplanned fluctuations and crises of confidence.

Thus both for domestic and, more important, for international reasons, economic planning has achieved far less than its advocates of both left and right hoped. It has been buffeted off course repeatedly by exchange rate and balance of payments crises and by failure to control either wages or prices (for a trenchant critique, see Budd, 1978).

This feeble record led directly to the monetarist and *laissez-faire* policies of the Thatcher Government. Indeed, now that the worldwide economic growth of capitalism is faltering, such policies are more popular among conservatives everywhere. But they cannot work. This is not primarily because of the technical difficulties associated with measuring or controlling the money supply or the like but because they ignore the growth of the corporatist economy.

The domestic market could only operate in a largely 'free' way if the welfare state were truly rolled back, if unions and professions were almost totally smashed, if agricultural prices were not politically negotiated, if corporate monopolies were broken up. Even the Thatcher Government possesses only the rhetoric, not the real political will, to undertake such a ferocious onslaught. Its hesitancy is perfectly understandable, for such action would precipitate crisis, electoral disaster and perhaps a good deal worse. This point is well understood by the Tory 'wets', who advocate a form of corporatism, 'one nation' consensus. Their policies do recognise the realities of the nation state. But they offer little to socialists (or to any democrat), for they would strengthen the non-democratic 'backstairs' control of corporatism.

## The reponses of the Labour Party

Labour Party reactions are still in a state of flux, but we can identify two main alternatives. First, the Labour centre and right. This faction merges with the Tory 'wets', as it is corporatist and accepts the external constraints imposed by international capitalism. For example, the right considers the terms of the IMF loan of 1976 to have been inevitable both then and — if circumstances repeated themselves — in the future. Domestically, these policies are based upon 'backstairs' corporatism, of the kind associated with the Callaghan social contract, which aims to persuade union leaders to accept wage restraint in return for some concessions on redistribution or welfare policies. Senior members of this faction argue that such policies 'almost worked' in the Callaghan years and that they have learned the necessary lessons to make them work properly in the future. Whether they would indeed work is uncertain. Even if they did, their contribution would be insufficient to turn the whole economy around. Even if they did this too, we would not be much closer to democratic socialism, largely because such policies accept the deflationary, reactionary terms imposed by international capitalism.

This point is clearly understood in all the various 'alternative economic strategies' being proposed by Labour's left. These propose an expansionist economic policy coupled with greater state direction of productive investment, either through direct nationalisation (for example, the famous 'list' of about twenty-five major companies that Labour Party documents of the early 1970s promised to nationalise), through an expanded National Enterprise Board or through 'planning agreements' between state and individual enterprise (Blake and Ormerod, 1980; Cripps *et al.*, 1981; Glyn and Harrison, 1980; Holland, 1975; Labour Co-Ordinating Committee, 1980; London CSE Group, 1980).

The authors of these strategies recognize that such policies would not be acceptable to many capitalist interest groups, whose main pressures would come through the City and through international 'confidence'. A flight of capital would ensue, starving Britain of investment funds from the market sector, forcing down the value of sterling beyond reasonable devaluation levels and fuelling inflation. They also recognise that the technical consequence of expansionist policies would be to increase imports at a faster rate than exports, leading to balance of payments difficulties. The left fears that these two pressures might force the British Government to capitulate to international capital, as it did in 1976.

Therefore, the left's alternative strategies *also* contain defensive policies against international pressures. There are three main ones, which involve restricting or banning the outflow of capital, coupled with varying mixtures of controlled devaluation and import controls. This is not the place, nor am I the person, to discuss the economic effectiveness of each of these. Politically, though, restrictions on capital flows and devaluation would not endear the British Government to international (or national) capital, but in moderation they are part of the normal rules of the game played by corporatist states today. Import controls, whether tariffs or quotas, are not. They contravene the letter of EEC rules and the spirit of GATT rules (non-selective general import controls would also contravene the letter of GATT). No one can predict at what point retaliation would begin. Doubtless Britain could get away with mild measures all round. But at some point retaliation *would* occur, and it would be considered legitimate by the international economy as a whole. That retaliation might destroy the alternative economic strategy.

Thus without some *other* international policies, all that would be safe would be mild defence of a mildly expansionist strategy. To have much effect it would probably require wage restraint. Thus the most realistic, attainable package of *present* policy alternatives is probably a centrist one, like that now advocated by Peter Shore. It is better than nothing, but it is not much of an advance towards democratic socialism. Only further internationalist policies, seeking to exert democratic controls on the *international* arena, can secure such an advance.

It is worth pausing for a moment to consider also the general spirit in which some of the alternative economic strategies have been expressed. Unfortunately, this spirit is a formidable obstacle to the new and necessary internationalism. Even internationalistic rhetoric is disappearing in some quarters. Let me instance the book *Manifesto: a Radical Strategy for Britain's Future* (Cripps *et al.*, 1981), written by a group of leading left Labour figures. They argue: 'The mechanisms of free trade and multinational business are destroying Britain's economy. Our present international relationships lock us into destructive patterns of trade and investment in many other countries and commit us to supporting an anarchic "free" world' (pp. 20–1). The solution is 'the case for national independence': *British* control over the British economy, withdrawal from the EEC and the Western alliance and national economic autarchy. Foreigners, aided by a fifth column in the City, are to blame. We must defend ourselves against them! This is also a persistent theme of Tony Benn. Towards the end of the deputy leadership campaign, when he was trying to speak to the electorate at large as well as to the Labour rank and file, his standard speech contained three main elements: first, a unilateralist defence strategy – defined as British, not American, control over our defence; second, withdrawal from the EEC, so that the British people, not Europeans, could set the price of their foodstuffs; third, the restoration of national control over the economy in place of the control of foreign bankers and the multinationals. The policies themselves are not objectionable (though I will argue below that they are not necessarily the most appropriate ones), but the tone of national chauvinism certainly is. It is well to recall here Tom Nairn's (1972) brilliant dissection of the anti-EEC case. For he showed then just how strong chauvinism had always been on the left of the Labour Party.

I do not wish to suggest that the whole of the left has abandoned itself to chauvinism. Some of the alternative economic strategies worry over the contradiction between internationalism and their preferred economic policies. Several on the left have also made the criticisms that I am repeating here (e.g. Bearman, 1979). But all would accept that these worries have not yet led to an international strategy as full or as coherent as domestic strategies. And so in the next section I attempt to sketch the outlines of such a strategy.

## Towards a new economic internationalism

The overall guidelines of our foreign policy should not be nationalist. As the international economy exerts increasing power over us, democracy involves controlling it, not turning our backs upon it. The latter would be the corollary of Mrs Thatcher's mistake: just as her policies cannot work because they ignore the power realities of the nation state, so nationalist policies cannot work because they ignore international power realities. But internationalism should also flow from socialism. The enemies of the British people are not foreigners. True, some of our most powerful enemies are internationally organised. But that means that our foreign policy should *always* distinguish between those international interest groups that are our enemies, those that are relatively neutral and those that are, or should be, our friends. Foreign policies that do not discriminate between different categories of foreigners are politically unacceptable.

So who are our friends, and how do we organize an alliance with them? There are two principal types of friend (and enemy too): classes and nation states. Socialists need little advice about class solidarity. In the present context that means strengthening international co-operation among trade unions and democratic socialist political parties, stiffening ILO codes of practice, establishing minimum labour standards and inserting social clauses in international trade agreements, importing only, or preferentially, goods produced by trade unionists, encouraging solidarity among the employees of multinational corporations, putting legal pressures on the European Court, etc., etc. But, being realistic, we must accept that this is not likely to achieve much in the near future.[2] Workers, unions and parties of the left are implicated so profoundly in their own corporatist states that they face inwards, not outwards. They are nationalist in their practices, if not in their rhetoric too.

International socialists have always deplored this fact. But perhaps it can be used for internationalist purposes after all by also developing alliances between the citizens of nations with similar (though not, of course, identical or internally homogeneous) interests. The principal similarities which matter are: domestically, a similar or higher level of democratic socialism; internationally, a similar or higher level of vulnerability to international capitalism. In Table 1, I have tried to present crude measures of these two indices of similarity for the main advanced capitalist nation states.

Table 1   Measures of level of democratic socialism and dependence on exports

| | Income distribution: Gini coefficient after direct taxes[1] 1975 | Socialist vote (%)[2] | Welfare spending[3] | Union membership[4] 1970 | Exports as % of GDP[5] 1978 |
|---|---|---|---|---|---|
| Australia | 0.31 | 47 | 23 | 53 | 15 |
| Canada | 0.34 | 18 | 35 | 33 | 26 |
| France | 0.41 | 43 | 37 | 20 | 21 |
| Germany | 0.38 | 36 | 35 | 37 | 25 |
| Italy | 0.40 | 42 | 31 | 57 | 29 |
| Netherlands | 0.35 | 35 | 43 | 41 | 47 |
| Norway | 0.31 | 52 | 45 | 67 | 42 |
| Sweden | 0.30 | 51 | 44 | 87 | 29 |
| UK | 0.32 | 46 | 35 | 49 | 30 |
| USA | 0.38 | 0 | 21 | 28 | 8 |
| Denmark | | 46 | 49 | 66 | 28 |
| Finland | | 47 | 38 | 62 | 31 |
| Austria | | 47 | 43 | 72 | 35 |
| Belgium | | 38 | 37 | 65 | 51 |
| New Zealand | | 45 | 30 | 45 | 27 |
| Ireland | | 10 | 36 | | 52 |
| Switzerland | | 29 | 24 | 31 | 35 |

Notes: [1]Sawyer (1976). Figures adjusted for the redistributive effects of public spending by Stephens (1979, 88–128).
[2]Percentage of total vote obtained by social democratic and/or communist parties 1945–1970, calculated by Stephens (1979).
[3]Percentage of GNI devoted to non-military public spending 1970 (Stephens, 1979).
[4]As percentage of non-agricultural wage and salary workers. New Zealand figure probably too low.
[5]UN (1979). Italy figure relates to 1977.

I have given four indicators of democratic socialism. First, public expenditure as a percentage of GDP, including transfer payments but excluding defence expenditures. This is strictly only a measure of 'state corporatism' and so has been supplemented by three more 'socialistic' indicators. Union membership density figures give us some indication of the general industrial strength of the working-class movement. Percentages voting socialist (or communist) give us an indication of political strength, and Gini coefficients give a crude indication of the results of such strength, a measure of the degree of income inequality in each country. The lower the coefficient, the more equal the distribution (a coefficient of 1 would mean that the top group possessed all the income, and 0 would mean that everyone received an identical income). All these figures have their imperfections. In particular, there is usually at least one country whose 'real' performance is not accurately measured by them. For example, the United States contains no significant socialist vote, though she contains some political pressure for welfare statism and redistribution, and France has a union movement that relies for its strength on factors other than simple membership density. However, the indicators will serve, provided we interpret them cautiously.

International vulnerability I measured only by exports as a proportion of GDP. To pursue the analysis would, ideally, require more sophisticated measures of international dependence and 'strength' (including direct foreign investment flows and the ratio of trading surpluses to deficits in trading flows between these countries). It would also have to control for regional trade alliances like the EEC. But this will do as a crude approximation with which the argument can begin.

We can see that many countries have roughly comparable levels of socialist achievement. They include the UK but not the USA (nor probably would they include Japan). All the Scandinavian countries and most of the Central European belt (Austria, Germany, Belgium and the Netherlands, but not Switzerland) are clearly either more socialist than the UK or at a comparable level. The two remaining major European countries are somewhat distinct. Thus France has lagged in equality (and union membership), but its present socialist Government may

change this. Italy still lags but may contain the political poten-
tiality for comparable changes. Outside Europe, the characteristics of Australia, New Zealand and Canada differ but not to the
same extent as those of the USA. Gini coefficients are dangerous
tools when applied internationally, but it is worth noting that
the most thorough comparisons to date of the eight countries
for which most data are available come to similar conclusions.
Britain, Sweden and West Germany are consistently more
egalitarian, then France (but she is apparently catching up on
Britain), then Australia and Canada, then Japan, then the USA
(Stark, 1977). In the final column we begin to realize the
impossibility, for *most* countries, of achieving 'socialism in one
country'. Even without adding direct foreign investment, the
international dependence is considerable (and is generally and
predictably the higher, the smaller the country). Note again the
exceptionally low vulnerability of the USA (and on this measure, Japan also appears surprisingly low, with exports at only 11
per cent of GDP). Britain is not alone in the extent and the
potential vulnerability of her democratic socialist aspirations.
Most of the other nation states are in a quite similar position.
Only the United States (and probably Japan) diverge significantly.

Many nation states can be expected to have a potential internal coalition of interests of a broadly Keynesian welfare-statist
type – more so than is acknowledged by the conventional wis-
dom of international capital or of the US Government. They
also intermittently, or even normally, elect democratic socialists
to power. There is enormous scope for political collaboration
with such parties. There is even scope for collaboration with
centrist and Christian Democrat Governments in some of these
countries – significantly more than for collaboration with *any*
Government of the United States for example.

Such collaboration does indeed occur, though as the normal
channels are diplomatic and secretive, it rarely breaks cover.
IMF loans are instances of visible negotiation. In the case of
Britain's loan in 1976 (described in newspaper articles by Fay
and Young, 1978), James Callaghan placed great hopes in
Chancellor Schmidt's influence on the IMF. These hopes were
not totally without foundation, but ultimately Schmidt listened

to more conservative advice from his bankers. In the same negotiations the US Government also feared that the IMF might be diverted from its normal deflationary policies by the pressure of Britain, Italy, Portugal and Mexico, which were all undergoing similar crises. But these pressures were never coordinated. Some years earlier Schmidt had intervened to moderate IMF terms to Portugal. In 1977 Callaghan and Trudeau successfully led pressure on the IMF to moderate terms to the Manley Government in Jamaica – but the IMF then retaliated with even severer terms in the next round. It is not a record of conspicuous success.

Why has international socialism been so feeble? It is my overall argument that as the pressures are new, they have not yet been fully appreciated by socialists and Keynesians. As yet, the international arena has been left to bankers, who also accept the leading role of the United States. The predominance of bankers is manifest in two ways. First, the permanent international secretariats are themselves almost invariably drawn from banking backgrounds. Second, although the final decisions are usually taken by politicians, their own principal national advisers are also bankers. The principal national adviser is usually the head of the central bank (e.g. the Governor of the Bank of England), together with men recruited from the leading private banks and career civil servants drawn from Treasury Departments. The economic advice of this advisory group is usually conservative – in recent years, monetarist. But on top of that they also defer to the principal conservative national Government, that of the United States. The United States is the dominant force in the IMF, as she is in all the international economic agencies. In practice, the USA dominates loan-giving. In the case of the 1976 loan to Britain, the negotiations were conducted jointly by an IMF secretariat team (six men, all professional bankers, drawn from Australia, New Zealand, the USA, Germany and Greece, with a British leader) and the top men at the US Treasury and Federal Reserve Bank (William Simon, Arthur Burns and Edwin Yeo – all bankers). This was a fairly typical set of negotiations, indicating consensus among bankers that the United States still rightly plays the leading role in the international economy, even if she has lost her actual hegemony.

This alliance between bankers and the United States Government embraces three things. First, it embodies a conservative economic philosophy based both on the primacy of ensuring profit to the private investor and on the belief that this is best guaranteed by opening up markets and class inequalities (or 'incentives'). Second, it is true internationalism, even if it has a pronounced American accent. Thus it is not merely *foreign* bankers who impose terms on national Governments. Blaming the foreigners is a smokescreen, for the IMF relies substantially on the advice of 'sound' financial circles within the country with which it is dealing. In fact, it generally asks domestic capitalists to detail the kinds of economic policy which would encourage and protect investment. Consequently, it receives extremely conservative political advice. Third, this international class interest is represented as *technically* necessary and is protected from political control on those grounds.

There is one broad answer to this: to *politicise the international economy*. It must be brought under political control. If it is not, it will always be able to outflank elected radical Governments which are seeking to redistribute power and rewards. Exchange rates, trade flows, tariffs, credit are not merely, or even principally, technical matters but political ones, affecting us all. In a democracy the people should be able to control them through their elected representatives. The principle implies two practices: the decision-makers should be elected politicians, not appointed bankers or other advisers; and there should be public debate between the principal opposed interest groups before decisions are taken.

The question of how to implement these practices is not easy, partly because present international institutions all have different structures and constituencies. Nevertheless, there are two main choices: to adjust to present structures or radically to reshape them.

The adjustive policy would accept the international economy as it is and would simply promote a concerted effort among sympathetic Governments, parties and unions to agree on common policies *vis-à-vis* the issues and the institutions. This would be better than nothing, and it is the only practicable immediate policy. It might imply the creation of a party spokesman/woman on the international economy, of Cabinet rank. This person's office could be a revived and reshaped Ministry of Overseas Development, though it would also assume certain tasks at present undertaken by the Treasury. While in Opposition, the shadow minister would principally propagandise and help to create institutions of international co-operation. While in Government, the Minister would be part of the Government's economic planning group and would deal with international economic negotiations. The role would be more political and less technical-administrative than is usual at Cabinet level, for the creation of a changed international political climate would still be the core of the task. This adjustive policy would preserve national sovereignty, but it might not be enough to ensure radical changes.

The more radical and inevitably long-term policy would be to reshape international institutions, probably into a single forum for political discussions with offshoot specialist councils like the IMF, the World Bank and GATT. There would be fierce resistance to this proposal from existing international agencies and from banking circles. Its implementation would symbolise (and perhaps even actualise) the breaking of the *organised* power of that class. Its market power would remain to be challenged by the new political agency, the institutions of which could take a variety of possible forms. One might be a small 'parliament', containing Opposition as well as Government party representation and a council of individual national Ministers. If this agency had teeth, it would reduce national sovereignty. But, then, so does the present unregulated international economy. It would also begin to interfere with international market pressures as soon as its debates became public (e.g. currency speculation could not continue as at present if changes in international economic regulation were discussed openly). These interferences are necessary to the forward movement of democratic socialism.

So far I have touched only upon the interests of the major capitalist nations of the North. But the developing countries of the South are also affected by the international agencies. They have actually gone further in arguing a new, politicised order. They demand reforms in voting and staffing of the IMF and the World Bank to give more weight to the countries of the South; they seek amalgamation of GATT and UNCTAD and the creation of a World Development Fund to replace the IMF, the World Bank and the IDA; and they want greater weight to be given to the political effects of deflationary policies. In these respects they are allies in the strategy here advocated. There is more in common between international democratic socialism and the kind of global Keynesianism advocated in, say, the Brandt Report (1980) than there is between either and the politics of fiscal conservatism.

The participation of the South would further complicate institutional arrangements, of course. For example, what about voting strength? Should the system be one nation, one vote (as in most UN agencies) or one vote per unit of economic power, which would give the advanced countries predominance (as in the main economic agencies)? Presumably this issue, and others, is capable of compromise.

The interests of these countries are not identical to our own, and there are many areas of conflict. On the other hand, the Southern countries are extremely varied. I have already argued that there are more potential internal divisions within the North than the present international economic order recognises – particularly between the USA and banking interests on the one hand and many of the more corporatist and/or democratic-socialist nation states on the other. To politicise the international economy would also be to open up divisions within the South. This development is to be welcomed: to politicise the order would be to allow real material interests to surface. There are not simply two 'quasi-classes', North and South, in international capitalism.

As the economic power of capitalism, as a single international system, now directly permeates two-thirds of the globe, it requires political regulation at the global level. Socialists should welcome that regulation, not complain about losses of national sovereignty.[3]


## Defence policy

My claim is that a broad internationalist strategy is relevant to all aspects of foreign policy. It is nowhere more applicable than to defence. At present the Labour Party, and the country at large, is riven by a dispute between what are generally called 'unilateralism' and 'multilateralism'. The aims of unilateralism are clear enough: Britain should go it alone, unilaterally, and there should be a progressive series of renunciation – of Trident, Polaris, all 'independent deterrents', Cruise and Pershing missiles, all American nuclear weapons on our soils and, finally, NATO. These various renunciations are usually advocated regardless of the policy of any other power, for the main supporting argument is that a unilateral gesture is needed to get the peace process moving. Multilateralism is not such a clear label. It usually refers to what is essentially *bilateral* negotiation between NATO, led by the USA, and the Warsaw Pact, led by the USSR. So, as in economic policies, the left advocates nationalism, the right USA-dominated internationalism. Thus the same counter-argument applies: that our real interests lie neither with a defence autarchy nor with an internationalism that remains subordinate to the USA.

However, there are also obvious differences between defence and economic strategy. The conditions of modern, especially nuclear, warfare mean that defence policy *must* embody a 'national interest' regardless of class. Bombs do not distinguish between classes – unlike most economic threats. Strategic considerations also involve a *regional* interest. And this means that our friends are likely to be defined regionally. Few now doubt that the European countries – caught between the USA and the USSR as the first candidates for their battleground – have a strong common interest in defence matters. Few would contest the nature of that common interest: primarily, to avoid nuclear devastation; secondarily, to avoid Soviet military domination (Better Red than Dead but Preferably Neither). But it is not as generally recognised that the common interest cannot easily be articulated by present institutions. Neither NATO nor the EEC can express it, for example. It involves Sweden, Switzerland and Spain quite as much as it involves Britain or West Germany; and it does not involve the dominant NATO partner, the USA. Nor is that common interest articulated by either unilateralism or multilateralism as those policies are generally formulated.

Multi-lateralism means subordination to the USA within the

NATO structure. It does not preclude constructive criticism, but its main goal is to steer the USA into essentially bilateral arms-control talks with the USSR. It is a naive policy because it ignores three salient features of those powers.

First, they are both extremely militaristic in their socio-political structure, though this is more erratic in the USA than in the USSR. The militarist pride of both the state and popular ideology in the USSR is obvious and well documented (Holloway, 1980). Militarism has also usually been a vote-winning strategy in US elections: the main 'liberal' response to the hawkish politician's demand for more military spending has been, 'We are *already* the number-one power.' Militarism in the case of the two super-powers is not confined to a narrow military-industrial complex but is a part of national pride, of the very sense of being a Soviet or an American citizen. This sense is no longer nearly as pronounced or as stable within Europe nations (Falklands frenzy notwithstanding). Hence disarmament negotiations between the super-powers present obstacles with which Europeans will always be impatient.

Second, the super-powers both use Europe as a buffer-state area and have a certain interest in its remaining one. They are not peculiarly evil in their use of Europe. They behave as great powers have always done when confronted by such plain geography. The USA has a strategic edge here because those of her nuclear weapons that are stationed in Western Europe can be used against the territory of the USSR, while Soviet missiles in Eastern Europe do not threaten US territory. This might not make a limited theatre nuclear war in Europe likely, as unilateralists sometimes claim (unless one takes a very jaundiced view of American aggression), for the USSR has no interest in this option. While US strategy presupposes Europe as a nuclear buffer zone, Soviet strategy presupposes a conventional buffer zone. It goes without saying that neither strategy corresponds to Europe's own interests.

This asymmetry is the third dangerous feature of US/Soviet relations. It prevents the emergence of a stable balance of power between them. Each side has different areas of vulnerability, and the arms race proceeds by a series of staggered escalations of weapons of different types responding to different threats. This also adds to the difficulty of bargaining for arms reductions.

If we consider multilateral progress to date, we cannot be reassured. After two decades of SALT treaties and their predecessors, each agreement has been reached only about 'yesterday's' weapons. On each side 'today's' weapons generally emerge at about the time that a treaty is concluded. They require a new arms response by the other power, and so the process continues on its asymmetrical path. At best — which is not the present situation — two détente-minded powers agree to trade off yesterday's threats. Have these multilateral negotiations made Europe or the world a safer place? Only in so far as it is better that the super-powers negotiate than that they do not. There is nothing in the process to *keep* them negotiating (as we have seen in recent years). They do not need to fear militarism as much as Europeans do. And the rational fear of Europeans increases exponentially with the annual exponential increases in the kill ratios of the weaponry. The risks of nuclear war, and the certainty of devastation that it would bring, make such leisurely progress increasingly inadequate as a guarantee of the survival of Europeans. Multilateralism, as it is conventionally understood, is not enough. Its inadequacy is a product only of the last decade, but European public opinion has already begun to perceive it.

Which brings us to unilateralism. Over the range of policy options covered by this label, there will inevitably be more disagreement. This is because of the very variety of the options and also because of the central moral dilemma that they highlight. Many unilateralists argue that as they themselves could never 'press the button' to inflict wholesale death on innocent people, it is morally wrong to have anything to do with an alliance which contemplates such an option. Such a stance naturally undermines all nuclear deterrence theory. If, in the last resort, we won't press the button, we cannot deter. That is also my own view. But to accept the essence of unilateralism is not to accept that it is sufficient as a defence policy. In fact, it is inadequate in two ways.

First, it will not necessarily obviate nuclear devastation for ourselves. Half-hearted unilateralism (for example, the rejection of nuclear weapons on British soil but the desire to stay in

NATO) would reduce the number of incoming Soviet missiles only by perhaps a half, for bases and communications systems would still be targets. Even withdrawal from NATO would be unlikely to protect us from the effects of a full-scale war in the European theatre. Geography again determines that our airbases and ports would be desired by both sides. In the short run, moreover, a policy of unilateralism would put greater pressure on other European allies of the USA to accept more missiles, submarines, etc. This would hardly endear us to the rest of Europe. It might be seen not as a moral gesture but as a hypocritical one. To hide behind continental Europe and the USA is not to set an example to the world! Something more is needed.

Second, unilateralism will do nothing to deter Soviet aggression. Many unilateralists do not accept this argument. They do not see the USSR as aggressive. This view seems naive, not because of any malignity peculiar to the USSR, still less because of anything to do with communism, but simply because the USSR *is* a great power. Great powers expand their sphere of influence as far as their power, and that of their rivals, allows. Such was the way in which all the Western European powers behaved until their power was taken away from them. Probably we should not envisage direct Soviet invasion (unless the consequence of a militarily weak Europe were that East European dissidents operated more freely from Western Europe), but greater Soviet influence over the terms of trade, the refugee problem and the internal affairs of neighbouring countries is a possibility, at the very least. That prospect is a great deal better than nuclear devastation, but is it avoidable by other means?

The hope is to achieve a Europe-wide disarmament strategy: to abolish nuclear weapons from the European theatre to the Urals, more or less as the European Nuclear Disarmament Movement argues (though removing the naivety that seems to colour the Movement's view of the Soviet Union), and to strive for the equalisation of conventional weapons. This objective is opportune because of the conjunction of three factors. First, all European states are experiencing the same geo-political vulnerability to nuclear weapons and they have also lost their traditional appetite for militarism. Second, the USSR's strategic vulnerability in the European theatre means that she has repeatedly advocated a nuclear-free zone in Europe. Her *militaristic* interests favour such disarmament. Third, the USA, unlike the USSR, leads an alliance of free, autonomous states. She could not, and ultimately would not wish to, prevent nuclear disarmament. If this latter were coupled with the equalisation of conventional forces, her own militaristic interests would favour it. This strategy represents a hope, but one based upon *realpolitik*. It could be achieved by hard multilateral bargaining between *three* sets of Governments, American, Soviet and European. It does not involve an appeal to common humanity or morality; still less does it reflect the forlorn unilateralist hope of appealing directly to the Soviet or East European peoples. It is based only on the nuclear fears and the geo-political opportunity of Europeans.

The principal stumbling-block to this policy lies probably not with nuclear but with conventional forces (the Soviet Union requires large conventional forces to crush dissidence in Eastern Europe, as well as for deterrence against the West). It might also be that we Europeans will have to increase our conventional forces in the short run. Nor would such a strategy eliminate all risks and threats. Naturally, some Soviet missiles east of the Urals could reach Western Europe or be speedily repositioned; naturally, the USA might seek to acquire around the southern flanks of the USSR what she has abandoned to the west. Having invented both great-power rivalry and nuclear weapons, we cannot abolish them. Who knows whether we can control them? But it is up to each nation and region to pursue its own salvation from them. Europe has a common geo-political interest and must therefore articulate a common salvation.

The essence of this strategy is to inaugurate a new multilateralism. The question of whether it should also include, to begin with, the traditional unilateral steps – the renunciation of nuclear weapons and withdrawal from NATO – is secondary and open to complex moral and tactical argument. More important should be an attempt to formulate a common European set of objectives *prior* to the involvement of the Governments of the USA and the USSR in negotiations.

# Conclusion

My argument is a simple one: that we are compelled to seek a new internationalism if we still seek economic growth, democratic socialism and freedom from nuclear devastation and foreign domination. Domestic socialism, coupled with international dependence on the USA, is nearing the end of its useful contribution to these goals. A crisis confronts British socialism and the British people. Luckily, we do not face it alone. Other people abroad have recently found themselves in similar circumstances. With respect to economic policy, they are the bulk of the citizens of most of the Keynesian welfare-statist democracies; with respect to defence policy, they are Europeans. Therefore we must ally ourselves with these groups and find new international institutions to cement our common interest. Internationalism is traditional (and tired) as rhetoric, but it has quite suddenly become an objective necessity.

# Notes

1  I would like to acknowledge the assistance of my fellow contributors and of John Stephens.
2  It must be stressed, for example, that the claims of international trade unions are almost always propaganda. Studies of their effectiveness show that they achieve virtually nothing in actual international disputes. See the devastating empirical detail contained in Northrup and Rowan (1979).
3  Arguments about national sovereignty inevitably raise the issue of the EEC. However, the EEC does not fit neatly into this discussion. This might seem odd in a paper devoted to nationalism versus internationalism within the Labour Party, for it is an issue which has deeply divided the Party, apparently on grounds of principle. But the EEC presently raises technical, not strategic, issues. If it had turned out as expected, it might have been, in Nairn's (1972) phrase, 'the terrain of the future'. Whether that would have been a future for socialism or intensified capitalism used to be a major issue of political principle. But it is now obsolete. For the EEC has turned out to be a far more idiosyncratic creature. Its budget is dominated by agriculture and by a small farmer lobby centred in France and West Germany. Its main extra-budget characteristic is that it is one of the world's principle low-tariff areas. Thus calculating the interests of the British people in the matter is a technical business involving assessment of agricultural costs versus the risks (and perhaps the costs) of excluding ourselves from this particular free-trade zone. I leave the calculation to economists.

# References

Bearman, J. (1979) 'Anatomy of the Bennite Left', *International Socialism*, Autumn, pp. 51–70.

Blake, D., and Ormerod, P. (1980) *The Economics of Prosperity* (London: Grant McIntyre)

Brandt Report (1980) *North-South: A Programme for Survival* (London: Pan)

Budd, A. (1978) *The Politics of Economic Planning* (London: Fontana)

Cripps, F., *et al.*, (1981) *Manifesto: A Radical Strategy for Britain's Future* (London: Pan)

Fay, S., and Young, H. (1978) 'The day the pound nearly died', *Sunday Times*, 14, 21, and 28 May

Glyn, A., and Harrison, J. (1980) *The British Economic Disaster* (London: Pluto Press)

Holland, S. (1975) *The Socialist Challenge* (London: Quartet)

Holloway, D. (1980) 'War, militarism and the Soviet state', in E. P. Thompson and D. Smith (eds.), *Protest and Survive* (Harmondsworth: Penguin)

Labour Co-Ordinating Committee (1980) *There is an Alternative* (London: LCC)

London CSE Group (1980) *The Alternative Economic Strategy* (London: CSE)

Nairn, T. (1972) 'The Left against Europe?' *New Left Review*, no. 75, pp. 5–120

Northrup, H. R., and Rowan, R. L. (1979) *Multi-National Collective Bargaining Attempts* (Philadelphia: Industrial Research Unit, University of Pennsylvania)

Sawyer, M. (1976) 'Income distribution in OECD countries', *Occasional Studies* (Paris: OECD)

Stark, T. (1977) 'The distribution of income in eight countries', *UK Royal Commission on the Distribution of Income and Wealth*, Background Paper No. 4 to Report No. 5 (London: HMSO)

Stephens, J. (1979) *The Transition from Capitalism to Socialism* (London: Macmillan), pp. 88–128

United Nations (1979) *Yearbook of National Accounts Statistics*, vol. II, International Tables 2A (New York: UN)

# 12

## Provision and Choice in Housing

Robert M. Power

There are housing needs and housing wishes. It is essential that people should be adequately accommodated in good-quality housing; it is desirable that they should be given meaningful and equal choice between buying and renting. These are two 'housing goals' which are to the fore of the British housing question and must be confronted by the Labour Party. They are not mutually exclusive, and I shall argue that positive policies designed to regenerate the public sector of housing, and thereby to rescue it from the danger of becoming a residual sector, will serve to tackle both housing need and the desire for choice between forms of tenures. Along with this, a revitalised public sector that provides and builds good-quality units of housing will succeed in alleviating other pressing housing problems, such as unemployment in the construction industry and the pitifully low levels of new starts in house-building.

Indeed, there can be no doubt that British housing is in a state of crisis. A conservative estimate identifies 62,000 homeless persons in England alone (the figure would undoubtedly be higher if 'sharers' and the ever-increasing numbers of single homeless were properly accounted for); well over 750,000 houses and flats are empty; 1,660,000 dwellings are classified as substandard, of which 916,000 lack basic amenities; and 1,623,000 non-substandard dwellings are in need of major repairs. Along with the general decline in the condition of the housing stock, house-building activity has fallen by 56 per cent over the past ten years; new housing starts in the UK fell by 38 per cent between 1968 and 1979; and after 1980's housing nadir, the 21,000 houses built in 1981 represented the lowest figure since records were first kept (*Roof*, March/April 1982, p. 7; Matthews and Leather, 1982, p. 12).

The House of Commons Environment Committee, which had a majority of Conservative MPs, predicted that Government policy would lead to a national shortage of 420,000 by the end of the current Parliament. And although John Stanley, the Housing Minister, boasted that the first nine months of 1980 had witnessed the commencement of improvement on 60,040 council houses (the best figures since 1973), the overall picture is indeed a desperate one (*Guardian*, 7 February 1981; *Roof*, Jan./Feb. 1981, p. 8).

Labour must resolve to use the public sector and direct intervention to boost the improvement and production of housing so as to bring about a situation in which housing needs can be met and meaningful choice realised. This will require a shift away from Labour's convergence with the Conservatives on the dominant role and fervent promotion of owner-occupation (see Griffiths, 1982).

Since the mid-1960s the Labour Party has accepted the Chamberlain philosophy of council housing as a provision only for those unable to solve their own housing problems (Merrett, 1979, p. 270). By 1970 some 50 per cent of the housing stock was owner-occupied, and there can be little doubt that the voting potential of this section of the electorate had a strong influence upon the housing policy of Labour throughout the decade. Indeed, although the Tories have always favoured owner-occupation, Labour's position until the mid-1960s was somewhat ambivalent as a result of its traditional support for the public sector of housing. However, by 1965 its White Paper on housing stated: 'The expansion of building for owner-occupation. . .is normal; it reflects a long-term social advance which should gradually pervade every region' (*Housing Programme*, 1965, p. 8). By 1977 Labour's Green Paper had gone further; it proclaimed that owner-occupation resulted from 'a basic and natural desire' (*Housing Policy*, 1977, p. 50).

Now is the time for Labour to divorce itself from this policy convergence and to redress the balance between the two main sectors (owner-occupation and council housing), both in terms of their respective roles in housing policy and with regard to financial and social equality across tenures. Once this has been accepted, central to Labour's housing programme must be the rejuvenation of our ageing housing stock, either by replacement or by improvement. This should be the base upon which any increase in the stock of housing is founded and the means whereby the public sector is revitalised.

The first half of this century witnessed a period in which successive Governments promoted either public or private solutions to the housing problem. Neither political party monopolised the championing of one sector to the exclusion of the other, but it has been strongly argued that the housing policy of the 1945–51 Labour Government (under the guidance of Bevan) was the last to view rental as the dominant form of tenure and the only administration to be dedicated unequivocally to the ideal of a public sector for 'general' rather than for 'specific' needs (Merrett, 1979, p. 236; Pawley, 1978, pp. 77–8).

There needs to be a return to such beliefs and convictions so that the public sector can offer a good standard of housing, of types appropriate to the needs of people wanting to live in them, and thereby offer a viable alternative to home ownership. As the National Executive Committee of the Labour Party (1981, p. 3) stated:

> In the longer term the only reliable defence for a major public sector within our housing system is to ensure that people want to live in it. That will require some substantial reforms in public housing to bring the housing rights and opportunities which it offers, and the social esteem which it enjoys, into line with home ownership at every possible point.

Therefore, it is essential that a Labour Government should intervene with money rather than good intentions and get a building and improvement programme under way, particularly in view of the lamentable failure, in recent years, of reliance upon the private sector to lead housing investment.

Michael Foot has stated that a Labour Government would provide £10 billion per year as a housing budget, and Frank Allaun has commented that a new building and improvement programme would make inroads into unemployment (*Guardian*, 20 April 1982). Indeed, as part of its 'socialist alternative', Labour views increased public expenditure on public housing as an integral part of its fight against monetarism and unemployment in its expressed endeavour to reflate and rebuild the economy.

Furthermore, alongside the inroads that an expanded building programme would make into the 500,000 unemployed in the construction industry, it would almost pay for itself through savings in unemployment and social security payments (Hilditch, 1981). In fact, a study by Cambridge Econometrics that was commissioned by the construction industry lobby, the Group of Eight, showed that of five different options for boosting the economy by £500 million, house-building, which would provide 64,000 jobs, would give the best 'overall performance' (*Roof*, Jan./Feb. 1982, p. 3). But – and it is a big but – a new Labour Government must give housing a priority claim on economic resources commensurate with the dimensions of the housing problem. Too often housing has been first in line for expenditure cuts, and Labour has been as reprehensible as the Conservatives in this respect (Berry, 1974, p. 223; Gould and Roweth, 1980). [1]

Housing cuts, and threats of cuts, have a disastrous effect upon housing programmes. Local authority schemes are halted altogether or held in abeyance; vacant jobs are frozen; and local authorities are reluctant to take on new workers who may be required only temporarily. Decisions by local authorities to supplement investment programmes must not rest upon the precarious business of spending against 'capital receipts' such as projected council house sales (as advocated by the Conservatives). Not only are these difficult to forecast, but also they may not be equalled in subsequent years, resulting in self-imposed future cuts over and above those enforced by central government. Labour must ensure that housing investment programmes return to being the three-year plans (rather than the present one-year plans) that were envisaged when the present system started, therefore allowing local authorities to go ahead with housing projects in a mood of confidence. With this in mind the next Labour Government must learn from the problems that beset the housing programmes of Bevan and Wilson and must guard against allowing economic contingencies and competing priorities to thwart its housing intentions.

For the public sector to offer a meaningful housing alternative to private sector owner-occupation, along with the essential improvement of the existing stock new units must be built. Shortage of land has always been a constraint, but the fact that Michael Heseltine was able to produce a land register of 52,287 acres of unused or under-used land owned by local authorities (which he wished to be put to use by private builders) indicated that the potential for new building still exists (*Guardian*, 26 April 1982).

However, it is not sufficient for Labour merely to 'build us out of the crisis', it must also 'build for choice'. That is to say, it must aim to offer units both for rent and for low-cost sale, and it must be sensitive to the housing needs of all sections of society, not just the nuclear family and the elderly.

The improvement, design and allocation of housing units must take into account changing demographic and social demands. The products of the baby-boom of the 1960s are coming of age; the divorce rate continues to rise; people are living longer and often alone – indeed, 24 per cent of all households consist of single people, most of them living in unsatisfactory private accommodation. If Labour is to offer choice in housing, single and multi-person units must be made available, and it is the public sector that should be taking the lead, as such diversity of units and occupants would greatly enhance the social mix and cultural heterogeneity of council estates. The private sector has long been aware of the market for single-unit accommodation. For instance, Barratt has built self-contained one-bedroom flatlets in small blocks and terraces, and Wimpey, Wilcon and Leech Homes all have their own versions, often produced to meet very basic requirements with minimal decoration. Such flexibility of design and furbishings should form an essential part of Labour's programme for the public sector. Not only would such a policy prove a cost-effective means of providing units for the homeless, but it would also succeed in offering meaningful choice in housing. To encourage more single and multi-person households to enter the public sector of housing, each case should be dealt with on its own merits, and housing need should be the primary criterion for admission.

Now, assuming that Labour works towards providing adequate accommodation for all, the secondary goal of equality in housing will mean that some will choose to rent and some to buy. Once there is financial equity between the two tenures (which I will come to below), and once the council house sales issue is confronted seriously (which I come to sooner), such a mix will become more acceptable.

Labour has never been against owner-occupation and has extolled the fact that it, as much as the Conservatives, has been responsible for establishing home ownership as the majority tenure. Indeed, the last Labour Government actively promoted a build-for-sale programme in the public sector. This scheme involved local authority collaboration with private builders in the supply of land, the provision of finance for development, the design of the schemes, the nomination of purchasers, the provision of mortgage finance and the sale of properties (Bayly and Swain, 1977, p. 9). For instance, in London, up to 1979 such schemes were being carried out by the Labour-controlled councils of Newham, Southwark and Tower Hamlets (although these policies were halted once the 1980 Housing Act made council house sales compulsory). If the role of private enterprise was reduced in this matter, and that of the local authority and its direct labour organisations increased, the public sector could play a significant role in the provision of good-quality, cost-price owner-occupation for the lower-paid.

However, it is one thing to permit local authorities to build a limited number of units for sale at cost price but quite another to allow them to sell off (at large discounts and often indiscriminately) council properties which were built for rent and which contribute, on aggregate, to the standardisation of council rents.

The debate about the financial effects of sales has a long history but can be summarised in terms of their impact upon individual buyers, local authorities and the Exchequer.

Individual council house buyers receive a capital asset priced at between one-third and one-half of the houses' market value. They stop paying rent, commence mortgage repayments and receive tax relief on their interest payments. They also shoulder the financial burden of the repair and maintenance of their properties. Whereas there is the undoubted attraction of entry to the owner-occupier sector on bargain terms, there are attendant dangers of mortgage default among those on the fringe of buying and the possibility that problems may arise when it comes to reselling.[2]

The Exchequer no longer pays a subsidy to local authorities for the units sold, but it loses tax revenue because the new cohort of owner-occupiers becomes eligible for tax relief on the interest on mortgages (see Dawson, 1977).

The position of the local authority is the most complicated. Sales mean that rent income is lost; central government subsidy is no longer paid on the sold units; mortgage payments or capital receipts are gained; and the maintenance and management of the properties are no longer the responsibility of the selling authority. The overall effect of sales depends to a large extent upon the age of the stock and the level of discount offered. When properties are sold below market price, the total potential capital receipts from sales and the scope for debt redemption are decreased according to the actual level of discount. The consequent loss of rent and subsidy income affects the Housing Revenue Account (HRA) and may complicate rent and rates decisions (Forrest and Murie, 1976, pp. 26–7).

Respecting the age of the stock, no matter how old a house is, when it is sold there is a reduction in housing expenditure in so far as central government subsidy is lost. However, because of the widespread adoption of pooled historic rents, older stock subsidises newer stock, and rent on older houses is set at a level higher (sometimes considerably higher) than their individual maintenance and debt charges. When these dwellings are sold with small outstanding debts, a further burden is placed on the remaining rental property, which benefits less from rent pooling. Fewer older houses exist with which the costs of any new or replacement building can be averaged. As 91 per cent of the council houses in Britain were completed before 1964 and carry a low historic debt, the concentration of sales within this group of housing means that the average outstanding debt to be serviced, and the average costs of maintenance and management (despite absolute decreases), are likely to rise (English and Jones, 1977, p. 99; Kilroy, 1977).

The net effect, at least in the short term, seems to be that the position of the HRA will improve unless modern properties, subject to cost rents, are sold. The extent of the benefit to the HRA depends crucially upon the amount of rent foregone on the one hand and the amount of debt that is redeemed on the other (Murie, 1977, p. 55). In the long term the HRA will suffer as rents increase with inflation whereas interest charges on the original debt do not (Hoath, 1978, p. 148; see also NAP, 1979).

Aside from the financial implications of sales at discount, evidence points to the fact that uncontrolled sales lead to the purchase of the best houses (usually those with gardens); that former council houses, when resold, are sold predominantly into the private market of owner-occupation and are therefore lost to the public sector for ever; and that sales tend to result in social segregation on council estates and the concomitant stigmatisation of council tenants (Kilroy, 1976; Forrest, 1980; Forrest and Murie, 1978). The real problem is that where disposed stock is not replaced an indiscriminate and largely unregulated council house sales policy relegates council housing to a residual and welfare role, trapping people in unsuitable accommodation and providing a second-rate service for those unable (or unwilling) to solve their housing problems in the private sector.

This is not to say that sales are necessarily unacceptable in all circumstances. Harloe (1982), for example, has called for social-ised owner-occupation within the public sector, with control over price and property disposal. However, sales can be permit-ted, under strict control and surveillance, only as an integral part of a comprehensive housing policy that develops and pro-tects the public rented sector and is geared towards equality between tenures.[3]

The Labour Party must take a much firmer line on this very important issue. Sales have come to form part of Labour's hous-ing policy and, except in the immediate postwar years, have been permitted by successive Labour Administrations, which have altered conditions regarding sales by means of Circulars and ministerial consent (see Murie, 1975; Power, 1982, pp. 115–57). In spite of Labour's ambivalence regarding sales, the 30,000 disposals under Labour in 1978 represented the third highest total since sales were first permitted in 1925.

Labour's acceptance of a moderate sales policy has resulted from its commitment to defend local autonomy from central government and from its belief that sales are electorally popular (Power, 1982, pp. 131–47). However, previous Labour Government attempts to control the level of sales by means of ministerial Circular have proved inadequate, and local authority discretion has resulted in practices that should be totally unacceptable to Labour. Aggressive sales policies, carried out predominantly by Conservative-controlled local authorities, have led to complaints from pressurised and harassed council tenants. Many local authorities have employed estate agents to boost sales, and a number have offered bonuses and commission to council officers who persuade tenants to purchase their homes (see Power, 1982, ch. 7).

Local discretion cannot be allowed to subvert national policy, and a Labour Government must introduce a 'code of guidance' to avoid the abuses outlined above. This should make clear the procedures to be followed by a local authority when processing a sale, ban the use of outside agents and the offering of bonuses and commission to council officers, stop sales at discounts, advise on the valuation of properties (taking into account improvements, etc.) and lay down strict controls regarding the proportions of properties to be sold in terms of location, type and age.

Currently, we find ourselves in a predicament. Public investment in housing was cut by some 40 per cent between 1978/9 and 1981/2; council house building has sunk to its lowest peacetime level for sixty years; and sales are outstripping new building, resulting in an unprecedented contraction of the public-sector stock. So there may well be a need to halt sales altogether for a period to allow the rented sector to recuperate and the damage caused by widespread sales to be assessed. Nevertheless, as part of a truly comprehensive housing policy, geared to satisfying basic housing needs and offering meaningful choice between tenures, regulated council house sales, other forms of home ownership (such as equity sharing), the provision of 100 per cent council mortgages and a limited build-for-sale scheme could mean that the public sector has a role to play in promoting home ownership among those lower-paid people who desire to buy. However, and particularly with regard to council house sales, such activity is totally unacceptable while the public rented sector is being allowed to diminish and fall into disrepair.

Interestingly, one argument on the left has suggested that any form of anti-council house sales stance is inappropriate, as it serves to reify council housing as 'socialist housing', leading to the fragmentation of the working class, while Labour is seen to take the side of the council tenant against the prospective working-class owner-occupier (Jacobs, 1981). Of course, were one to be complacent about the content and the administration of the public sector, Jacobs would have a point. However, my argument is for equality and choice in housing. That being the case, along with improving and augmenting the public sector, Labour will need to address the question of bureaucracy and paternalism that has for so long been associated with council housing. Although it is no longer the case that handbooks are produced that advise tenants to sit up at the table for meals, get to bed early and wash regularly (in the bath and not in the coal shed), if equality is to exist between the two major tenures, council tenants must have real control over their lives (see Power, 1982, p. 246). At the same time, local authorities must be instructed to break down the barriers that so often exist between themselves and their tenants.

This latter objective could be achieved by encouraging the adoption of the methods used by local authorities such as Kirkless and Walsall, which have made bold attempts at decentralising and rehumanising their housing departments.

In Kirklees in 1981 pre-fabricated cabins were installed on the largest estates so that tenants requiring repairs came into direct contact with the local building superintendent and foremen, who then arranged for someone to carry out the work. As a result, the waiting time for repairs dropped from four to three weeks. Other benefits of the decentralisation of the housing department were that tenants came to know and to respect members of the council's direct labour organisation, which became profitable. There was a 50 per cent drop in absenteeism and a resultant 27p *decrease* in council rents. Also the council's decision to alter its system of estate management, so that rent collectors became 'estate stewards' who covered fewer houses and were encouraged to spend more time discussing individual tenants' problems, proved successful in breaking down further the division between 'them' and 'us' (Wheen, 1982).

At the same time, in Walsall the Labour council determined to reduce town-hall officialdom, identifying this as one of the biggest barriers to the implementation of radical policies. At a cost of £1,700,000, it dismantled the old housing department and sent 150 of the 200 civic centre staff out to thirty-four local neighbourhood offices. These carried out the normal housing functions but were also involved in advisory work and community development and in schemes as diverse as running five-aside football competitions, setting up unemployment projects and organising mother-and-baby groups and jumble sales. As in Kirklees, the direct labour organisation responded well. Mobile caravans toured the estates, and radio-linked tradesmen carried out on-the-spot repairs; demarcation between workers was broken down, and a 130 per cent increase in productivity was achieved, with a 30 per cent pay increase (Sharron, 1982; *Guardian*, 16 March 1982).

I am not suggesting that such cases offer a panacea for housing management: indeed, a further positive step would be for the tenants themselves to control the offices and organise repair programmes. However, they do at least point in the right direction.

Regarding tenant participation in public-sector management itself, a certain degree of convergence has taken place between the Labour and Conservative Parties, and this represents another area in which positive steps need to be taken by a Labour Government.

What is noticeable about the Conservative Party's tenant charter (as embodied in the 1980 Housing Act) is that it emphasises the individual rather than the collective rights of tenants. Likewise, and in spite of the Labour 1977 Green Paper's notion of 'full participation' for council tenants in the management of their affairs, a move towards individual rather than collective rights is discernible in Labour's policy. Indeed, this shift can be traced back to a 1978 consultation paper, in which it was suggested that tenants should be allowed some 'involvement in management', and to the Party's 1979 Housing Bill, in which 'involvement' was diluted to 'consultation' (Schifferes, 1980, pp. 10–12).

More recently, Labour's *A Future for Public Housing* (Labour Party, 1982) gives some reason for optimism in this regard. It states that representative tenants' organisations could be given certain rights: for instance, to be consulted, to take control of the budget for minor works and possibly to set up co-operative self-management schemes where desired. However, if equality and choice in housing are to become a reality, the move must be towards full participation in the management of council housing, with tenant representatives playing a full part in all aspects of the running of their estates and working alongside the professional bureaucrats rather than existing together in an atmosphere of mutual mistrust and suspicion. Moreover, if groups of tenants wish to set up housing co-operatives, they should be encouraged and aided to do so, as this will create further diversity in the housing choices available to individuals.

Along with full participation in management, council tenants should be relieved of restrictions regarding alterations and improvements to their homes; indeed, they should be financially assisted to carry these out. The remaining petty restrictions on their lifestyles should be lifted, and a workable mobility and inter-regional transfer system must be devised.[4] Only then will the privileges and social esteem associated with owner-occupation accrue to council tenants.

Labour must ensure that these council tenants live in an expanded and revitalised sector. To further its dual goals of adequate provision and meaningful choice, alongside a building and improvement programme Labour should be positive in promoting municipalisation and compulsory purchase of properties from the privately rented sector. Where landlords are allowing their properties to fall into disrepair, local authorities should be provided not only with the power but also with the resources to purchase and rehabilitate them. Compensation could be paid to the landlords in the form of government stock, which would yield an income related to the value of the property with a sitting tenant.

Under-occupancy has always been a thorny problem in the

owner-occupier sector, and has resulted in the serious under-use of housing resources. Labour Party policy should encourage the purchase of these properties where the occupant is willing to sell. Many such people are elderly and are often struggling to maintain their properties. Consequently, the opportunity to sell their properties to local councils, who would offer in turn more appropriate accommodation in a public sector in which people would choose to live, would be welcomed by many. Such a policy was put to good effect by the 1971–4 Labour Administration in the London Borough of Havering, where approximately 1,000 properties were purchased by means of a positive municipalisation policy, which included the opportunity for owner-occupiers to offer their homes to the council (Power, 1982, pp. 327–30). As well as providing new homes, Labour must be prepared to take responsibility for the efficient use of the existing stock in the public and, where appropriate, in the private sector.

However, all that has been said so far will be so much whistling in the wind if Labour fails to commit itself to a radical reform of housing finance. There can be no equity between tenures and no real choice while owner-occupiers enjoy privileged financial benefits. With respect to housing costs and subsidies, home owners clearly receive a better deal than those who rent their housing, either in the private or in the public sector (see, for example, Clark, 1977; Robinson, 1979, pp. 127–40; Robinson, 1980, p. 19; McIntosh, 1982, p. 12). As a result of such inequality, investment decisions and tenure preferences are distorted, and income is distributed in an indiscriminate way. Consequently, we have witnessed the ever-increasing absorption of home-loan funds into an exchange process of very little benefit to real housing needs. Indeed, overall patterns of distribution of public housing expenditure favour better-off owner-occupiers and higher-income socio-economic groups (Robinson, 1980, tables 3–6). Such inequalities in costs and subsidies exist primarily because home owners are exempt from capital gains tax, are no longer liable to taxation on imputed income and enjoy tax relief on mortgage interest payments.

The present Conservative Government has intensified existing inequalities and inefficiencies by cutting subsidies to tenants while protecting the tax concessions enjoyed by owner-occupiers. If meaningful choice is to exist in housing, what is needed is greater financial equity between households in different tenures and a more progressive distribution of subsidy by income level (Goss and Lansley, 1981, p. 30).

To this end, one need on which recent commentators concur is a reduction in, or the elimination of, the tax expenditures associated with owner-occupation. Le Grand (1982, pp. 100–3) proposes that capital gains tax could be introduced along with the reintroduction of taxation on imputed income or, alternatively, that mortgage interest tax relief could be eliminated. Likewise, SHAC's report calls for the reintroduction of a tax on imputed income from home ownership. It suggests that there should be exemption from, or at least a reduction in the level of exemption from, capital transfer tax, and that although the £25,000 limit beyond which mortgage tax relief is inapplicable should be retained and allowed to be eroded by inflation, mortgage tax relief should be replaced by a system of interest rate subsidies similar to the option mortgage subsidy. This would mean that the value of relief would not increase with a taxpayer's marginal rate of tax. Indeed, tax relief could be faded out altogether and could be replaced by a system of income-related subsidies similar to rebates for tenants. As with a recent CIPFA study, the SHAC report sees the necessity for gross rents in the public sector to rise and for private rented and housing association rents to come into line with these (with housing association subsidies being adjusted accordingly). However, according to SHAC, the introduction of a universal housing allowance could encourage further the move towards equality across tenures by providing assistance in both major tenures and eradicating the problem of non-take-up of rebates (Grey *et al.*, 1978; Goss and Lansley, 1981; McIntosh, 1982).

Kilroy (1981) believes that mortgage tax relief should be reduced to standard rate, that the £25,000 ceiling should be lowered, that tax relief should be tapered over the life of the mortgage and that a single annuity system should be introduced. In the longer term, he argues, the rate at which tax relief is allowed should be reduced, and capital gains tax should be paid on the death of householders.

Shelter (1982) has come out firmly in favour of a radical reform of housing finance. Its report estimates that in 1981/2 mortgage tax relief was worth £1,985 million, exemption from Schedule A tax about £6,000 million and exemption from capital gains tax about £2,400 million. Shelter suggests that a version of Schedule A should be reintroduced so that home ownership would be taxed like any other form of investment and that maintenance and repairs could be made tax-deductible. Its plan would include protection for elderly home owners, large families and first-time buyers, with the yield from the new tax being sufficient to allow the base rate of income tax to be lowered to 25p.

So a number of options are available to Labour; but one that can no longer be contemplated is evasion of the issue. To carve out a progressive and radical housing policy Labour must face the responsibility of drastically altering the system of subsidies that perpetuates inequality between housing tenures.

Whereas Labour's main concern must be the pressing need for adequate housing for all and the establishment of meaningful choice between tenures, it must also tighten up some existing legislation that is open to abuse.

- To begin to tackle the alarming increase in homelessness, Labour must make clear local authority responsibility. The Housing (Homeless Persons) Act of 1977 must be extended to cover all homeless people, including the single and childless. Additionally, the 'code of guidance' which was initially issued in tandem with the legislation should be reinstated to prevent local authorities from abnegating their duties.
- Although there is no reason to lament the continuing demise of the private rented sector, while such a sector remains in existence (and, indeed, houses some of the poorest and most vulnerable members of society), its occupants must be protected.
- Quite plainly, the invidious shorthold tenancy provisions of the 1980 Housing Act must be repealed, even though they have been relatively ineffective, and full security of tenure must be given to all existing 'shortholders'.

- The much abused common law distinctions between 'tenancies' and 'licences' must be ended and all residential occupiers given common legal rights. Similarly, Rent Act evasions such as bogus 'holiday lets' and 'bed and breakfasts' must be clamped down on, along with the misuse of the definition of 'resident landlord'. Such changes have been campaigned for by organisations like Shelter and CHAR and must constitute part of Labour's short-term housing objectives.

- Labour must ensure that the scandal of empty properties is not allowed to continue. Shelter's survey of the 1981 Housing Investment Programmes showed that at least 600,000 properties were empty in England alone. This represented 3.3 per cent of total stock: 97,000 of these were in the public sector, of which a fifth were empty awaiting sale and a quarter had been empty for over a year. Additionally, 285,000 council dwellings in England were defined as 'hard to let'; they represented 5.8 per cent of local authority stock (Matthews and Leather, 1982, p. 12). Labour must instruct local authorities to include in their HIP submissions to the DOE plans to make use of all the empty properties in their areas, both public and private. It would be efficacious to impose a 100 per cent rate levy on private owners who refuse to bring their properties into use (*Roof*, Jan./Feb. 1982, pp. 21–3).

So it may well be necessary for Labour to introduce early emergency legislation to deal with pressing issues such as the sale of council houses, empty properties and Rent Act anomalies. However, the Party's overall objective must be to introduce comprehensive, not piecemeal, legislation; to inaugurate a radical and progressive housing policy that will at last mean adequate provision, equality in housing and real choice between tenures.

It is incumbent upon the British Labour Party to recognise and attack the housing crisis as it occurs in Britain. To fail to do so will not only mean that individual housing problems are compounded and that the public sector of housing is doomed to a residual role, with its stock falling into disrepair and decay; it will also mean that Labour will be responsible for sponsoring and perpetuating inequality and privilege.

## Notes

1  For a review of public spending in general and the consequences for housing between 1950 and 1977, see Gould and Roweth (1980). Indeed, the Conservative Government of 1979 showed a particular eagerness to reduce spending on housing. This sector of public spending was to take the burden of three-quarters of all cuts planned for the first four years of its rule. Although public spending as a whole was to be reduced by only 4.1 per cent, spending on housing was to be cut by as much as 50 per cent (Marks, 1981, p. 225).

2  An article entitled 'Mortgage dangers' (*Roof*, May/June 1982, p. 8) notes that mortgages resulting from the right to buy are being given to families not thought to be safe borrowers by other lenders. An analysis of 2,200 sales in eighteen London boroughs showed that mortgages which extended into retirement accounted for 55 per cent of sales and those involving family groupings (almost exclusively parents and their working children, and often the children's spouses) for 18 per cent of mortgages. The article warns that tens of thousands of people on the fringe of buying are putting themselves at risk. Equally disturbing is the difficulty that some council house buyers are experiencing in reselling their properties. A Conservative MP, John Heddle, has disclosed that many who bought 'Airey houses', built between 1946 and 1955 for short-term need, are now finding that estate agents are refusing to offer them for resale and that building societies are refusing to lend mortgages on them (*Guardian*, 25 June 1982).

3  The old idea (originally suggested by Peter Walker) that council houses should be given to sitting tenants, thereby solving the problem of equity between tenures, has been floated once again (*The Times*, 11 May 1982). Aside from the fact that this would make a mockery of any notion of tenure choice in housing, it would also lead to serious problems, such as rentless local authorities with enormous outstanding debts on their council houses, ever-increasing waiting lists but nothing now for people to wait for, families trapped in high-rise and unsuitable accommodation with no chance of transfer and inevitable unemployment among local authority housing workers. For a succinct outline of the case against giving away council houses, see Aughton (1979).

4  The current National Mobility Scheme has been open to abuse by authorities unwilling to take advantage of the potential it has for allowing freer movement within the public sector of housing. For instance, one authority has represented the scheme as a labour mobility scheme, open only to those needing to move because of their jobs. Others are ignoring the fact that any families exported by the scheme should be balanced by an equivalent import of families (*Roof*, March/April 1982, p. 5). Labour must tighten up this scheme and may find it necessary to introduce a statutory, rather than the present voluntary, mobility scheme.

## References

Aughton, H. (1979) *Why not Give Council Houses Away?* (London: Labour Party Research Department)

Bayly, R., and Swain, A. (1977) *Local Authorities and Building for Sale* (London: DOE)

Berry, F. (1974) *Housing: the Great British Failure* (London: Knight)

Clark, S. (1977) *Who benefits? A Study of the Distribution of Public Expenditure on Housing* (London: Shelter)

Dawson, D. (1977) 'The sale of council houses and local government finance', in J. English and C. Jones (eds.), *The Sale of Council Houses* (Glasgow: University of Glasgow), pp. 46–53

English, J. and Jones, C. (1977) 'Reflections and conclusions', in J. English and C. Jones (eds.), *The Sale of Council Houses* (Glasgow: University of Glasgow), pp. 90–100

Forrest, R. (1980) 'The resale of former council houses in Birmingham', *Policy and Politics*, vol. 8, no. 3, pp. 334–40

Forrest, R., and Murie, A. (1976) *Social Segregation, Housing Needs and the Sale of Council Houses* (Birmingham: CURS, University of Birmingham)

Forrest, R., and Murie, A. (1978), 'Paying the price of council house sales', *Roof*, December, pp. 170–3

Goss, S., and Lansley, S. (1981) *What Price Housing?* (London: SHAC)

Gould, F., and Roweth, B. (1980) 'Public spending and social policy: the UK 1950–77', *Journal of Social Policy*, vol. 9, no. 3, pp. 337–57

Grey, A., Hepworth, N., and Odling-Smee, J. (1978) *Housing Rents, Costs and Subsidies* (London: CIPFA)

Griffiths, D. (1982) 'Housing: Labour's tangle over tenure', *New Socialist* no. 5, pp. 50–2

Harloe, M. (1982) 'Towards the decommodification of housing? A comment on council house sales', *Critical Social Policy*, vol. 2, no. 1, pp. 39–43

Hilditch, S. (1981) 'Build homes, build hope', *Roof*, Nov./Dec., p. 16.

Hoath, D. (1978) *Council Housing* (London: Sweet and Maxwell)

*The Housing Programme 1965 to 1970* (1965) Cmnd 2831 (London: HMSO)

*Housing Policy: A Consultative Document* (1977) Cmnd 6851 (London: HMSO)

Jacobs, S. (1981) 'The sale of council houses: does it matter?', *Critical Social Policy*, vol. 1, no. 2, pp. 35–48

Kilroy, B. (1976) 'Free the serfs – but keep our priceless council houses', *Roof*, May, pp. 66–7

Kilroy, B. (1977) 'No jackpot from council house sales', *Roof*, May/June, pp. 74–81

Kilroy, B. (1981) *Housing Finance – Organic Reform?* (London: Labour Economic Finance and Taxation Association)

Labour Party (1981) *Re-purchase of Council Houses Sold* (London: Labour Party)

Labour Party (1982) *A Future for Public Housing* (London: Labour Party)

Le Grand, J. (1982) *The Strategy of Equality* (London: Allen & Unwin)

Marks, S. (1981) 'Numbers games', *New Society*, vol. 57, no. 977, p. 225

Matthews, R., and Leather, P. (1982) 'Housing in England the view from the HIPs', *Roof*, May/June, pp. 11–13

McIntosh, N. (1982) 'Owning-up', *Roof*, March/April, pp. 10–12

Merrett, S. (1979) *State Housing in Britain* (London: Routledge & Kegan Paul)

Murie, A. (1975) *The Sale of Council Houses: A Study in Social Policy* (Birmingham: CURS, University of Birmingham)

Murie, A. (1977) 'Financial aspects of the sale of council houses', in J. English and C. Jones (eds.), *The Sale of Council Houses* (Glasgow: University of Glasgow), pp. 54–60

NAP (1979) *Where Have All the Assets Gone?* (Nottingham: Nottingham Alternative Publications)

Pawley, M. (1978) *Home Ownership* (London: Architectural Press)

Power, R. (1982) 'The Sale of Council Houses in Britain, with Special Reference to London' (unpublished Ph.D. thesis, University of London)

Robinson, R. (1979) *Housing Economics and Public Policy* (London: Macmillan)

Robinson, R. (1980) *Housing Tax Expenditures, Subsidies and the Distribution of Income*, Urban and Regional Studies Working Paper no. 19 (Brighton: University of Sussex)

Schifferes, S. (1980) 'Housing Bill 1980 – the beginning of the end for council housing', *Roof*, Jan./Feb., pp. 10–15

Sharron, P. (1982) 'Walsall: out of the civic centre, into the field', *New Statesman*, 19 March, pp. 11–12

Shelter (1982) *Housing and the Economy: A Priority for Reform* (London: Shelter)

Wheen, F. (1982) 'Kirklees: more speed, less waste', *New Statesman*, 19 March, pp. 10–11

# Index

Advisory, Conciliation & Arbitration
    Service 137
Allaun, F. 209
Alternative Economic Strategy (AES) 35,
    47–60, 130, 189–90
    and spatial policy 149, 152–3
Austria
    public expenditure 14

balance of payments 2
bankers
    influence on international
        socialism 196–7
    post-war status 44
Benn, T. 191
Beveridge, W. 8, 114
British Medical Association and
        monopoly 68
Bullock Report 139–40
bureaucracy
    and social services 71

Callaghan, J. 38, 120, 195
    and the social contract 189
capitalism
    failures of 3–4
    international power of 184, 185,
        187–8
central government
    access to decision-making 135
    and local government
        spending 15–18
child care
    lack of facilities 102, 109, 110–11
    welfare benefits 116–18
citizenship
    concept of 15–16
common culture
    concept of 28–9, 32
community
    encouraging sense of 19–20, 70–1
Concerted Action 134–5
Conservative Party
    economic policies 1, 37–8
    family policy 120
    housing policy 208, 217
    immigration policies 164–5
    social policies 1–2, 3
'contracting out'
    and public services 65
cost-benefit analysis
    and subsidies 74–5

council housing 208
    empty 222
    sales 210, 212–15
    tenant participation 217–18
Crossman, R. 162

defence policy 199–204
democracy 184
Department of Education & Science 65
Department of Employment
    survey of sex segregation in labour
        force 109
disarmament see multilateralism;
        unilateralism
'dualism' 16

economic policy 2
    and labour relations 129–30, 134
    and post-war reconstruction 42–3,
        186, 187
    corporatism 186–7, 188, 189
    Liberal/SDP Alliance position 29
    monetarism 10–13, 29, 188
    see also Alternative Economic Strategy
education
    anti-industrial bias 40
    case against subsidies 78–9
    case for state 70, 74
    standards 9
    tax losses and private schools 73
    'vouchers' 65, 79
    see also nursery education
efficiency
    and state provision of services 71, 77,
        78
egalitarianism 28–30
employment
    and housing programmes 209–10
    and income maintenance schemes 84,
        86, 92–3
    and spatial planning 146–7, 153–4,
        158–60
    of women 102–3, 105–12
    part-time 111–12
    see also full employment; manpower
        policy
Equal Opportunities Commission 108,
    109
Equal Pay Act 1970 103, 105–8
Equality
    and Labour Party policy 22–3, 30–1,
        120, 216

and sexual divisions 102–5
and world redistribution 35–6
objectives of 23–30
politics of 119–21
Europe
and defence policies 200, 201, 202
disarmament strategy 203–4

family
and policy making 119–21
conflicting obligations to 102, 111
models and women's inequality
112–19
finance
housing 18, 219–21
local government 12, 16–18
of income maintenance
schemes 88–92
Foot, M. 209
France
Mitterand economic policy 54
union movement 194
freedom
and effects of welfare state 71, 72
full employment 125
and the alternative economic
strategies 48–9, 51, 52–3
and growth 38–9
strategy for 32–3, 60–2

GATT 187, 198
and import controls 190
GDP
and growth 11
Group of Eight 210
growth
decline 37, 40, 45
indicators of 11
presumption of 7
projection plans 61
stagnation 39

Havering, London Borough of housing
municipalisation policy 219
health care
and women 119
charging for 12
subsidies 74
see also National Health Service
Heath, E. 38, 133
Heseltine, M. 211
homelessness 207
and local authorities 221
housing
cooperative estates 20
crisis 207–8, 210
finance reform 18, 219–21
legislation reforms 221, 222
owner-occupied 73, 208, 212

public sector 70, 211, 215–16
purchase from private sector 218–19
rent controls 69–70
single unit 211
standards 9
statistics 207, 222
subsidies 75
see also council housing
Housing Revenue Account 213–14

immigration
as an electoral issue 162–3, 167–9,
178, 180
attitudes to party policies 164–73
Labour Party policy 161–3, 166–7
public concern over 163–4
strategies for 173–7
import controls 49, 51, 54, 55–6, 130,
190
income distribution
guidelines for 32–3
statistical information on 31
income maintenance systems
aims 81–2, 83
employers's contributions 94
strategies for 94–9
techniques of 84–92
see also pensions; social security benefits
incomes policy
and labour relations 130, 133–6
and public spending 14
and reflation strategy 51
and strategy for equality 33
voluntary 2
India
and British economic growth 40, 44
Gold Standard 41
industrial democracy 139–41
industrial organisation
and distributions of resources 33
and growth 39–40
industrial relations
and international economy 126–8,
141–2
legislation reform 136–8
industry
decline of 144–6
location strategy 147–54
inequality 31
and race 173–4
and women 102–3
in the workplace 13–14
inflation 2
information
consumer access to 68–9
inner cities 145
problems 146, 154–7
strategies for 157–60

international economy
  and decline of British economy   45–6,
    144
  and industrial relations   141–2
  and world redistribution   35
  factors influencing   126–8, 187,
    196–7
  strategy for political control   197–9
internationalism
  and economic strategies   190–9
  and foreign policy   199–205
  traditional   184, 185
International Monetary Fund   187, 189,
    197, 198
  influence of USA   196
  loans   195–6

Japan
  state expenditures   186
Jenkins, R.   107
Joseph, K.   65

Keynesian economic theory   6–7, 125,
    126, 186
Kirklees
  housing department restructuring
    216–17

labour movement
  closed-shop   136–7
  political strategy   128–41, 142
  shop-floor   125–6, 139
  see also trade unions
Labour Party
  and immigration issues   161–9
  and 'participation' standards
    policy   25–6
  and women's rights   120–1
  anti-sex discrimination legislation
    103
  economic strategies   6–7, 32–3,
    54–5, 188–19
  housing policy   208-10, 212, 214–15,
    218–19
  industrial relations strategy   136–41
  social policy   7–10
law reforms
  in housing   221–2
  in industrial relations   136–8
Liberal Party
  immigration policies   165
Liberal/SDP Alliance
  economic policy   29
  policy on inequality   32
local authorities
  and devolved responsibility for local
    services   18–21
  council house sales   213–15

homlessness responsibilities   221
  housing programmes   210
local government
  finance   12, 16–18
  see also local authorities
local needs
  and central controls   15–16
  and housing departments   216–17
  and inner cities policies   158–9
  and social services   19–21
Low Pay Unit   108–9

MacDonald, R.   113
manpower policy   138
Manpower Services Commission   138
Maudling, R.   39
means tests   35, 78
micro-processor technology   126
'monetarism'   2, 10–13, 188
monopoly power   68–9
multilateralism   200–1, 202

National Council for Civil Liberties   108
National Health Service
  local administration   19
  privatisation of   65
  value of state provision   70
nationalism
  and socialism   185
NATO
  and defence policies   200
  and multilateralism   202–3
neighbourhood committees
  and local needs   19–20
'new technology'
  and economic strategy   56–8, 126
  and employment   154
'night-watchman' state   27
nursery education   110–11

participation
  and council housing tenants   217–18
PAYG scheme   88–9
pensions   87, 95
  and female dependency   114–15
  'contracting-out'   93
  improvements   98
personal social services
  and women   119
  charging for 12
police
  and race relations   175–6
poverty
  and 'minimum standards' policy   26–7
  and social justice theory   27
  concept of   24–5
  'relative'   28–9
Powell, E.   162, 166–7, 172
Price Commission   133–4

privatisation schemes 65–6
  and exploitation of monopoly
    power 68–9, 77–8
  types 66–7
profit
  and the AES 54–5
  control in monopolies 69
public expenditure
  cuts 2, 14, 210
  Marxist approach to 13, 14
  monetarist approach to 11–12
public transport 74
  subsidies 75, 79

race relations
  and police 175–6
  Labour policies 175–6
  strategies for 173–5
  *see also* immigration
racial incitement 174
rates reform 18, 20
reflation strategy 48–51
regional policy 145, 150–2
  and AES 152–3
  and employment 153–4
  and ownership and control 153
rentier economy 40–1, 46
  effects of war 42–4

savings schemes
  and tax discrimination 96–7
Schmidt, H. 195–6
sex discrimination
  legislation 103, 105–8, 109–10
Shore, P. 190
Smith, A. 187
social contract
  and industrial relations 133, 135, 189
social contract theory 27
Social Democratic Party 23
  incomes policy 33
  *see also* Liberal/SDP Alliance
social insurance 8–9, 86
  and the dependent subsidy 95–6
  and strategy for equality 34–5
  *see also* income maintenance systems
social justice 27
  and the case for subsidies 76–7, 78
social policy
  lack of 1–2
  Labour Party 6, 7, 8–10
social security benefits 9, 84
  and female dependency 114–16
  paying for 85–92
  protection of 97–8
social services
  and economic growth rates 11, 13
  and local diversity 19–21
  reduction of 2–3

state vs. private provision 67–72,
    77–8
  subsidising 72–7, 78–9
  *see also* education; health care; housing;
    personal social services
social wage 26, 62
socialism
  and principles of welfare state 66
  philosophy of 4
  international 192–8
spatial policy 145–50
  *see also* inner cities; regional policy
standards of living 8
  and concept of poverty 24–7
  rising 9
statistics
  and extent of inequality 31
  of housing 207, 222
subsidies
  and social insurance schemes 95–6
  and the social services 67, 72–7
  'industrial' 83
  reduction of 78–9
Sweden
  parental leave 112
  public expenditure 14

taxation
  and owner-occupiers 73, 79, 219–21
  and private schools 73, 79
  and welfare benefits 86–7, 90
  and the welfare state 9–10, 15, 82–3,
    96–7
  and women 118–19
  reform strategy 34
Thatcher, M. 1–5, 65, 164, 168
Third World
  industrialisation 127
trade unions
  and incomes policy 134–6, 142
  decline of power 124–5, 126, 128–9,
    132–3, 136–8
  goals of 125
  politicisation of 131–2
Trades Union Congress 108

unemployment
  and capitalism 3
  and economic policy 1, 27
  and geographical inequality 146, 155,
    156
  and trade union policies 56
  *see also* employment
unilateralism 200, 202–4
Union of Soviet Socialist Republics
  and bilateral defence policies 200, 201
  policy of aggression 203

United States of America
  and international economy    187,
    196–7
  and international relations   184, 200
  and technology revolution    40
  defence strategy   201
  militarism   201
  regulation of monopolies   69
  socialist vote   194
universality   8–10

values
  and democratic socialism   14–15, 20
  and welfare state   70, 71

wages
  equal pay   105–6
  'family'   113, 114
  *see also* social wage
Walsall
  neighbourhood housing offices   217
war effort
  and full employment   38, 42
wealth
  inherited   33

welfare benefits
  and married women   103, 116–18
  as a right   35
welfare state
  and centralised planning   186
  and sense of community   70–1
  decline of   37, 38, 66
West Germany
  unions and economic policy-
    making   134–5
Wilson, H.   2, 38, 133, 162
women
  and 'caring' roles   102–3, 113, 119
  and the family   112–19
  and paid employment   105–12
  and reorganisation of work process   58
  and taxation   87
  *see also* sex discrimination
work
  conditions and inequality   13–14
  process reorganisation   58
  *see also* employment
World Bank   187, 198
world economy *see* international economy